MEDICINE IN THE MEANTIME

CRITICAL GLOBAL HEALTH: EVIDENCE,

EFFICACY, ETHNOGRAPHY

A Series Edited by Vincanne Adams and João Biehl

MEDICINE IN THE MEANTIME

The Work of Care in Mozambique

RAMAH McKAY

DUKE UNIVERSITY PRESS

Durham and London

2018

Library of Congress Cataloging-in-Publication Data
Names: McKay, Ramah, [date] author.
Title: Medicine in the meantime : the work of care in Mozambique / Ramah McKay.
Description: Duke University Press : Durham, 2018. | Series: Critical global health |
Includes bibliographical references and index.
Identifiers: LCCN 2017029951 (print)
LCCN 2017042416 (ebook)
ISBN 9780822372196 (ebook)
ISBN 9780822370109 (hardcover : alk. paper)
ISBN 9780822370192 (pbk. : alk. paper)
Subjects: LCSH: Public health—Mozambique. | Public health—Mozambique—
International cooperation. | Medicine—Research—Mozambique. | Medical care—
Mozambique. | Non-governmental organizations—Mozambique.
Classification: LCC RA552.M68 (ebook) | LCC RA552.M68 M353 2018 (print) |
DDC 362.109679—dc23
LC record available at https://lccn.loc.gov/2017029951

Cover art: Hygiene kits for distribution, Morrumbala, Mozambique.
Photo by Ramah McKay.

CONTENTS

ACKNOWLEDGMENTS

————————————

I acknowledge with gratitude the generous teachers and caring friends who have sustained me over the long period of writing this book.

My thanks to the many people that made my fieldwork possible. Institutional support from the NGOs and clinics described in this book and the support and approval of the Mozambican Ministry of Health were critical to my research, as was an institutional home in the Department of Archaeology and Anthropology at the Universidade Eduardo Mondlane.

I am grateful to the staff and patients at the clinic I call "Clínica 2," and the other clinics I visited in Maputo, for their assistance and support. I thank the staff I refer to as Dr. Joana and Raquel, and especially Dr. Luísa and her colleagues, for their patience and kindness and for sharing their challenges, aspirations, and frustrations with me. I also thank the Davane family; the openness with which they shared their thoughts and experiences constitutes one of my biggest debts.

My thanks go equally to "GCF," in Morrumbala, for allowing me to accompany their projects and I give special thanks to the volunteer I refer to as Pastor Tomás and to his family for making me so at home. I am grateful as well to Violeta, Renato, and other project staff, to the many community volunteers that talked with me, and to those enrolled in the program who shared their experiences, especially Susana and her family.

For their guidance through the world of Mozambican NGOs, public health histories, and the predicaments and rewards of providing health services in Mozambique today, I wish to thank many people in Maputo and beyond. Paula Vaz offered her insight into the transformation of the health system in Mozambique and inspired me with her commitments to care. James Pfeiffer and Kenny Gimbel-Sherr have been generous guides to the world of NGO "partners." Julie Cliff has generously shared her knowledge and experience. Beatriz Thome and Beatriz Rocha offered friendship along with insight, welcome, and hospitality. For their guidance and help at many stages of this project, but especially with helping me get started, I offer special thanks to Euclides

Gonçalves, Sandra Manuel, Carla Braga, and Teresa Cruz e Silva, as well as to Ivo Correia, Kenly Fenio, Erling Hog, and Ilana Kirstzjain. In Quelimane, Daphne Sorensen, Flavia Porto, Monica Carvalho, and Troy Moon offered help and hospitality as well as fun. To my research assistant, Arcanjo de Jesus Silva, I am most grateful, as well as to Dulce Pereira for her help.

As a graduate student, I benefited from the generosity of many teachers. I am tremendously grateful for Jim Ferguson's patient engagements with this project over many years. I have learned from him not only much about Africanist ethnography but also, I hope, something of how to be a teacher. Sylvia Yanagisako always pushed me to be analytically sharp and clear, and has taught me the value of feminist ethnography—for scholarship and for being in the world. Liisa Malkki has offered intellectual friendship that has sustained me through the frustrations of fieldwork and writing. I am grateful too for the insights and help offered by Matthew Kohrman, Lochlann Jain, Miyako Inoue, Paulla Ebron, and Tanya Luhrmann as I formulated the dissertation on which this book is based. I acknowledge with happy gratitude my fellow members of the monster cohort—Rachel Derkits, Oded Korczyn, Tania Ahmad, Serena Love, Stacey Camp, Zhanara Nauruzbaeva, Kevin O'Neill, Erica Williams, Mun Young Cho, and Thet Win—as well as Nikhil Anand, Hannah Appel, Austin Zeiderman, Maura Finkelstein, Elif Babul, Robert Samet, Lalaie Ameeriar, Rania Sweis, Hilary Chart, Jocelyn Chua, Jenna Rice, Samantha Gottlieb, and Tomas Matza. I thank Shelly Coughlan and Ellen Christensen. Support for the dissertation research from which this book draws was provided by the Social Science Research Council, the Wenner Gren Foundation for Anthropological Research, and the Fulbright Hayes program, as well as by Stanford University.

I found a generative and supportive intellectual home as a postdoctoral fellow at the Woodrow Wilson School in Princeton. My deep thanks to João Biehl for his patient support of this project, for creating an intellectual space in which I could find the narrative voice of this book, and for helping me to think more carefully about the critical and political stakes of ethnography. I am grateful too for the wider community of anthropologists, graduate students, and postdocs I encountered at Princeton, including Peter Locke, Betsey Brada, Heath Cabot, and Amy Moran-Thomas, as well as Carolyn Rouse, Lisa Davis, Carol Greenhouse, Rena Lederman, and Carol Zanca. Funding from the Woodrow Wilson School also made follow-up field research possible.

As a faculty member at the University of Minnesota, I was fortunate to have wonderful colleagues to whose creative insights I hope I have done justice. Thank you to Karen Ho, David Valentine, Karen-Sue Taussig Jean Langford, David Lipset, Peter Wells, Hoon Song, Stuart McLean, Bill Beeman, Kat Hayes, Martha Tappen, Michael Wilcox, Kieran McNulty, Steve Gudeman, Allen Isaacman, Rachel Schurman, Michael Goldman, and Vinay Gidwani.

I am grateful to Didier Fassin for the opportunity to be a visitor at the Institute for Advanced Study in 2013–14. The community there helped me to refine the ideas in this manuscript, especially my conversations with Nitsan Chorev, Joseph Hankins, Jeff Flynn, Vanessa Ogle, Lisa Davis, Joe Masco, Manuela Picq, Omar Dewachi, Noah Salomon, and Amel Gorani. I appreciated the care with which Joan Scott and Danielle Allen worked to create a welcoming intellectual community.

Generous colleagues have offered their insights, criticisms, suggestions, and friendship through the course of my writing this book and refining the ideas in it. I thank Nikhil Anand, Hannah Appel, Crystal Biruk, Claire Wendland, Stacey Langwick, Zeynep Gursel, Christy Schuetze, Euclides Gonçalves, Brian Goldstone, Juan Obarrio, Ippy Kalofonos, Dave Morton, Abby Neely, Tomas Matza, Alex Nading, Sarah Besky, Bianca Dahl, Rebecca Warne Peters, Sherine Hamdy, Peter Redfield, Charlie Piot, Susan Reynolds Whyte, and Harri Englund. For extremely helpful suggestions concerning chapter 4, my thanks go to Tobias Rees, Carlo Caduff, and Miriam Ticktin, and audiences at McGill University. For offering feedback on chapter 6, I thank Ravi Sundaram and participants in the Center for the Study of Developing Societies workshop on information.

Most recently, this book has been informed by my colleagues at the University of Pennsylvania. My thanks go to my colleagues in History and Sociology of Science, who have provided a generous and generative welcome across disciplinary lines. Thank you to Robby Aronowitz, David Barnes, Etienne Benson, Sebastian Gil-Riaño, Ann Greene, Susan Lindee, Harun Kuçuk, Beth Linker, Jonathan Moreno, Projit Mukharji, John Tresch, Heidi Voskuhl, Stephanie Dick, and Steve Feierman for creating a generative and supportive departmental home, and to Pat Johnson and Courtney Brennan for all their help. Outside the department, my sincere thanks go to Adriana Petryna, who has generously engaged with the ideas in this book over many years and to Deb Thomas for making me welcome in Anthropology.

At Duke University Press, Ken Wissoker offered early support and helpful advice for the writing of this book. Elizabeth Ault offered generous editorial insight, advice, and support that got this book to fruition. I thank the series editors, Vincanne Adams and João Biehl, for their support. The time and effort of reviewers who offered much thoughtful and constructive feedback is acknowledged with gratitude. In addition, some of the material in chapter 3 appeared as "Afterlives: Humanitarian Histories and Critical Subjects in Mozambique," in *Cultural Anthropology* 27, no. 2 (2012): 286–309. Some of the material presented in chapter 4 appears in a different context in *Critical African Studies* 8, no. 3 (2016): 278–90 as "The View from the Middle: Lively Relations of Care, Class, and Medical Labor in Maputo," and some of chapter 5 appeared as "Documentary Disorders: Managing Medical Multiplicity in Maputo, Mozambique," in *American Ethnologist* 39, no. 3 (2012): 545–61.

In Maputo, *a chefe,* Marta Nhanice de Sousa, and her extended family have given me a home on many visits over many years, and have provided me with insights and care without which this project would not have come to be. Obrigada.

In Mumbai, Roshni and Surinder Anand have graciously supplied many hours of babysitting (and many reams of printer paper), resources without which whole chapters would remain unwritten.

In the United States, I thank my loving family, Jill, Ron, Alisdair, Lisa, Owen, and Adrian; I am the lucky anthropologist whose family has maintained unflagging support of my unlikely plans and projects. This book is dedicated to my parents, whose care—for me and those around me—has made this possible.

Finally, I thank Nikhil Anand, whose love for and curiosity about the worlds we travel through have helped sustain this work. And I thank Kabir and Neel, who have accompanied, supported, and interrupted this process with their loving and joyful spirits.

Introduction

Care and the Work of History

In May 2013, doctors in Mozambique's Serviço Nacional de Saúde (National Health Service) went on strike. In the capital city, Maputo, emergency services remained open, as did private clinics, but many public health services were limited or closed completely. The strike was the culmination of months of slow-burning frustration over raises—many doctors in the public health service earn as little as $500 to $600 a month—and benefits, especially access to state-owned housing. Within days, footage of doctors marching from Maputo's Central Hospital was broadcast on media and circulated via text message, Facebook, and blog posts. Images showed strikers with tape on their mouths to symbolize the government's lack of response. Many protestors carried paper plates inscribed with the words "hunger" and "empty" or signs with slogans like "We are tired of counting our coins at the end of the month!" The South African newspaper the *Mail and Guardian* quoted a frustrated health worker who said, "We are exposed to a lot of sicknesses. Every day we are covered in blood, piss, and everything. But the president doesn't respect what we do" (AFP 2013a).

In June 2013, not long after the strike ended, I arrived at Clínica 2 for the first time in over a year. Centro de Saúde da Cidade 2 (or Clínica 2) is a small, busy public health center on the northern edge of Maputo where I have conducted research since 2006. Set behind a brick wall and just off a main road, near a popular open-air market and a roundabout that serves as a public transport hub, the clinic is both centrally located and tucked away. When I began research there at the end of 2006, the clinic buildings had been newly painted with funds from UNAIDS and the European Union. The new paint job, however, failed to hide noticeable differences between the older buildings—built in the early 1990s, when funds for postwar reconstruction rehabilitated many public infrastructures—and a slick new building at the back that housed the clinic's HIV/AIDS program. There, a big-screen television played the Cartoon Network in a colorfully appointed waiting room, patients relaxed on comfortable chairs, paintings hung framed on the wall, and wide windows allowed dappled sun to spill through cheerful curtains. Reflecting the prominence and inequalities of transnational funding for medicine, clinic infrastructure also pointed to a paradox at the core of this book: the unequal and uneven material and social ramifications of "global health."

That afternoon in 2013, however, it was public, rather than transnational, health funding that was a topic of conversation when I sat down with Dr. Luísa, a staff psychologist with whom I had spent many hours over the course of my research, she immediately remarked, "I suppose you've heard about the strike." In her late fifties, Dr. Luísa had salt-and-pepper hair that was always neatly set. Her sensible blouses, skirts, and shoes peeked out from beneath a precisely pressed white coat. Reading glasses and a small gold cross hung around her neck. Dr. Luísa's persona was far from the image of rabble-rousing recent medical graduates or disgruntled *serventes* struggling to make ends meet; she often seemed to me to be an exemplary civil servant. Moreover, the last time I had seen her, she had been working with an American non-governmental organization (NGO) partner that supported Clínica 2. I hadn't expected to hear her articulate support for the strike. But when I asked her about it, she exclaimed, "The government is always talking about how we already have annual raises . . . but these raises, really! For someone who is earning all right, to get an additional 500 MT [US$20 a month], what is that? And for someone earning little and who receives an extra 50 MT [US$2], an extra 100 MT [US$4], *what is that?* 100 *meticais* [US$4] when you have to pay for milk, for bread, for transport. . . . That doesn't help at all." These small amounts were not just useless, she went on to say, but "insulting" and "disparaging," evidence of how the government "discounts" the value of public health work. These insults were all the more acute given celebratory headlines, in national and international newspapers alike, that trumpeted Mozambique's booming resource economy and rapid economic growth. Signs of new wealth were visible everywhere in Maputo's landscape—from expensive new cars to luxury ocean-view apartment buildings. In this context, the government's claims that doctors' salary demands were unsustainable rang hollow.

Despite my initial surprise, talking with Dr. Luísa about the strike helped me to understand how medical practice, career opportunity, and professional desire are being transformed by Mozambique's changing economy and by the changing institutional and aspirational context of medicine in Mozambique. Much attention has been paid to the role of NGOs and global health projects in Mozambique, where more than half the national health budget is provided by foreign donors and organizations (Pfeiffer 2013). Aiming to provide and extend care to patients, especially those with HIV or other chronic diseases, NGOs have facilitated a dramatic expansion in access to medication in Mozambique over the past decade.

Clínica 2 was just one example of how transnational funds have created partial transformations in the provision of public health. When I first arrived, for instance, NGO-sponsored programs supported patients with HIV/AIDS, tuberculosis, and malaria, and provided food support to eligible families, while basic and emergency medical services were provided through the National Health Service. Yet for all the visibility of transnational organizations, resources, and projects, the passion with which clinic staff responded to the strike served as an important reminder that long histories of health work, public employment, and earlier governmental projects continued to inform how health has been delivered at Clínica 2 and by whom. As I conducted fieldwork, first in Maputo and then in rural Zambézia province, I came to see how Dr. Luísa and others drew on their own experiences with caregiving, support, and medical treatment as they worked amid transient transnational medical regimes.

Stories of global health have often focused on epidemiological experience and on the therapeutic materials (like medications) that enable physical wellbeing, extending life expectancies as they do so. Medical care at Clínica 2, however, was facilitated not only by pharmaceuticals, X-rays, and medical tests, but also by relations among family, friends, colleagues, and neighbors; by norms of public employment and practices of market exchange; and by the prices of milk and transportation. These relations are the subject of this book.[1]

A proliferation of health entities was easily visible in the landscape of central Maputo during the time of my fieldwork. A brief walk down the leafy streets that surround the Ministry of Health, for instance, takes one past the headquarters of development and relief organizations such as Doctors without Borders, World Vision, the Red Cross, Samaritan's Purse, Save the Children, and the offices of newly established "global health organizations," as well as a host of smaller medically oriented NGOs from the United States and Europe. In some ways, this abundance of agencies reflected the expansion of funding for "global health," which grew from approximately $6 billion worldwide in 1990 to almost $30 billion in 2013 (IHME 2014).

Many of the NGOs whose offices line Maputo's streets receive (or have received) funding from the United States' Presidents Emergency Plan for AIDS Relief, known as PEPFAR—a package of U.S. government funding mechanisms that deliver clinical support, medical goods, and services to Mozambican clinics via nongovernmental organizations. In 2007, for instance, PEPFAR distributed more than $200 million in Mozambique, an amount equivalent to 60 percent of all total spending on health (Pfeiffer 2013), in addition to funds provided by other large transnational agencies and organizations, such as the Global Fund for AIDS, Tuberculosis, and Malaria and the Gates Foundation. In those years, as much as 50 percent or more of the national budget came from transnational donors (S. Jones 2009), and many aspects of medical care were facilitated by transnational funding. The abundance of organizations also reflected Mozambique's position, since the mid-1980s, as one of Africa's major recipients of foreign aid, particularly for health (Cunguara and Hanlon 2012; World Bank 2015; Vassal, Shotton, and Reshetnyk 2014).

More broadly, the surfeit of organizations reflected how sub-Saharan Africa has become an important site of nongovernmental, bilateral, philanthropic, and private investment and extraction, responsible for both new medical resources and the creation of deeply unequal market opportunities. Aiming to provide and extend care to patients, especially those with HIV or other chronic diseases, nongovernmental interventions facilitated a dramatic expansion in access to medication in Mozambique during the first decade of the twenty-first century. Though efforts were made to integrate these resources into daily practices at the clinic, the lines between NGO projects and public health were easy to discern. When I first arrived, for instance, NGO-sponsored programs supported patients with HIV/AIDS, tuberculosis, and malaria, and provided food support to eligible families, while other programs and basic and emergency medical services were only available through the National Health Service. As transnational and nongovernmental dollars flowed to neatly circumscribed programs that were implemented in—but often administratively separate from—public hospitals and clinics, public and nongovernmental visions of care sometimes seemed uncomfortably entangled under the same clinic roof.[2]

Among the most visible of transnational interventions at Clínica 2 was the Psychology Office where I first met Dr. Luísa, a sunny room compactly organized around a four-person table. Glass-fronted bookshelves ran along one side, and a cache of worksheets, books, papers, and office supplies were stacked inside them. The triplicate forms, full bookshelves, and smart new furniture gestured immediately to funding from an American NGO whose logo was emblazoned across all of those three-part forms. In addition to underwriting medications, diagnostic tests, lab supplies, and office staff, the NGO paid the salaries of three psychologists, who occupied the small office at the end of the hall. The funding that made the Psychology Office possible also distinguished the clinic from otherwise similar public health spaces elsewhere in the city. Indeed, Clínica 2 was sometimes described as exemplary among clinics in Maputo. Just before I began my research, one of their American NGO partners had hosted a visit from Laura and Jenna Bush, wife and daughter of then U.S. president George Bush, during which the First Family had played and cuddled with young patients who were carefully screened to ensure a vision of healthfulness and success. If these particular visitors were illustrious, such visits were not unusual. In fact, images of American students, researchers, "voluntourists," and celebrity visitors to African hospitals have become somewhat ubiquitous (Benton 2016); I imagine many readers can recall similar images.[3]

At Clínica 2, transnational connections were evident in the presence of expanded staff, better diagnostic equipment, and a wider array of social and psychological as well as medical supports. In an interview, a Dutch woman called Ena, who lived in the neighboring city of Matola, and who brought her adopted daughter to the clinic for treatment, commented, "When I was told there was a Psychology Office, I couldn't believe it. I thought, 'I am in Holland.' I have never seen anything like this [in Maputo] before!" Ena's surprise seemed a reaction not only to the clinic's relative material plenty but also to the provision of—or the aspiration to provide—high-quality care and mental health services to relatively poor patients more frequently targeted by programs to control infectious disease.[4] Just a few minutes away, in the Department of Mental Health at the Ministry of Health, staff members decried the lack of transnational interest in their work and the absence of resources. As if the Psychology Office itself were not unusual enough, Ena told me that she was impressed by the range and ready supply of medications at Clínica 2; though she used to import medications from Holland, she was now confident that she could get what she needed there, or certainly at a private pharmacy downtown.

Despite the overwhelming presence of NGOs at Clínica 2 when I first arrived, over time I saw that it no longer hosted such a wide and robust array of nongovernmental programs. Amid a contraction of health funding around the world, in Mozambique new health policies reasserted state authority, while corruption scandals, political conflict, and allegations of state violence called broader aid projects into question. By 2011, the physical structure of the clinic no longer conveyed the transnational abundance visible on my first visit. First the cable hook-up, then the television itself, disappeared. The waiting room and consultation spaces began to show signs of wear. The computer that had temporarily facilitated office work was taken to higher-priority settings. More urgently, the smooth and untroubled delivery of medications that recalled "Holland" for Ena had been interrupted. As PEPFAR funding to the clinic dwindled and then abruptly ended, public health staff were dispersed across the center or sent to work at other health clinics and hospitals in the city; some left for jobs with other organizations. Remaining staff grumbled about the increased workload and restricted resources.

These transformations were particularly striking since, in interviews, NGO staff consistently spoke of expansion, of "scaling up" their programs to encompass more and more patients. By 2013, however, the clinic's main source of support had switched its attention from Maputo's urban clinics to health centers in rural districts, and many NGO personnel had moved on. Within a decade, many transnational actors had shifted to concerns with "health systems strengthening" and noninfectious disease, and some programs moved away from interventions in health altogether. Yet the conditions that had motivated them to intervene in Clínica 2 to begin with—high rates of HIV and TB infection, poor capacities for diagnosis and treatment, poverty in surrounding neighborhoods, and inadequate staffing—remained. Despite some infrastructural improvements, the clinic was now comparable to most other public clinics around Maputo. Before long, the clinic was being run entirely through the public system and with public sources of funding.

Over time, I came to see how the sedimentation and erosion of nongovernmental resources, practices, and even clinical norms shaped the experiences of workers and patients, as well as the meanings of labor and care that were instantiated at Clínica 2. I began to understand how clinic staff and patients worked between the (often transitory) resources of nongovernmental intervention and longer experiences of medical labor and alternative forms of care. Not only did these rapid shifts pose challenges to health workers and patients; they also made clear how public policies, state spaces, and market forces were central to the provision of care and thus to the strategies of patients as they moved in and out of the clinic. As I returned to interview, observe, and simply chat with doctors, nurses, psychologists, and patients over time, I was reminded not only of the entangled public and nongovernmental nature of medicine in Mozambique—as transnational NGOs provided care in public spaces, and a multitude of agencies and institutes intervened in care in different ways—but also of the quickly shifting nature of interventions in a context of political uncertainty and recurrent crises. In 2015, I stopped by Clínica 2 one day to find, unexpectedly, the clinic's head nurse, a fifty-nine-year-old woman named Elsa, and Nilza, a younger colleague, poring over portraits of clinic patients taken during Laura and Jenna Bush's visit in 2007. Ignoring the celebrity visitors, Elsa and Nilza were discussing patients who had died in the intervening decade. As transnational resources flowed and ebbed, and the lives of those under treatment were sometimes shortened as a result, seasoned medical workers at the clinic, like Elsa, drew on their long experience to navigate the vicissitudes of clinic practice.

This book traces the lives and afterlives of two medical projects in Mozambique. During the last two decades and through the course of my research, efforts to enhance "global health" expanded the medical resources available to patients and workers in Mozambique, yet these projects often gave rise to deeply divergent understandings of what care *means,* what it *does,* and *who* does it. Central to these competing visions were differing ideas about the kinds of relations—among staff, patients, medical technologies, friends, kin, organizations, food, and pharmaceuticals—that were involved in the provision of care, and about the spans of time (acute or sustained, short-term or cyclical) over which care might endure. Whereas health regimes prioritized individualized and bodily definitions of health, patients were also enmeshed in webs of relation that made their medical care possible. While nongovernmental projects envisioned discrete interventions shaped by short-term (if repetitive) funding cycles, the resources they made available were shaped by past experience and by future imaginations of health and well-being.

To explore this constellation of issues, the book draws from fieldwork conducted at a variety of public health sites and with two organizations—the International Center for Health Care, or ICHC, an NGO formed in the year 2000 that supported care at Clínica 2 and at other sites in Maputo, Mozambique's capital city; and the Global Children's Fund or GCF, which had, since the 1980s, managed health and development projects in Morrumbala District, in Zambézia Province.[5] It also follows the patients and workers who moved through and beyond these clinical spaces. Through their experiences, the book investigates how global health NGOs shaped the work that care requires. The work of care was transformed, I show, by the sudden influx of resources

Map Intro.1 Mozambique, with the capital, Maputo, to the south and Morrumbala District to the north.

that NGOs brought with them; it was also molded by historical experiences that many Mozambican health workers (and patients) have developed in encounters with the state and NGOs over decades and by the relations, and practices of labor and livelihood, in which patients and workers have long been enmeshed. These relations have emerged through transnational processes, national health policies, and historical experiences alike.

The question with which this book is fundamentally concerned, then, is how care is made when medical materials, knowledges, and practices are shaped by a range of interventions constituted through diverse actors, aims, and temporalities. How do diverse modes of biomedical care articulate with one another? What do such articulations make possible and for whom? What complications do they introduce? How can attention to the relations through which care is made possible help us to understand the effects and limits of transnational medicine today?

Care, Work, and Multiplicity

Why care? I use *care* in this book because of its proliferation as a technical term. The assemblages of pharmaceuticals, medical knowledges, social and nutritional supports, and community interventions deployed by AIDS organizations in Mozambique were known as "care and treatment" programs. Care, in this formulation, encapsulates all the material, social, epistemological, and medical work that accompanies pharmaceuticals. This work is my object of analysis. However, care also makes clear the close proximities between anthropological and global health vocabularies. In both, conceptualizations of care not only draw attention to health inequities and serve as calls for action; they also reflect normative political claims about what the state is or should be (see also Redfield 2012) and serve to index caring subjects and subjectivities in ways that are raced, classed, and gendered (Bailey and Peoples 2017, Benton 2016, Page and Thomas 1994).

Many anthropological accounts of humanitarianism, welfare, development, and global health have shown how efforts to "care" have unintended effects: they may entail the surveillance or policing of those they aim to assist (Donzelot 1979); they may forestall political claims or demands for recognition in ways that are ultimately problematic or counterproductive (Fassin 2011, Ticktin 2014); they may reflect the "need *to* help" rather than the desire *for* help (Malkki 2015). Though care is often assumed to connote an emotional orientation and moral value, caring—especially care offered to "distant strangers"—may also presuppose and reinforce inequalities of race, class, and national origin (Boltanski 1999).

One approach to navigating the uses and limits of care comes from scholars working in the tradition of feminist science studies have written that care is better seen not "as a (preferably 'warm') relation between human beings" but rather as a "matter of 'tinkering'" (Mol, Moser, and Pols 2010). Care, in this view, is embedded in situated practices and processes through which interrelatedness is made possible, "a matter of various hands working together (over time) toward a result" (Mol 2008: 18). Amid the diversity of caregiving actors in Mozambique, who is to say that the various hands of Jenna Bush, Elsa, Ena, and Dr. Luísa, even my own, are working toward the same end? Still, I share this approach to care as a matter of practice. I too am interested in how care comes to matter, for whom, and in what ways. While critical accounts have shown how subjects of care are constructed through processes of class formation, gender identity, and race, so too are *caring* subjects. Caring—in global health imaginaries but also in the clinics I studied—was often most easily embodied by foreign or expatriate, often white, middle class, and professional women (Page and Thomas 1994, Benton 2016). As a result, as transnational medical economies intersected with public and state-run medicine, clinics were partially and temporarily "white public [health] spaces" (Page and Thomas 1994; see also Brodkin, Morgen, and Hutchinson 2011).[6]

To understand the experiences of Dr. Luísa, Nurse Elsa, and others, then, I focus on two aspects of care. One is the *work* that enables care and that care enables. Spaces like Clínica 2 were simultaneously sites of nongovernmental and public health interventions, and they were locations in which a variety of caregiving strategies were enacted: from the access to pharmaceuticals that Ena and her daughter valued, to the new forms of professional practice available at the clinic, to the forms of long relation that marked Nurse Elsa's contemplation of the photograph. Different modes of seeking care, or of caring for others, required different kinds of work. Like the emphasis on improvisation and tinkering that have characterized many understandings of care, in and beyond Africa, my ethnography emphasizes care as a set of practices—yet these practices were structured by health systems and interventions, incentivized through salaries, gifts, or relations, and shaped by the material resources that they enabled. As a result, I focus on *work* to highlight how care was entangled with, not separate from, economic processes and to show how medical resources and caregiving practices were situated in relation to broader projects of making lives and livelihoods.

Second, in the chapters that follow, I conceptualize this plurality of relations to and of care in terms of *multiplicity*. Multiplicity describes how singular objects and practices (a written diagnosis, a clinical archive, an old photograph) may enact multiple and sometimes competing modes of care: Does a diagnosis enable prescriptions and rest, or promises of profit and the market? Does the photograph depict a former first lady or a former patient? How is care itself at once public and nongovernmental, medical and more-than-medical? I use *medical multiplicity* to describe how diverse, deeply unequal actors and institutions come to be invested in the objects, actors, and practices of medical care. Medical multiplicity thus describes how transnational medical projects are structured by and produce practices of care (enacted, for instance, by public health workers, family members, or friends) that are simultaneously rendered external to it. Frequently, these actors and practices are perceived as a threat to the modalities of care that NGOs advanced; absent or incompetent public health employees, unreliable family members, or truculent community volunteers were seen as putting NGO interventions at risk. Yet these social relations were necessary to and frequently produced by health interventions themselves. In other words, multiplicity is not an idiosyncratic aspect of Mozambican medicine—an "African" aberration. Rather, it is central to transnational biomedicine today.

My approach draws from recent attention to ontologies of medical practice around the world. Scholars, for instance, have recently argued for attention to the ontological multiplicity and instability of medical objects (Street 2014) and diseases (Livingston 2012). Annemarie Mol (2002), for example, has demonstrated the multiplicity of the body, suggesting that an ostensibly stable object—such as the leg of a woman or man suffering from atherosclerosis, who will need surgical interventions and daily care—is in fact multiply and differently constituted for the patient, the surgeon, the domestic caregiver, and other actors who experience, diagnose, or treat atherosclerosis. These approaches emphasize how health objects are folded together with other objects of healing (e.g., Langwick 2011); for instance, a photo comes to be at once a memento and a clinical record. They also draw attention to how the material infrastructures of global health create new possibilities for health and care, for instance, by making new therapies available (e.g., Nading 2014; Redfield 2008). Rather than simply describing a diversity of medical practices and actors in the clinic, then, multiplicity shows how care emerges when patients and workers bring medical goods, categories, and materials into relation with political institutions, practices of livelihood, and even emotions.[7]

The existence of many modes of healing is also a central theme of Africanist literature on medical pluralism (Olsen and Sargent 2017).[8] On the one hand, biomedicine has a long history in Africa, not as a foreign import but as a field of practice; medical and development practices are as "African" as they are "Western" or "global" (Comaroff 1993). On the other hand, literature on medical pluralism has shown how patients, families, and health workers have long moved between diverse systems, epistemologies, and practices of care in a search for therapeutic efficacy (for instance, Feiermann and Janzen 1992; Granjo 2009; Janzen, Leslie, and Arkinstall 1982; Langwick 2008; Meneses 2004). This literature has shown how "health" is not limited to physical well-being, but encompasses financial, domestic or relational, spiritual, and bodily experiences. These accounts make clear that the health of individuals is inseparable from the relations in which those individuals are embedded.

While the literature on African healing and medical pluralism makes these relational dynamics of health particularly prominent, similar attention to relations was not entirely absent from biomedical practices at Clínica 2. When staff asked patients about their families and resources for support, they too embedded care in relations, and they too, as I show in chapters 4 and 5, had to account for the economic and social constraints that patients faced. In other words, biomedicine, too, makes room for relations. Together, ontological and pluralistic approaches highlight how "medicine" is never a singular ready-made thing but is always enacted through situated practices informed at once by transnational flows of funding, materials, and knowledge, and by located (not necessarily "Mozambican") practices of care.

By characterizing the institutional scene of this book as multiple, I focus on the ways that the state public health structures, and transnational practices are entangled. Rather than describing a quality of "Mozambican" or "African" medicine, multiplicity describes how transnational medical actors presume and rely upon, while also distinguishing themselves from (and even compromising) public health systems. It describes how the public system comes to be at once necessary and rendered external to transnational projects. A specific example may make this clear. From one perspective, the apparent fragility of public health services at Clínica 2—crowded facilities, a lack of space and staff—appeared to demonstrate the need for transnational assistance; from another point of view, public health centers are necessary locations in which "global health" care can be delivered.[9] The ICHC could focus on select diseases and populations *only* by presupposing other, more capacious, and usually more public entities within which their interventions could be staged. No one would advocate for a health system that treated only a single disease, unless they assumed other entities would provide other forms of care, and no one would advocate for short-term interventions unless other structures provided more enduring forms of care. It was only because Elsa *remained* that NGO staff could come and go. Health projects thus both relied on and presupposed institutions, actors, relations, and entities that were rendered external to transnational processes and projects. This way of providing medicine, in other words, takes for granted *and* produces a temporally and institutionally plural field.

Despite the transnational nature of these politics, however, "African" examples proliferate in both ethnographic and health literature. The persistence of "African" representations of global health speaks not so much to epidemiological "facts on the ground" as to historical processes of pathologization that have long figured Africa as a site of difference, disease, and lack (Chabal and

Daloz 1999; Comaroff 1993; Meyers and Hunt 2014). Ethnographers, though critically attuned to the historical conditions through which these representations are produced, have also played central roles in generating these representations and images. Alongside my attention to health work in and out of the clinic, then, I also show how anthropological engagements help to stabilize the forms of difference that distinguish care in Philadelphia, Maputo, or Morrumbala. How and when does ethnographic research disentangle those who are assumed to provide care (global experts and NGOs, for instance) from those who receive it (patients, public health systems)? How is ethnography, and how are ethnographers, participant in the practices of care that make up transnational medicine today? Attending to care as relational work, I hope to keep such stabilizations in abeyance.

Finally, throughout the book, I attend to how time shapes both the work of care and ethnographic practice.[10] On the one hand, as I returned to interview, observe, and simply chat with doctors, nurses, psychologists, and patients over time, I saw how practices of care both shifted and persisted despite the institutional instability of many health projects.[11] On the other hand, even as NGOs like the ICHC made medical resources available in new ways, they also frequently evoked a future without aid. In these imagined futures, certain kinds of medical care were imagined as fully public, the domain of a capacious and caring state.[12] To my surprise, these futures converged with and even reflected critical political sensibilities that have animated ethnographic and journalistic assessments of the problems of transnational assistance (Easterly 2006; Moyo 2009). In so doing, these narratives constituted state and transnational actors as separate and easily distinguishable. Attending to time therefore helped me to see not just temporal change but temporal politics (Gonçalves 2013), as invocations of past and future helped to shape the politics of care, and of ethnography, in the meantime.

Time, Care, and History in Mozambique

Why were staff and patients navigating between different kinds of public health institutions with such different and transient possibilities for care? How did the institutionally multiple landscape of care at Clínica 2 emerge? The historical, political, and economic forces that gave rise to the landscapes of care that Dr. Luísa and others now traverse were topics of frequent discussion, debate, and analysis—not only by anthropologists but also by medical practitioners and policymakers in Mozambique. Early in my fieldwork, for instance,

I spoke with Joe, the expatriate country director of an American philanthropic foundation. Sitting at a pleasant sidewalk café around the corner from the Ministry of Health, Joe described how he had participated in writing early drafts of Mozambique's "Strategic Plan" for HIV/AIDS, which delineated plans for treating and caring for AIDS patients. It also outlined the assemblage of institutions, including the public health system, international NGOs, and local associations that would participate in the provision of care. It described both what was to be done—providing access to medication—and how that was to be accomplished: through a consortium of local, national, and transnational organizations and institutions. In this way, the document reflected and enacted the kinds of institutional multiplicity that came to characterize global health interventions in Mozambique.

Many observers, including Joe, noted to me that Mozambique's strategic plan was different from (and an improvement on) strategies enacted in neighboring countries because it emphasized Ministry of Health spaces, such as Clínica 2, as sites of care, even when that care relied on funds, drugs, and doctors provided by NGOs. Though the Strategic Plan aimed to organize and entrench multiple actors within the public health system, it also demonstrated what Joe described approvingly as an "ideological commitment to a single national health system, not divvying up the health system between different NGOs and missions." In this way, public systems remained discursively and spatially important, even as the forms of care they were providing relied ever more heavily on nongovernmental and transnational resources.[13] That Joe praised this commitment, I would later come to see, was not too unusual. Many observers, Mozambican and expatriate, saw transnational medical interventions as eroding public health capacities and they valued efforts to enshrine and promote the Ministry of Health as the ultimate health authority. As the director of Clínica 2 put it, "In the name of supporting . . . [many NGOs] are just weakening an already-weak system."

These debates were shaped by high levels of donor spending on health in Mozambique and a national history in which nongovernmental and foreign actors have played important roles. Explanations for the high levels of foreign assistance the country has received have included political stability and high rates of economic growth. With headlines like "The Mozambique Miracle" (Kaminski 2007), the country has often profited from an image of "hope" and "potential" (see, e.g., USAID 2008) in much media reporting about transnational aid. The International Monetary Fund named Mozambique one of a handful of "frontier economies" in recognition of its low levels of development and rapid economic expansion (Lagarde 2014).[14]

This narrative was shaped by Mozambique's emergence, in the early 1990s, from two successive and brutal wars. The first, against Portuguese colonial rule, came to an end in 1975. Shortly thereafter, fighting emerged between the then-socialist ruling party, FRELIMO, and an opposition group, RENAMO, supported by apartheid South Africa and white minority-ruled Rhodesia (now Zimbabwe).[15] I describe the legacies of the war in more detail in chapter 3. With the signing of peace accords in 1992, Frelimo (formerly FRELIMO) and Renamo (previously RENAMO) became the ruling party and major opposition party, respectively, a transition in which transnational and humanitarian actors played crucial roles.

In subsequent years, the narrative of a successful transition to peace and democracy reinforced foreign aid investments, and Mozambique would be frequently described as a "donor darling." This narrative often overlooked the inequalities that accompanied and have been exacerbated by the processes of economic reform and development that donors and NGOs promoted. For instance, a report by the United States Agency for International Development (USAID 2008; see also S. Jones 2009) opens by citing Paul Collier's notion of the "bottom billion," a term he coined to describe inhabitants of countries that experienced no or negative income growth during the 1990s (Collier 2007). It shows how donor narratives often framed Mozambique as at once successful and desperately poor.

> Mozambique resides near the bottom of the bottom billion . . . [and] is still recovering from the effects of a protracted civil conflict that ended sixteen years ago and destroyed much of the country's key infrastructure while delaying investment and development of basic services. Continuing peace and stability, however, coupled with economic growth averaging nearly 8% for the last five years, offer hope for a more prosperous Mozambique. . . . Relative to governance problems in many countries in Africa and judged by its record of stability and growth since the end of its civil war in 1992, Mozambique appears to be a success story. (USAID 2008: 1)

From this vantage point, Mozambique's "success" appeared to coexist seamlessly with its spatial localization near "the bottom of the bottom billion." The contradictions this entails, however, profoundly shape the struggles of public workers like Dr. Luísa and of the patients she served.

Recently, these celebratory narratives have collapsed. New horizons of capital investment and the intensification of inequalities of wealth and power not only sparked resentment among health professionals like Dr. Luísa but also rekindled political animosities. In 2012, fighting began between Renamo forces and the Mozambican military and paramilitary forces in central Mozambique. In July 2015, residents of some districts fled to Malawi in fear of political violence, echoing experiences during earlier iterations of the conflict (which I describe in chapter 3). Political conflict, human rights abuses, a debt scandal, and the suspension of international loans and assistance have called narratives of success and state transformation into question. For more than three decades, however, donor literature described Mozambique as a "poster child" of international reform and a safe and attractive site for philanthropic investment. Indeed, as I show in chapter 2, a great deal of work has gone into making health projects and health workers the "right place" for donors to put their money. As a result, for more than a decade, global health investments seemed to offer important possibilities for constituting care in ways that were at once public and "global."

Glory Days of Public Health

Such imaginings were deeply shaped by the medical and political history of Mozambique. Central to Joe's assessment of the Strategic Plan was his conviction that locating transnational interventions in existing public health programs and spaces was important. He noted that the plan's emphasis on the Ministry of Health was "a good long term—like 30 year—strategy." He also linked the ministry's strong sense of national autonomy to legacies of the "civil war, when health centers were completely trashed . . . targeted, plus a legacy of 'the glory days of Samora,' who was very anti-mission." Joe thus situated contemporary health practices within a historical frame shaped by conflict and by the lingering influence of Mozambique's charismatic first president, Samora Machel. His comments recalled historical aspirations to state-run health care provision as well as legacies of restrictions on the activities of religious missions that have long been central actors in the provision of medicine in southern Africa (Comaroff and Comaroff 1991; Ranger 1992). In this recounting, Mozambique's centralized, socialist past created the infrastructures and political orientations on which the country's biomedical future could be imagined.

Invoking the "glory days of Samora," nongovernmental actors like Joe (and his expatriate and Mozambican colleagues) demonstrated political commitments to the state. They recalled an inspiring, if partial, historical narrative that emphasized not only "Samora" but also a moment of hope in efforts to expand primary health care in Mozambique and around the world. By 1978, for instance, more than 90 percent of Mozambique's population had been vaccinated. This feat was particularly remarkable since, by 1976, only a year after independence, the country had only an estimated 60 medical doctors, down from 289 just four years earlier (Vio 2006).[16] Reflecting this lack of medical capacity, FRELIMO's initial plans for the health service emphasized an expansion of health posts into rural areas, the training of midlevel medical staff, and the promotion of community health workers. In the era of the World Health Organization's 1978 Alma Ata Declaration with its campaign to realize "Health for All" and to promote primary and preventative care, these efforts reflected not only a socialist vision of public health but also an internationalist ideal that privileged state responsibilities for medical care and grassroots services. By the early 1980s, the World Health Organization had recognized Mozambique as a model of primary health care (Walt and Melamed 1983).

Referencing this hopeful historical moment, Joe's comments showed how the history of medicine in Mozambique created ideological and concrete structures that remain important to the provision of care. Recalling the past, Joe articulated an appealing (if nostalgic) vision of, or ambition for, national, autonomous, and grassroots medical services that captured nationalist aspirations of the time (Prince and Marsland 2014). The "glory days of Samora" could thus be heard as a sincere invocation of a moment when primary health care ideals offered new hope for international population health. This nationalist vision was shared by health workers like Dr. Luísa and Elsa for whom medical service had offered an opportunity for both professional and national advancement. This history also informed Joe's sense of the past as glorious and his conviction, which I shared, that public commitments to primary health care were "a good long term—like 30 year—strategy."

Yet to invoke the "glory days" was also ironic. First, because the horizon of public commitment seemed to be continually receding, and seemed to offer little now, in the meantime. Second, because these efforts were almost impossible to extricate from bitter, contested, frequently violent struggle over the politics of health. Indeed, the history that Joe offered in our conversation was a relatively partial or truncated account. In Mozambique, nongovernmental institutions—from corporations to churches—have played significant roles in areas such as health, education, and labor regulation (even tax collection and law enforcement) since the colonial period. A tenuous, decentralized, and privatized system of administration aimed at the brutal extraction of wealth has been described as a hallmark of the colonial Portuguese administration, from the landing of the first Portuguese soldiers and traders in northern Mozambique in the late fifteenth century.[17]

More critically, legacies of governmental intervention and socialist governance, sources of nostalgia for some, are recalled ambivalently or resentfully by many who experienced this period as one of violent governmental intrusion. While the medical achievements of the socialist state were impressive by some public health measures, they were also part of a brutal remaking of daily life that many Mozambicans feared and resisted. Many socialist projects, such as efforts to resettle rural populations in planned communal villages, were resented (West 2005). Communal villages, for examples, were not just new ways of constructing rural towns but were also locations in which campaigns against "traditional" thinking could be waged (Borges Coelho 1998; Israel 2014). These efforts engendered bitterness among citizens who found their ways of living, forms of authority, practices of healing, and spiritual beliefs subject to criticism, violence, and reform in the name of a socialist ideal. Recalling past "glory days" thus overlooked how legacies of state intervention in Mozambique were received with ambivalence and resistance by the populations to which they were directed.

These struggles were compounded by Mozambique's position on the violent fault lines of the Cold War. Apartheid-era destabilization policies made the socialist project particularly volatile (Minter 1994), and health practices were at the heart of both revolutionary (socialist) and counterrevolutionary politics.[18] By the late 1970s, RENAMO had begun attacks on sites of governmental authority, including health posts.[19] The war disrupted salaries, medical supplies, and infrastructural support. Staff shortages left those who remained with increasing workloads even as wages fell precipitously. With neither salaries nor medical tools to support them, many health centers were abandoned and others were physically destroyed.

By the mid-1980s, less than a decade after it had received WHO accolades, concerned observers described the public health system as in a state of near total collapse (Cliff and Noormahomed 1988). Rural populations were affected not only by war but also by conditions of extreme drought that coincided with the worst years of fighting (Macamo 2006). By the time peace accords were signed in 1992, it was estimated that two million Mozambicans had died and more than six million people had been displaced from their homes (Finnegan 1993; Lubkemann 2008). Subsequent efforts to repatriate refugees were, at the time, the largest planned movement of refugees in the world (Crisp and Mayne 1996).[20] The traumatic impacts of displacement and violence remain evident in many places, including Morrumbala, one of few district capitals to have been controlled by RENAMO military forces.

Historical legacies also informed the experiences and aspirations of health workers in Mozambique. Nurses like Elsa, who entered nursing school at the beginning of the socialist period, had witnessed both the birth of the public health system and its dramatic transformation over the course of their medical education and careers. Some spoke proudly of how their contributions to the socialist project had been recognized by the state in public ceremonies and awards. Some recalled the material constraints and ideological rigidity of the early health system. Many recalled how the urgent need for care during times of war opened unexpected opportunities for training and experience— for instance, as doctors trained nurses in techniques and practices beyond standard nursing curricula in order to expand possibilities for care.[21] Despite the sad context of this education, such experiences also represented moments of professional accomplishment and were sometimes recalled with pride. More commonly, though, legacies of conflict are recalled with sorrow, anger, or disgust (Gengenbach 2005; Schuetze 2010).

Remaking Health

The war also had indirect reverberations in health policy. Institutional reforms, enabled by the conflict, reorganized political and social life in ways that dramatically affected possibilities for health and medicine. By the late 1980s, the conflict was drawing to a close. Soviet support for socialist projects in Africa, including financial and military support for FRELIMO, was dwindling. The devastating effects of a drought further stretched FRELIMO's political and economic resources. At the same time, foreign support for RENAMO similarly declined. By the late 1980s, FRELIMO signed international agreements that would restructure the state and economic policy in exchange for loans from the International Monetary Fund (Chingono 1996).[22] Though international development and media narratives described Mozambique as a "miracle" and "poster child" for economic reform, such claims also belied the highly mobile and repetitive nature of such imagery and of International Monetary Fund policies and their effects across multiple countries.

These processes of structural adjustment entailed the remaking of public medical programs. Amid efforts to "shrink" state budgets, public services were curtailed. Medical services, once free though often underfunded, now required payment on a "fee-for-service" model. Patients were required to pay larger fees to receive even primary and preventative care, and free and low-cost medical programs were to be phased out (Cliff and Noormahomed 1993). Salaries for public workers, including health workers, were cut. Funds for hospitals, clinics, and equipment were restricted. In retrospect, it is clear that these cuts had devastating consequences on health in the southern African countries that adopted these policies. These policies both weakened health systems and exacerbated the spread of disease, including HIV/AIDS, tuberculosis, and malaria—the very diseases that global health agencies would later emerge to combat. They institutionalized and intensified medical and social inequalities (in the case of Mozambique, see Pfeiffer and Chapman 2010, 2015), worsened public health outcomes, and reduced life expectancy (Deaton 2013).

In this context of curtailed public spending, new agencies, from Pentecostal churches (Pfeiffer et al. 2007) to nongovernmental organizations (Duffield 2001),[23] came to play larger roles in the provision of care. Indeed, NGOs were central to the vision of care that emerged through and in the wake of these political changes. In the year 2000, newly adopted international frameworks, such as the Millennium Development Goals (MDGS), which aimed to halve world poverty and halt the spread of HIV/AIDS, gave renewed impetus to transnational investments in health. A growing number of global health agencies, and the expanded and dominant role played by financial institutions such as the World Bank and the International Monetary Fund in setting world health policy, further linked new economic approaches to health outcomes.[24]

Global Health and the Futures of Care

The story of care in Mozambique is thus a transnational one, driven by international financial policies and transnational agencies. Yet, as I show in chapter 1, it is also a story of the state. Even as NGOs took on new roles in medical provision, national health policies were also transformed. Efforts to expand services to rural populations and to calculate and extend life expectancies not only improved population health but also demonstrated Mozambique to be an appropriate site for transnational investments. In some cases, the state seemed to no longer aspire to the provision of care but rather to make populations available for humanitarian intervention.

These new aims were reflected in changing norms and practices of public health. For example, instead of training cadres of medical workers as in the late 1970s, NGOs expanded the use of community volunteers. As described in chapters 1 and 2, "community-based" and "grassroots" projects promised low-cost distribution of medical information and goods, but did so by multiplying the channels through which care was delivered. Expertise and authority often remained in the hands of expatriate doctors and aid workers. At the Ministry of Health, the work of managing donors and meeting multiple, often conflicting, donor requirements took time and energy away from the implementation of health services (Brugha et al. 2004; Biesma et al. 2009), as staff had to prepare unique plans for each donor or agency (Oomman et al. 2007). And as shown in chapter 6, new regimes of evidence-based medicine, rooted in global metrics rather than in local standards or expectations of care, not only accompanied but often seemed to *drive* the forms of care and intervention that NGOs made available (Adams 2016).[25] These changes in health policies and actors made important treatments accessible. Yet for many medical workers, they entailed mixed consequences. Employees of and actors involved with NGOs expressed an uncertain perspective on how their work contributed to and profited from the problems of primary health care that they also aimed to ameliorate.

In my conversation with Joe, for instance, he not only reflected on the positive aspects of working in Mozambique; he also described the work of supporting public health as riddled with practical ambivalences. Though he asserted forcefully that medical care "*should* be driven by the Ministry of Health," he pointed to political and technical constraints on the ministry's ability to do so, exacerbated by donor institutions' demands that initiatives expand rapidly despite overstretched public health resources. "For example," Joe explained, "In our rural initiative, wanting to get five hundred people on treatment—you have to be able to say [to your donors] 'it's not gonna happen.' When you have one doctor for 300,000 people and he's hardly there anyway 'cause he's going for training and conferences [sponsored by NGOs] and the nurses are taking bribes and you have people dying in their beds . . . , you *can't*. But because there are [donor] commitments, you *do* it."

Later in our conversation, Joe elaborated on this theme, commenting that "funders don't get it. Development organizations might, but these are the people—like the Norwegians—we like to lambaste for lacking innovation." Yet if donors didn't "get it," Joe was also skeptical of the approach taken by the minister of health at the time, who was known for taking a critical public stance toward the activities of NGOs. The minister, he noted, "wants a completely independent health system, with no foreign support. He basically acts like it is *already* 2030." Contrasting the technical and financial demands of donor programs (which he described as pressure to "save lives and report numbers") with the real conditions of his work, Joe located the limits of good intentions in the space between unreasonable donor expectations and an almost apocalyptic portrayal of rural health centers. In his view, there was little room in global health for persistent and time-earned attention to local projects.[26]

On the one hand, the contradictions that Joe identified were scalar—processes of rapidly increasing and expanding the scope of programs were known as "scaling up." But they were also temporal, located between what Joe described as a seemingly nostalgic public imaginary rooted in "the glory days of Samora" and a future horizon marked by aspirations for "a completely independent health system, with no foreign support" that Joe saw as an unreachable, subjunctive future condition—as if it were "already 2030." Despite Joe's ideological sympathies, then, he seemed to see global health as precariously situated between nostalgic echo and future horizon, and his sympathies did little to change his practices now, in the meantime.

In his example, Joe illustrated how political and economic inequalities complicate the provision of public health via transnational interventions. Taking a perspective frequently understood as progressive and self-critical, Joe imagined a public future—"2030"—in which the provision of care was disentangled from the vicissitudes of intervention and in which NGOs no longer "call[ed] the shots" (Hanlon 1991). Such a position was not uncommon among thoughtful nongovernmental actors, as well as policy-makers, medical practitioners, and scholars with whom I spoke. Yet the temporal horizons of these critiques were often shaped by a sense of urgency (patients "dying in their beds") that both obscured the longevity of NGO intervention and disavowed transnational responsibility for the future. This book is ultimately concerned with an account of health work and care that does not rely on the disentanglement of institutions, the purification of public health, or the end of intervention, as in the dream of "2030." Rather, it asks about the possibilities that are made in the meantime.

About the Book

Ethnographic Locations
Over the course of my fieldwork, I interviewed, talked with, and accompanied medical staff (expatriate and Mozambican), community health and develop-

ment workers, and patients and their families. In Maputo and Morrumbala, I aimed to understand how the presence of new transnational medical and scientific regimes articulated with long-standing political formations, public health practices, and livelihood strategies. In both places, by engaging the disparate workers—such as nurses, psychologists, and data entry clerks—as well as the patients and family members that these projects assembled, my fieldwork traced how a range of actors moved between, sought help from, and made claims upon the dynamic and multiply-constituted field of transnational health intervention in Mozambique.

In Maputo, I followed the work of the International Center for Health Care, an AIDS care and treatment organization started in the year 2000 by faculty at a large midwestern U.S. school of public health. Operating in eight countries around the world, the ICHC provided visiting and permanent medical, psychosocial, and supervisory staff along with funding for resources such as medical materials, treatment plans, and protocols (as well as everyday clinic items such as computers, photocopiers, paper, and pens) in a dozen clinics in Mozambique, where most of their activities were funded by PEPFAR. I conducted fieldwork in two of these, an urban hospital and Clínica 2, a peri-urban clinic, following programs that included pediatric and family care as well as the affiliated community interventions that were tasked with evaluating, monitoring, and sometimes intervening in the "social determinants" of health such as poverty and with providing moral support for the ill.

In Morrumbala, I accompanied the Global Children's Fund, a European development organization that had recently taken on new global health practices, transforming itself from a broadly focused aid agency to a more narrowly focused medical organization. Supporting both the local hospital and community-based health programs, the Global Children's Fund, or GCF, similarly provided staff, training, supervision, and material resources to support AIDS programs and psychosocial interventions in Morrumbala District, as well as intervening in a broader array of community- and child-based health issues. Like the ICHC, the U.K.-based Global Children's Fund was part of a national pilot program to formally incorporate child and family-friendly health policies into Ministry of Health programs.

Ethnographic mobility—moving between programs as well as through and *out* of clinical and institutional spaces—was important for ethical and pragmatic reasons as well as for analytic ones. For instance, engaging patients and workers outside clinical spaces allowed for more wide-ranging (and sometimes more nuanced) conversations. These helped me to situate medical practices within broader domestic, social, and political arrangements, and also helped to distinguish my small-scale, ethnographic study from some of the larger scientific and clinical studies also conducted in clinical places. Following two projects and thinking across multiple sites also allowed important contrasts to emerge—in Maputo, for instance, "global health" often seemed to be the provenance of mostly white, transnational, well-educated and well-paid medical experts (see also Crane 2013); in Morrumbala, expatriates often played walk-on roles within a wider range of Mozambican staff (not necessarily "locals"), many of whom had come from the public health service.[27] It also pointed to commonalities. For instance, in both places, health "projects" assembled a diversity of often cosmopolitan workers (whether nurses, technicians, doctors, administrators, or janitors) and enacted a surfeit of relations (treatment, surveillance, exclusion, governance, employment, claims-making, or profit-generating).

Moving across my fieldsites, then, I have focused less on clinics and projects as bounded units of analysis, nodes for comparison, or instances of a top-down "logic" of global health. Rather, I've considered them as partially connected ethnographic sites. The practices I observed in Maputo mapped fairly neatly onto many critical definitions of global health—many clinic practices focused on select, diagnostically bounded conditions, emphasizing the provision of treatment and of medical expertise, and driven by HIV/AIDS care as a point of departure. By contrast, the care I accompanied in Zambézia was much more ambiguous or intermediary, informed by the development history of the district and of the organizations working there as they sought not only to tackle new medical problems but also to recruit new sources of funding and opportunities for intervention through "global health" projects. Thinking across programs and locations thus helped me to see how transnational and humanitarian biomedicine takes a global health form at some moments and in some places, but may also look more like humanitarianism, development, or public or private medical care at others. A multi-sited perspective therefore helped me to see how new and transfigured ways of evaluating, diagnosing, and responding to problems of poverty and ill-health were historically imbricated with preexisting approaches. As a result, this book highlights the *difference* it makes to realize development, welfare, and humanitarian projects through medical interventions. What does it take to realize medical projects within a global health rather than a developmentalist, humanitarian, or public health frame? What does such a frame enable, and what does it forclose?

Structure of the Book

The remainder of the book unfolds in six ethnographic chapters. Chapter 1 introduces GCF's community health projects as a means of exploring the entanglements of public, para-public, and nongovernmental health entities in Morrumbala. Despite the outsize impact of NGOs in the district, public institutions remained important, not only to patients and public health staff, but also to GCF. Yet the role of the state in the day-to-day work of providing care was not always or not only to provide health services. Rather, the state was often an important location for and coordinator of interventions, charged with making subjects and populations available for intervention. Because transnational concerns with global health have introduced notions of "vulnerability" as key means of distributing and accessing care, often in ways that depart from earlier models, this availability was frequently constituted in terms of epidemiological populations and humanitarian assessments of vulnerability. In a context of political entanglement, recognition by humanitarian actors came to be a central means by which patients and community members were "seen" by the state.

Chapter 2 extends this attention to community health projects, focusing on how ideas about "community" transformed local political and social relations into NGO resources. "Community" was a central concept through which global health projects were enacted. Envisioned and described as a seemingly "natural" social arrangement, community in Morrumbala has long been conceptualized on the basis of specific political histories. As a result, just as global health projects are entangled with contemporary political relations (as described in chapter 1), so too do they rest on political legacies of colonial rule and socialist liberation and contestation. For volunteers, "community work" meant mobilizing and packaging social relations in ways that were historically resonant, highly specific, and deserving of remuneration. Generating, mobilizing, and documenting community became a site of intense struggle between Morrumbala residents and volunteers who understood their participation *as work*, and therefore deserving of salaries, and global health projects that imagined community as a site of solidarity and voluntary labor.

While the second chapter highlights the longevity of state discourses of community, chapter 3 demonstrates the longevity of humanitarian medical interventions as well. Despite the insistence of NGOs that their interventions were short term, "not forever and not for everyone," the experiences of many volunteers, health workers, and patients suggested that NGO projects were in

Intro.1 Clinic courtyard on a quiet afternoon.

some ways "perennial" (Fassin and Pandolfi 2010), recurring frequently over decades. By drawing on historical experience of and engagements with NGOs, I show that NGO recipients demanded interventions that facilitated (rather than interrupted) the social relations on which they relied.

Chapter 4 focuses on the provision of food support to the ill in Maputo and Morrumbala. As food moved between clinic and kitchen, household and market, it illustrated how patients and workers worked to produce robust and meaningful forms of well-being. These forms of well-being went beyond a physical conception of health (a concern with the biological or bodily life) to encompass instead life as it is lived. In this context, cultivating health meant enabling and facilitating the relations through which the daily work of care was provided and nurturing the (often deeply gendered) bonds through which claims to care could be made. This work of cultivation was particularly important because of the ease with which organizations and projects arrived and departed. In such a context, relational labor transformed temporary interventions into future possibilities.

In addition to transforming possibilities for access to care, NGOs can also transform the experiences and aspirations of medical workers and the subject positions that medical labor entails. For many public health workers, new opportunities for employment coexisted with new frustrations and challenges. In chapter 5, I contrast the experiences of differently situated health workers to show how the transformation of public health is also remaking the aspirations, class positions, and professional hierarchies of medical labor and produces rapidly shifting professional identities.

In the final chapter, I return to consider how multiplicity is situated in relation to transnational investments. Through a focus on the informational and knowledge-producing practices of NGOs in Maputo and Morrumbala, I show that the multiplicity of medicine—at once public and nongovernmental—also produced important gaps in the generation of knowledge and attendant possibilities for care. In the end, attention to how care and medical resources flowing in one direction were supplanted by information and data—including ethnographic data—flowing in the other demonstrates that the entanglements of medicine in Mozambique are deeply unequal; those best positioned to make use of interventions are often those who are already in positions of power. Throughout, and in the afterword, I also aim to critically interrogate the role of ethnography and of anthropology as fields adjacent to and often deeply implicated in these practices of humanitarian biomedicine and global health, sometimes in ways that unsettled my analytical and ethnographic comfort zone.

CHAPTER I

Governing Multiplicities

Morrumbala Town, the capital of Morrumbala District in Zambézia Province, stretches for a couple of kilometers along a main road. Entering along the unpaved thoroughfare that connects to the north-south highway, the road passes a cotton-processing plant, an expansive industrial warehouse, and a small market. As it approaches the town, the road becomes busier and is soon lined with stalls, shops, and markets. The town's commercial center is situated around a crowded intersection, where *chapas* wait for passengers and dry goods stores sell clothes, agricultural supplies, bicycles, and food. To the left, the road drops steeply downhill past the old municipal market, housed in a colonial-era tile building, before descending to a small creek. It then crosses a bridge and rises again to the administrative part of town. At the top of the hill is a secondary school, newly built with European funds. The old boarding school that serves as a hostel for students from more rural parts of the district hovers close by, as does the community radio station. Behind these, the offices of the municipality are clustered together with the bulky Catholic cathedral, the police station, the Social Services (MMAS) office, and the district hospital, renovated with funds from a variety of NGOs and set around a breezy courtyard. Situated even higher up a small hill, the white wedding-cake home of the district administrator looks down on the activity below.

The offices of the Global Children's Fund (GCF) are here too, in a dusty compound between the municipal administration and the hospital. A large international NGO headquartered in Europe, GCF has been present in Morrumbala since the early 1980s. Ringed with a five-foot cement wall and accessible through a creaky metal gate, during the time of my research, the offices occupied two permanent structures and a trailer. The rest of the compound was filled with a small cement guest house, an outhouse, a garage, and a large warehouse, all set around a large, partially paved courtyard. To the side of the main trailer, a small verandah covered in green plastic sheeting had been constructed to provide shade for a set of wooden benches and worn plastic chairs.

It was here on the verandah that GCF community activists, or health workers, met each month with their supervisor, Violeta. Focusing on support for patients with chronic diseases and their families, the program was part of a national pilot program to formally incorporate "child-friendly" health policies into Ministry of Health spaces. The volunteers were residents of the seventeen neighborhoods in which the program operated, and they were trained to identify and care for patients with chronic illness, to distribute public health goods (such as water purification solution), conduct health awareness campaigns, and accompany GCF-enrolled patients to the hospital. Though GCF did not pay them for their efforts, the volunteers received small and intermittent subsidies and were given the material tools of their work: a T-shirt, a pair of canvas sneakers, a backpack, notebooks, pens, and a bicycle. In the absence of a salary, these benefits motivated many of the activists and were also a significant point of tension between the volunteers and the program organizers.

Benefits were also a point of tension between local health authorities and the volunteers who frequently accompanied patients to the hospital (as GCF policies encouraged them to do). Frequently, volunteers arrived at the hospital only to be told that the patient would need to pay for the consultation, tests, or prescriptions. As one volunteer put it, "We end up paying out of our own pockets, even though we don't have any money either. Because otherwise we are just wasting our time sitting there [at the hospital] for nothing. And then how can we make someone go home without medicine when they are ill, when we have told them to go there? In this way we are losing money." To these complaints, Violeta replied that the volunteers were not supposed to pay for patients. If the patients are unable to pay, she regularly repeated, they should be referred to the local authorities to apply for a Statement of Poverty, with which they can have their hospital fees waived. The complexities of accessing such a statement, or the fact that many hospital "fees" were actually informal payments, went unaddressed in Violeta's reply. Herself hamstrung by GCF policies, Violeta could do little in response to the volunteers' frustration.

How did GCF staff, volunteers, and patients negotiate the resources and practices of care that GCF made available in Morrumbala? How did distinctions between "local authorities" and "community actors" work to shape the forms of care and governance that GCF enacted in these encounters? What kinds of claims are possible in this context? This chapter introduces one NGO, the Global Children's Fund, as it worked to enhance access to health care in Morrumbala by directing patients to the hospital, extending community health programs, providing food support to the chronically ill, and expanding programs supporting children in the district. I focus on how entanglement with and distinctions from state programs and practices came to be a focus of many GCF activities and a central point of contestation among the volunteers who enacted GCF programs and the community members to whom these programs were directed.

When I began my research, I expected that the proliferation of nongovernmental projects to expand access to medical care would lead me away from public institutions and from salient political categories of "rights" and "claims." I imagined that, as nongovernmental projects defined and intervened in medical and social problems in new ways, humanitarian categories would override public health projects and social services. Yet, following GCF staff and volunteers, I soon found that NGO practices and public institutions were entangled in surprising ways; the story of humanitarian aid in Morrumbala was a political story, too. Attending to these entanglements, I aim to show how humanitarian *and* public forms of government come to be at work, together but unequally, in projects of making community health. As NGO staff like Violeta worked within entangled fields of governmental practices, time and the future became key means through which they worked to delimit care and to disentangle nongovernmental practices from imagined public futures. As a result, temporality was a key means by which inequality and exclusion were built into everyday NGO practices.

Being attentive to how public policies, actors, and institutions are entangled with—or inseparable from—GCF practices and to how humanitarian categories come to be built *into* public practices offers two important insights. It alerts us, first, to how political claims and practices are made *through* humanitarian words, concepts, and practices in ways that may narrow as well as extend opportunities for care. This is what I refer to as a *politics of multiplicity*, rooted in unequal, inextricable, and frequently obscured relations between public and nongovernmental institutions, actors and concepts. Such multiplicity, I suggest, emerges from the long history of nongovernmental intervention in Morrumbala District. Second, keeping the public in our peripheral vision as we trace the political life of global health also helps make clear how efforts to help "the most vulnerable" may fail to assist some of those in need—may sometimes, in fact, fail the neediest—as claims to public and nongovernmental services alike come to depend on singular processes of humanitarian recognition.

Locating Volunteers

One sunny May morning, about three dozen people, most wearing bright red GCF T-shirts, pulled up wooden benches and chairs in a semicircle in the yard outside the office. After welcoming the volunteers, Violeta asked who would like to begin. One of the volunteers raised her hand and said, "I told you about the problem we were having with the son of Pascua [one of the patients], that he had left home. So, we went to the house and talked with the grandmother, and with Pascua and her daughters, and we talked with him. He has already returned home to his mother's house." Violeta nodded in approval. Another volunteer raised his hand and complained that new volunteers had not yet received their "kits"—the backpack with basic medical supplies, a pair of sneakers, and a bicycle. A third voice chimed in, commenting that the bicycles in their neighborhood had been in need of repairs for many months. To these complaints, Violeta responded wearily that another program officer, Edilson, was in charge of kits and transportation. There was a routine quality to these comments; they had all been discussed many times before. As more volunteers trickled in and joined the group, chairs and benches were shifted around to make room for the latecomers and to avoid the swarms of ants that streamed out of the dry, cracked earth, climbing up chairs and benches, pouring over toes and ankles, sometimes biting and leaving large, stinging welts. Our location in the yard seemed to match the volunteers' sense that they were marginal to the organization, and it contributed to the frustration with which volunteers sometimes voiced their complaints.

Volunteers were primarily tasked with conducting visits at the homes of community residents who had been enrolled in GCF's community health and home-based care projects. These were most often patients who had been diagnosed with HIV/AIDS or other chronic diseases, and a typical visit was expected to last between fifteen and thirty minutes. In practice, since the enrolled patients were sometimes relative strangers and sometimes close friends, the content, tone, and style of visits varied; some visits entailed little more than a brief chat while others involved lengthy conversations on a wide range of topics. On arriving at a patient's home, volunteers and I would generally greet the patient and any family members. Chairs and stools might be organized or a woven reed mat spread on the ground so that we could sit nestled against the shady wall of the house. When patients were very ill, we might sit indoors, at their bedside, but for the most part, we chatted outside with patients and their families, inquiring about the patients' health and perhaps asking for medication bottles to see whether or not they were properly taking their pills.

Although GCF policies emphasized medical interventions, in practice most volunteer visits combined gentle surveillance (asking about the patient's health, for instance) with companionship and practical advice. Often, it was not only the patient who was the object of encouragement and surveillance. Family members and others were also pushed to take on appropriate roles as caregivers, and suggestions that patients might be excluded or marginalized within the household were cause for concern. Despite rules concerning medical confidentiality, it was not uncommon for volunteers to enlist the help of patients' relatives in caring for patients or performing other kinds of work. This work ranged from the medical to the practical. For instance, in one case, hospital staff asked a volunteer to visit a particular patient to find out why he had not been coming for his tuberculosis treatment lately. At his house, we found only his sister, who was hanging washing out to dry. "We are here for your brother," one of the volunteers announced, "we're here from the tuberculosis program to find out why he hasn't gone to the hospital. Tell him to come to my house when he returns." In another instance, at the house of a woman who had lost the use of her legs, volunteers organized the children to clean up a mess of dirty dishes and leftovers that were piled haphazardly in the yard. In addition, volunteers were expected to inquire after and help resolve any difficulties that might interfere with treatment or contribute to illness, including providing referrals to other public or nongovernmental services that offered additional support. In practice, volunteers most frequently referred patients to family members, suggested that they pray or ask church groups for help, and encouraged efforts at independence. Finally, volunteers used the social connections they developed through their work to help others. For instance, the adult daughter of a terminally ill patient asked volunteers to help her find good domestic help to look after her mother while she was away. Volunteers drew on their knowledge of other neighbors in need of work to help arrange a suitable person. In a context of weak social services and narrowly defined nongovernmental interventions, volunteers served as a social "parainfrastructure" (Biehl 2013) through which practices of care, medical goods, and institutional referrals were distributed.

As these examples show, volunteer work entailed a familiarity with not only basic medical practices but also familial, institutional, and neighborhood relations through which patients were identified and resources located. This mastery was particularly salient when volunteers were charged with generating "local knowledge." Community participants were important, I was told by program staff, because the volunteers "live in the community, so *they* know who is the most vulnerable. To us, each house may look the same, but they know what is happening *inside* the house." Yet even as community participants persisted in observing and recording health information about their neighbors, identifying and singling out the vulnerable, they often complained that their observations went unheeded.

Principal Cases

During one of GCF's monthly meetings, Pastor Tomás, one of the most outspoken and dedicated GCF volunteers, raised his hand and spoke to this question of recognition. To the issues already raised by his colleagues, Pastor Tomás added: "There is another thing too. We see things in the field, we report these things, and we are not heard." Pastor Tomás gave the example of a patient who had recently died. The patient's wife, Paula, was visually impaired and, now a widow, had been left alone with two small children. "These are principal cases for GCF," Tomás said, raising his voice:

> This man already died. He had TB associated with HIV and his wife is blind. The children are small, they are eight and ten years old, and they are already trying to do something to help the family—to carry bricks and sell plastic bags in the market, but this means they are missing school. I asked if they could become beneficiaries of the *cesta básica,* but [the provincial GCF supervisor] said that they can't. But this man already lost his life because he had medicine but he didn't have anything to eat. No one gave him anything to eat, just medication only. He died the week before last. The kids and the wife are bad. And this woman will die too if we don't give her a hand!

As Pastor Tomás described this "case," he was careful to emphasize the variety of ways in which Paula might qualify for GCF programs: her deceased husband's HIV status, the risk to the children's education, and their status as paternal orphans. In doing so, he argued for providing a *cesta básica*—a food basket composed of beans, sugar, flour, and salt, as well as soap and chlorine solution to purify drinking water.

Like many similar programs, GCF food baskets were initially designed to support HIV patients in the early stages of treatment and followed national guidelines on the composition and distribution of food baskets. In early 2007, food support policies had been expanded to cover patients with a broad range of "chronic illnesses," including but not limited to HIV. In keeping with national guidelines, GCF had adopted the language of "chronic illness," a category elaborated not only by the Ministry of Health but also by the National Social Welfare Institute, or INAS. In practice, however, GCF's food program was housed under the organization's HIV/AIDS project and AIDS patients were the most common beneficiaries of food support. This reflected both the comparatively ample funding available for HIV/AIDS programs, relative to GCF's other initiatives, and a broader practice of emphasizing discrete illness categories in organizing interventions and projects.

As a result of these organizational priorities, Violeta's next question for Tomás was obvious: had Paula already been tested for HIV? She had not, and did not want to be. This was not necessarily grounds for excluding her from GCF assistance; not infrequently, Violeta and her colleagues included disabled, visually impaired, or chronically ill residents in GCF programs. Sometimes, these cases were considered exceptional and the circumstances that motivated them were clear; a child with spina bifida, for instance, was included in the program after one of the GCF drivers, who had been named as the child's godfather, had advocated on her behalf. Many others, however, were unremarkable, including the almost twenty elderly patients whose GCF enrollment cards listed only "cataracts." Elderly and impoverished, these patients could perhaps be more easily seen as suited to the broad mission of supporting vulnerable community members with chronic conditions. It was often assumed in such "borderline" cases that patients were sharing food they received with the staff and volunteers who enrolled them.

Today, however, Violeta was unwilling to hear Tomás's complaint and, dismissing Paula's case, she returned to Tomás's initial assertion—that volunteers hear and report cases that go unrecognized by GCF. "We report these cases and we know these cases," Violeta told him, "but the donor gives until six months [whether or not they are better]."

"That is the problem," Tomás agreed. "We are working in accordance with the law. That is, with the rules of GCF. But we feel these situations . . ." Tomás trailed off.

"I'm not saying you don't feel it," Violeta replied sharply, adding:

We feel it too. Children usually don't have the *cesta básica*. Those who receive a basket are orphans who live with their grandmother. But there are children that receive who have a father and mother, or who have a mother, but we close our eyes to this! We evaluate the conditions in that house, for instance, if they live with an extended family—as in the case of [another recipient]. The provincial coordinator said that you have to see which are the cases in which it's possible to give. Everything is with a justification. There are even times when patients abandon [their treatment] and we still concern ourselves with the family. But GCF is not everything! It's just one project that could end. It's just giving a mouthful to give strength, to help people make an effort. *It's not forever, and it's not for everyone.*

Responding to Tomás, Violeta acknowledged that she was able to bend the rules—"we close our eyes to this"—as long as she had appropriate "justification," but she reminded him that GCF was only a single project, necessarily selective, and never intended to be universal or "everything" to "everyone."

Anthropological literature on transnational governmentality (Ferguson and Gupta 2002) has described how NGOs, over the course of the 1990s and 2000s, came to take up practices once associated with the state (such as providing medical care or poverty relief) but without the forms of accountability or aspirations to universality associated with public systems. Instead, critics of humanitarian governmentality (e.g., Ticktin 2011) have shown how humanitarian projects build selectivity into the distribution of care, privileging those who meet appropriate categories of vulnerability (such as an HIV diagnosis) while denying services to others. These perspectives help to make sense of Violeta's words; they demonstrate that when care and support are distributed as humanitarian goods rather than political entitlements, they are often framed in exceptional and selective terms. They require "justification." They are "not forever" and certainly "not for everyone." Moreover, even as Violeta acknowledged that the program sometimes included people who did not meet relevant, mostly medical, criteria, she also distinguished the efforts of humanitarian projects from more expansive government programs. Describing her work as "just giving a mouthful," or "lending a hand," Violeta expressed a view I heard stated by program supervisors in Quelimane and Maputo, by visiting European donors, and even by the organization's director on a site visit to Zambézia: "We are *not* the government; we are just one project that will one day end."

Perhaps Tomás recognized that his argument was not progressing, because he suddenly changed tack. In a more energetic voice, he exclaimed: "But the situation here is really the worst!" Referring to the intense hunger that often accompanies antiretroviral therapy, Tomás noted that "Even for people who are doing treatment, the very pills eat away at you. And this case . . . you know how our tradition is here: when people are sick, they are isolated. And this woman is not from here, she is from [the nearby city of] Beira, and now the family of the deceased [husband] want to take the house from her."

Hearing this, Violeta suddenly perked up as well, exclaiming, "Oh! They want to take the house?!" Then she continued, "Listen, you guys are the *authorities*! When it's like this, we have to *act*! That woman is going to *continue* [living] in that house!" Then she paused, as if conscious of her own transformed demeanor, and said: "But that is different than the *cesta básica*. You see that we have to treat each thing on its own. Do you understand?" Suddenly, Artur, an older and experienced volunteer from another neighborhood in town interrupted the conversation. With an air of impatience, he asked Pastor Tomás, "Is this because she is from the program or because she is blind? Because you should take this to the vulnerable children committee [in your neighborhood] or to the [neighborhood] secretary." Artur took a breath and continued: "Just take her to the secretary and put her on the road to INAS [the government social services agency]. But GCF doesn't have anything to do with this. It's INAS and the [neighborhood] authorities. . . . You should make a report to hand in to the secretary. The government has money for this, for cases like this. . . . Listen, you help them for two months afterwards and then you close the file and transfer them to INAS." Like Violeta, Artur insisted that this was not a case for GCF. Instead, he suggested, Tomás needed to take the case to the neighborhood secretary. The secretary, Tomás suggested, was responsible for affirming a Statement of Poverty, with which Paula could apply for support from the government social services agency known as INAS.

In response to this suggestion, Tomás looked resigned. "With these things, it's difficult," he said. The secretary in Tomás's neighborhood, Sr. Mavote, was not well liked; self-interested and difficult to work with, he was unlikely to provide assistance for free, something that Violeta and Artur surely knew. A few months later, Tomás would succeed in enrolling Sr. Mavote, who had tuberculosis, in the food program, thereby enlisting his support for other patients as well. In the meantime, however, efforts to obtain Statements of Poverty for needy patients were slow and thankless. The argument came to a close as Artur said short-temperedly: "Look, it's the responsibility of the volunteer to direct them [patients] to the neighborhood secretary."

Nongovernmental Histories in and beyond Morrumbala

Portraying GCF assistance as temporary and transitory, as "not forever and not for everyone," Violeta and her supervisors obscured the historical durability of GCF's presence in Morrumbala District, which dated to soon after independence. Both the town and the rural areas of Morrumbala had been sites of particular violence during the war. As early as 1980, GCF had been involved in supporting refugees from Morrumbala who fled the district's intense fighting to seek refuge in camps across the Malawian border. In 1986, Morrumbala was occupied by RENAMO fighters, and many residents moved to the bush, to Malawi, or to the provincial capital, Quelimane (Hall and Young 1997).[1] Even after the town was reoccupied by FRELIMO in late 1987, many residents remained displaced (Finnegan 1993). As fighting diminished over the late 1980s, GCF played a prominent role in government reconstruction projects— rebuilding the hospital and the local school, as well as constructing the first office of the Ministry of Women, Children and Social Action, as it was then known, to which INAS would later be affiliated. Not only did some Morrumbala residents thus have decades of involvement with GCF, but GCF programs predated many comparable governmental initiatives.

Although GCF had a particularly long history in Morrumbala, such longevity was not unique among NGOs. From groups of socialist-sympathizing *cooperantes* who came to support the new government in the 1970s and 1980s to humanitarian organizations like GCF that arrived in the 1980s and 1990s, war relief and postwar reconstruction projects provided an entry point for many organizations and actors in Mozambique. Many of these initiatives were mobilized not only out of a desire to offer impartial or apolitical relief to suffering Mozambicans, but also out of a sense of commitment to or solidarity with the socialist-leaning government. Following the World Health Organization's 1972 commitment to primary health care and "Health for All," the promotion of community health and a commitment to expanding access to primary health care services briefly became a cornerstone of public services and an arena for international intervention and support.

These commitments were short-lived. Beginning in the late 1980s, IMF-sponsored structural adjustment programs cut funding for public institutions, including health care. These policies reinforced and created room for programs such as those promoted by GCF, which expanded from emergency relief services into a wider range of development interventions in fields such health, agriculture, and education. By the mid-2000s, as GCF initiatives continued, a majority of their projects in the district focused on health interventions organized around responses to HIV/AIDS and to the burgeoning field of "global health" more broadly. Community mobilization projects once focused on public health were retooled to deal with HIV/AIDS, even as many of the projects continued to provide material supports (such as small grants or food baskets) to the patients they enrolled. However, many critics argued that, despite their new focus, "global health" interventions continued and even magnified some of the difficult aspects of nongovernmental involvement in international health (Pfeiffer 2013).

These tense histories were manifest in the trajectories of GCF staff, many of whom had been accomplished public servants before taking on employment with GCF. Violeta, for instance, had worked as a nurse in the public health sector for almost ten years before leaving, two years earlier, to assume her position with the NGO. Her immediate supervisor, Ester, also a nurse, had worked in the public sector for more than two decades, while Ester's supervisor, Reginaldo, had directed the public tuberculosis control program in the province. As was true of his wife, now an administrator at a nearby ICHC office, Reginaldo was widely recognized as a particularly skilled practitioner and administrator. His strong commitment to improving public health was evident in the energetic enthusiasm he displayed on frequent visits to the district and the warm greetings he offered to district hospital staff, many of whom he had trained. In many ways, GCF exemplified the kinds of brain-draining practices for which NGOs have been criticized (Sherr et al. 2012), and they were known locally to be both especially well-paying and particularly demanding employers. It was therefore almost ironic to hear Violeta and her supervisors articulating careful nongovernmental stances on the importance of the state and reminding Tomás that GCF's mission was to "lend a hand" while the government did the rest.

The historical overlaps between public and nongovernmental institutions and actors were also evident in the experiences of the community members and volunteers that GCF sought to mobilize. Tomás, for instance, was often recognized, by his colleagues and by GCF staff, as energetic, enthusiastic, and smart—one of the most successful and dedicated GCF volunteers. When the GCF program in Mozambique participated in an "exchange program" with a project in Kenya, no one was surprised that Tomás was invited to be the volunteer representative. In addition to volunteering for GCF, he also worked intermittently for government health teams, such as the mosquito spraying brigades sponsored by the malaria control program, and, as a pastor, he ran his own small church. On the edge of his property, next to the house where he lived with his wife and three young sons, was a thatch-roofed adobe hall where he held services each week. The son of well-respected *curandeiros,* or healers, who lived in the agricultural zone alongside the Zambezi River tributary marking the southern border of the district, he had converted to Christianity as a high school student. He told me that he was one of the youngest people to be made a church leader. He was a member of a number of pastors' networks and had previously worked for a children's rights program run by World Vision, a Christian transnational organization, which paid him 500 MT (US$20) a month to organize community activities. The same charismatic charm and pastoral interests that made him an excellent volunteer at GCF also shaped his involvement in a range of faith-based, secular, and public projects, aimed at providing care to the community around him. This range of activities also enhanced his standing as a pastor. In reaching out to Paula, then, Tomás drew not only on his position as a GCF volunteer but on a range of experiences, motivations, and pastoral identities. He also illustrated the diversity of pastoral projects, even fragile ones, that were available in Morrumbala. While Violeta's response to Tomás emphasized the newness and temporary nature of the community health initiative, the presence of GCF in the district and the individual biographies of actors involved revealed the deep historical roots of nongovernmental action in Morrumbala.

The Politics of Vulnerability in Morrumbala

In the weeks following the GCF volunteers' meeting, Tomás and I visited Paula a number of times. Seated on a wooden chair in front of her house, Paula explained that she had come to Morrumbala relatively recently. She had previously lived with her husband, Castigo, in Quelimane, the provincial capital, where he worked as a cook. A few years previously, he had fallen ill and, eventually, lost his job. Anticipating that he would soon recover, Paula and Castigo used the 4,500 MT (US$180) he received as severance pay from his former employers to buy cement to build on land he owned in Morrumbala Town. Paula found work pounding maize for her neighbors to raise the money for bricks, a sturdy wooden door, and wooden window frames and shutters. The house they built was large and comfortable, and they imagined renting it out for a good income when they returned to Quelimane. But instead of recovering, her husband became sicker. As Paula's persistently failing eyesight worsened, a return to the city seemed out of reach. Eventually, they decided to move into the house themselves.

The move compounded Paula's poor relationship with her parents-in-law, who blamed her for their son's illness, and when Castigo died, Paula's relationship with his family deteriorated further. Lacking familial support in Morrumbala and unable to manage on her own, Paula decided to sell the house and travel with her children to Beira, where she had grown up and where she hoped to find her father and brothers. Moreover, Paula assured me that in Beira "the government is not like the government here. They'll see that I'm a widow, a disabled person [*deficiente*], and they will pay some of my expenses, at least to send the children to school." Paula's plans to move provided more fuel for conflict, however, as her parents-in-law contested her ownership of the house and her right to sell it.[2] It was this incident that Tomás had relayed to Violeta during the GCF meeting.

As it turned out, GCF did not get involved, nor did they need to. Paula solicited help from the local police unit that focused on women and victims of violence and was directed to the Human Rights League's branch in Morrumbala, which argued that the property belonged to her.[3] In the end, Paula and her brother-in-law devised a compromise. Upon selling the house, for which she was asking 17,000 MT (US$680), she would give almost a third, or 5,000 MT (US$200), to her husband's family. She would use 2000 MT (US$80) to make the 185-mile journey to Beira together with her three children and her youngest brother-in-law (who would accompany them), and would save 10,000 MT ($400) to settle in Beira. In the coming weeks, I would learn that Paula had arrived in Beira only to find that her father had died the previous year. Nevertheless, she decided to stay on and look for her brothers. In contrast to Morrumbala, where she felt that neither the government nor her family ties provided support, Beira offered the potential for claiming care across a variety of registers, familial and governmental.

Anthropologists have explored how disease categories and diagnostic technologies mediate access to resources in contexts where institutions of care, including the state, are absent or unstable and where access to medical treatment is tenuous. Analyses of biological and therapeutic citizenship (see Petryna 2002 and Nguyen 2010, respectively) have demonstrated that linking social supports to medicalized categories of vulnerability, such as HIV infection, privileges some forms of bodily suffering over others. They show how people come to access supports—whether food baskets, medicines, or welfare benefits—on the basis of biological conditions rather than political rights. Violeta's concern with Paula's diagnosis and Tomás's careful mention of the categories employed by GCF (that her husband had HIV, that her children were orphans, that they were not attending school) illustrate how medical knowledge and humanitarian categories were central to the distribution of care at GCF.

Describing similar processes in West Africa, Vinh-Kim Nguyen (2010) uses the term *therapeutic citizenship* to describe how AIDS medication was made available to some patients and not others in the era before global treatment programs, showing that resources were "triaged" to those patients who best matched not only biological categories but also the social imaginary of good patients. These theorizations link, in Didier Fassin's words, "the matter of the living (biological) and the meaning of politics (citizenship)" (2009: 51). They illustrate how lives are accorded (different levels of) value, meaning, and legitimacy through biological, scientific, and diagnostic processes.

Reflecting on similar programs elsewhere, anthropologists have contrasted rights and humanitarian benefits. In his book *The Politics of the Governed,* however, Partha Chatterjee argues that many, even most, people in the world are "only tenuously, and even then ambiguously and contextually, rights-bearing citizens" (2004: 38). Rather, people are more often included in politics not as members of population groups defined in terms of multiple technologies of governmentality.[4] As individuals and groups come to identify with populational categories, they invest these identities with the moral attributes of community. For instance, if being recognized as a widow or an AIDS patient is central to the process of political recognition, membership in those categories comes to mediate or constitute one's relation to the state.[5] Moreover, in Mozambique, scholars have described how distinct and disconnected governmental regimes, including humanitarian regimes and transnational practices of rule and care, have become intertwined and entangled with local and national political forms (Santos 2006).[6] New modes of citizenship have emerged from this plurality of authorities and institutions (Buur and Kyed 2006, Gonçalves 2006 and 2013, Obarrio 2014), and some scholars have emphasized the multiplicity of sovereignty itself in a context where many formal and informal political practices extend beyond the state (Bertelsen 2009).

Together, these perspectives can help to make sense of how Paula's claim to assistance was mediated across a variety of state and nonstate institutions and by way of medical terms and objects (such as HIV tests) and legal categories (such as her rights as a widow) that aligned imperfectly. Paula's applications to

GCF's food program or to the government social services benefit were treated not as rights but as vulnerabilities. It was as a potential patient, a mother of orphans, and a wronged widow that Paula tenuously—and not very successfully—sought recognition of a multivalent vulnerability from a range of institutions: GCF, public social services programs, the Human Rights League, and ultimately family relations. These diverse terms, objects, and categories worked together to mediate her claims, but they enabled different kinds of political and humanitarian recognition.

More crucially, with or without an HIV test, Paula could gain access to both GCF and public supports only through relations with others—principally Tomás, along with Violeta, Artur, and Mavote, as well as members of the police and the Human Rights League. Among these relations, Tomás was central. It was through his advocacy that Paula might access GCF community services, and the public-NGO health assemblage of which they were part. It was *also* through Tomás's efforts that she might access the neighborhood secretary and the governmental programs to which he held the documentary and bureaucratic keys. In other words, in order to claim care, Paula had to be recognized (as vulnerable or ill) in the right ways by the right people (Tomás and then Mavote and Violeta). Claiming care required membership in, and had to be mediated by, a collectivity that was at once humanitarian and governmental. Because these collectivities were constituted in ways that blurred distinctions between public authorities and the state, enrolling as "a GCF patient" entailed processes of recognition that extended into both nongovernmental and public institutions. It was not as undifferentiated and individualized citizens but as members of a spatially organized, socially recognized, and ultimately vulnerable community that Morrumbala residents were expected to claim and access care—not from the state *or* humanitarian agencies, as Violeta suggested, but through locally situated volunteers who, like Tomás and Mavote, moved across and between these diverse institutions.

Representing Vulnerability

Paula's situation not only shows how claims to care are mediated by relations that are at once humanitarian and political. It also shows that the assumption that community members share social ties as a result of their geographical proximity misses how many Morrumbala lives were assembled by way of mobility. Paula, for instance, described how her life had taken her from the city of Beira to her grandmother's rural home to the city of Quelimane and eventually to Morrumbala. As we will see in later chapters, the complex mix of familial ties, financial opportunities, and legacies of violence that shaped Paula's trajectory were not at all uncommon. Moreover, assumptions that community residents had strong geographical and social ties obscured how women's trajectories, in particular, were often shaped by the expectation that a woman would live near her husband's family (and not vice versa).[7] As a result, efforts to assemble social and political relations in order to be recognized as community members and to make claims were multifaceted and often deeply gendered. Neither therapeutic nor community categories seemed to fully capture the flux of social relations that shaped Paula's life.

However, while the lives of residents such as Paula traversed geographical boundaries, GCF notions of vulnerability were highly spatialized. This was particularly evident in periodic "vulnerability mapping" exercises that GCF conducted in Morrumbala neighborhoods. A few months after the contentious meeting in the GCF courtyard, I accompanied one of Violeta's colleagues, Felisardo, to the Patrice Lumumba neighborhood where Tomás lived. GCF had constructed meeting areas in many Morrumbala neighborhoods, often open-walled brick *paiols* that created a shady, partially enclosed gathering place for meetings or for staging events. In the long-established and more crowded Patrice Lumumba neighborhood, however, there was little room for new construction, so meetings often took place at Tomás's house, where we pulled up chairs under the spacious branches of the tree that shaded his front yard or gathered together in the cozy hall of his small church. That afternoon, we met in the church, where Felizardo unrolled half a dozen large sheets of paper taped together into a large, six-by-six-foot square, and then distributed a set of blue, red, green, and black felt markers.

As he set things up, Felisardo explained the mapping exercise to the group, all of whom seemed familiar with the process. The first step, using black markers, was to map the boundaries and infrastructure of the neighborhood—the roads that marked the western border, the school and covered market, and the creek and riverbed that sliced the town in half. Then, using the variously colored markers, we were to begin filling in the houses. Black for houses in which people were "not vulnerable," green for homes of volunteers, blue for homes of orphans or children who are vulnerable—"that is, those who don't have a father or don't have a mother, those who are not studying, or those who really don't have material conditions," Felisardo reminded the group—and red for those who were ill. Because the assembled group included the members of both the child rights or "children's" committee and the "health" committee, Felisardo moved quickly through the definitions of vulnerability.

The rapidity with which the exercise started suggested to me that participants understood, or were assumed to understand, how vulnerability was being defined. It also seemed to be implicitly understood that they could identify local vulnerability and render it visible. When Felisardo had first mentioned the mapping consultation to me, for instance, one evening as we walked together to the local municipal hall, he explained that the committee members "know who is vulnerable, because they know what people's lives are like. So, for us," Felisardo said, gesturing to himself and me, "*we* see that *all* these houses are vulnerable." He indicated the houses we were passing, built of mud brick and sometimes thatched with reeds, unlike the cement and tiled homes in which he and I lived. "But, for *them* [committee members], they know that the children in 'Mario's' house eat two meals a day, but the children in that other house eat only one meal a day. So who is more vulnerable? It has to be that house there." Explaining it this way, Felisardo suggested that recognizing vulnerability entailed both local and comparative knowledge. Yet while Felisardo seemed to imply, through his example, that vulnerability was transparent to those who were "*in* the community," at other times he recognized vulnerability as a process of negotiation. Thus he reflected that I might find the mapping process interesting, since in the process of making the maps, "there's a lot of discussion about where things are actually located."

I first interpreted Felisardo's comments to mean that the discussion or debate would center on *who* was vulnerable to *what*. I soon came to see that the problem was not in recognizing but in spatializing relations. This surprised me. As the argument over Paula's case had already made clear, it was not always easy to determine whether or how a person or household might be considered vulnerable or to whom responsibility for the designation should accrue. Moreover, critical perspectives on development have offered harsh critiques of "participatory," "bottom-up," or "indigenous" models of NGO practice, such as GCF's attention to community mapping. Scholars have shown that these practices not only represent but also *create* local social worlds by constituting and arraying people, places, and things in ways amenable to nongovernmental action (Li 2007; Mosse 2005). In "mapping vulnerability," for instance, GCF processes left little room for participants to identify forms of vulnerability that did not correspond with the four-color schema even when lived realities seemed more complex. How to color Paula's house, for example? Was it the house of a patient? Of orphans? How to represent the gendered processes of governmental, nongovernmental, and familial abjection that had led her back to Beira? With their black, red, green, and blue pens, participants could not represent other forms of vulnerability, such as the ways that possibilities for work, life, and livelihood had been transformed through, and in the aftermath of, bitter forms of corporate colonialism and postwar economic restructuring. They could not render their neighborhood visible in terms unrelated to vulnerability. Nor could they spatialize their social and experiential worlds in ways that exceeded the municipal neighborhoods around which GCF programs were structured, despite the obvious ways that family and friendship stretched back and forth across the town, reinforcing and complicating the ideas of "neighborliness" that GCF sought to mobilize. The limitations of the exercise seemed numerous and almost self-evident.

Precisely because of predicaments like these, anthropologist David Mosse and other critical theorists of development have shown that participatory planning models often "turn out to be dangerous counterfeits," promising to offer a "bottom-up" corrective to top-down planning methods but instead serving to reinforce development or humanitarian interventions as sites of rule (Mosse 2005: 4). Though mapping was presented as a tool of transparency whereby GCF made use of the local knowledge of committee members, the forms that local knowledge could take—neatly divided into red, blue, and green houses—were predetermined in ways that did not encompass the variety and complexity of problems facing Morrumbala residents. Instead, the markers corresponded to and therefore facilitated exactly the kinds of interventions that GCF prioritized. Following Paula's experience, having witnessed not only Tomás's advocacy but also Artur's response, I imagined the mapping processes might offer a similar site for contestation, as committee members worked to expand or delimit humanitarian and developmental categories that matched only imperfectly committee members' experiences and those of their neighbors. In doing so, I thought, committee members might expand or contract the forms of exceptional care that GCF projects made available.

Just as Felisardo had anticipated, though, as the mapping session unfolded, the debate intensified over where to place local landmarks such as the creek and the road, with the artistic and spatial abilities of those holding the markers loudly criticized by onlookers. Yet as Felisardo had also implied, the discussion of vulnerability and the decisions about which houses to represent in what colors was amiable and disinterested. The group seemed to agree with relatively little discussion, only pausing occasionally to consider whether someone was ill, whether the children were orphans, or whether the household was in some other way in need of assistance. Expecting contestation, I found that there seemed to be a surprisingly self-evident sense of transparency to the process, as if the group really *did* "know who is the most vulnerable." I was puzzled by the contrast between this and the earlier debate, but my questions, when I asked Tomás and others about the process, yielded little clarification. "No, if you know who lives in each house, and their conditions, then it is just a question of including each one," participants told me vaguely, echoing Felisardo's instructions.[8]

Another clue as to how and why the mapping process unfolded so smoothly came shortly afterward, when I saw the maps from Patrice Lumumba and other neighborhoods taped up on the wall of the GCF program office. On the assumption that they were part of an ongoing project, I asked how the information was used. "Oh, in this way, we can see the neighborhoods we are working in," a GCF staff member named Wilson commented to me, "and we can send the numbers to donors of how many vulnerable houses there are in each category." In this description, the local knowledge of committee members was easily translated into a literally top-down view of the neighborhood and a demonstration of generalized need. Yet while some of the information on the map might be circulated to regional offices or donors, and while it provided a bird's-eye view of the neighborhoods, Wilson assured me that the information was not used to guide program implementation. For this reason, the stakes regarding the choice of one color over another were low. There was no "upper limit" to how many houses could be marked as vulnerable, and Felisardo and Wilson had little reason to contest the representations given to them, beyond assuring the basic accuracy of the map—that the creek was in the south, and the road was running east-west. There was little contestation in the mapping process because there was little at stake and little, other than the map itself, to contest.

Why then spend the time to generate the map? Many other, more accurate maps of the district and the town existed, and there were already many surveys of community needs. Estimates of HIV and TB prevalence, studies of access to prenatal care, and calculations of children at risk were constantly being generated by the government, GCF, and other nongovernmental agencies. Moreover, as a guide for intervention, the map was used only in the vaguest, most general way. Another way of thinking about the map, then, is not as an object, but as a process. It was the mapping, not the map itself, that was necessary. Along with locating and representing vulnerability, the mapping process also served to legitimate GCF practices "in the community," especially to those

1.1 Map produced through community mapping exercise, Morrumbala District.

who donated their time, labor, and social capital to GCF projects. By generating evidence of the very vulnerabilities that GCF wanted to address, the map engaged GCF staff and volunteers in the practice of modeling the vulnerable community in which they would later intervene. In this way, the map enacted and represented not just vulnerability but also "community participation" in a context where community participation was both a foundation of GCF's continued success and, as Tomás argument with Violeta made clear, a site of frustration and struggle.

Mapping and Making Community in Maputo

The programs I accompanied in Maputo also made use of volunteers and relied on "mapping" projects aimed at identifying and documenting different forms of medical and social vulnerability—from food shortages to orphan-headed households—in certain neighborhoods. Here, such renderings often *were* complex processes of translation, as volunteers debated whether a patient who had gone to work outside Maputo had "abandoned treatment," "missed an appointment," or even "recovered." Despite the epistemological uncertainties, this data ultimately became a key component of donor reports and a source of information provided to the Mozambican Ministry of Health. As in Morrumbala, practices of community labor and processes of community-mediated recognition stretched across political institutions and historical modes of governance. In some cases, these connections were quite literal; for instance, of the six volunteers I worked with most closely in Maputo, one was the daughter of the head of the politically affiliated women's group in the neighborhood, another was the sister of the neighborhood secretary and former socialist cadre, while still others were active in other party activities and associations. In fact, it was largely on the basis of earlier experiences with community work and neighborhood volunteering, often with political organ-izations, that these volunteers had been chosen. These structures and relations shaped and were reinforced by everyday "community" work; for instance, we took breaks from walking the neighborhood streets in the hot sun to sit and watch Brazilian *telenovelas* in the living room of the local party secretary.

The role of volunteer work was also distinct in different programs and locations. Unlike the GCF efforts in Morrumbala, where community programs were a cornerstone of medical treatment, the community visits I witnessed in Maputo were at best a supplement to care centered on clinic services. This distinction between (relatively) rural and predominantly urban models of public health reflect much longer histories of privileging "community" mod-els of governance in rural areas in ways that both extend services and pro-duce ambiguous forms of political subjectivity (Kyed and Buur 2006; Obarrio 2014). Yet in both places, by focusing on discrete "neighborhoods" framed by the boundaries of the national health system and its hospital catchment areas, a transnational apparatus of care did much to reinforce and replicate a national, political frame—rendering visible local residents, reinforcing local political structures, and producing public and national health data—even as it competed with state-making practices by transforming service delivery into a matter of humanitarian and transnational intervention.

Registering Vulnerability

That the participation of community embodied by committee members and neighborhood secretaries was important to GCF's activities—and that it was important for these neighborhood and political authorities to see themselves as representing and acting on behalf of a community in ways that necessitated GCF interventions—became evident in a final workshop. Held not long after the mapping exercise, this workshop, too, took place in Tomás's small church, late one Sunday afternoon. Tomás had run an extension cord from his house across the neatly swept yard to power a light bulb that hung from ceiling, illuminating the benches and chairs where we sat and the large flip chart that Wilson, the GCF children's rights coordinator, had installed on an easel next to him.

Aimed at informing neighborhood volunteer committees and leaders— in this case, pastors and neighborhood authorities—about child registration, the workshop helped make clear how governmental and nongovernmental political practices converged in Morrumbala. In so doing, it shed light on a lingering conundrum of the mapping exercise: why, if the map was of such little consequence, did anyone bother to participate? In considering the child registration workshop, I want to return to the question of how distinctions between government and "organizations" were enacted in everyday GCF practices. Mundane practices of mapping, representing, or registering communities tied GCF agendas, resources, and activities together with other political practices, including governmental practices of registration and enumeration and local relations of distribution, advocacy, and care. Thus, they worked to articulate—both in the sense of giving voice to and in the sense of connecting (Choy 2011)—diverse practices of government and care.

Writing "child registration" in large capital letters on the top of his paper, the workshop leader, Wilson, explained that the workshop aimed to address the importance of filling out and filing birth certificates at the Morrumbala municipal offices. Emphasizing the crucial role played by attendees in "spreading the word" about the government's registration campaign to their neighbors, he began with registration basics: "What is child registration? It is registering the birth of each new child, so that the government can know how many children there are in Morrumbala, in Mozambique, so that the government can know what is the population of our district." Volunteers and other members of the community had a particularly important part to play in the current campaign, Wilson said, letting people know that registration was free within ninety days of a child's birth and that it cost 5 MT (then about 20 cents) after that. After setting up the campaign in this way, Wilson emphasized the role of the organization and its volunteers in helping citizens navigate the state bureaucracy and comply with public regulations, thereby assisting the government to enumerate its population. A correct assessment of population size was particularly important, Wilson noted, because "if the government doesn't know how many we are, they can't know what we need." Referencing the floods that had caused mass evacuations along the Zambezi River during the previous year, he suggested that it was only through practices of registration that the government could know how much assistance to offer the district. In this way, the mapping exercise served as a classically biopolitical example of how governance operates by way of enumerating populations and individuating bodies.

In addition to these examples of population management, however, Wilson went on to suggest that registration was also of potential humanitarian importance. For instance, he explained, it was important to know how many children were in each house: "Because tomorrow there may appear someone who wants to help and in order for us to be prepared for this help, it's necessary to have a data base, with numbers, to be well organized. Since if they were to arrive and ask how many children we have and we say, "We don't know . . ." Well, then, they might just pass on to the next community!" As he introduced the campaign, Wilson had focused on the rights and responsibilities of the state and its citizens. However, in elucidating the process through which the campaign would be realized, he presented a different model of governance, one in which state practices (such as registration) facilitated access to an undefined, transitory, and mobile "someone," who might help, but who might just as easily "pass on" to the next "community." In a context where NGOs and "projects" made available important resources, from food to medicine to material goods, the implications of "be[ing] prepared for . . . help" were clear. Registering citizens was thus also a work of making residents and neighbors available for future intervention.

While Wilson's initial comments had been greeted with polite attention, the notion that governmental processes might articulate with nongovernmental projects of distribution seemed to pique the interest of a number of participants. This was underscored when he told the group that their first task today would be to select a "management committee" to supervise the campaign. An audience member and neighborhood secretary, who had been listening silently up to this point, raised his hand to get Wilson's attention, stood up abruptly, and said, "This management committee. I think it's a good idea. And one thing that the management committee can do is establish contacts with NGOs in order to get funds, and to do all the documentation associated with this. As well as registering children and making reports." Wilson nodded tentatively before Sr. Mavote, also present at the meeting, interjected, "I have a question, which is this: in the community here, there is Project RITA [a project run by the US-based organization World Vision], there is Association KEWA [a local NGO], there is Save the Children, there is Oikos, there is GCF, and there are churches. And they all support children. I would like to know whether you can mix all the children together in the registration or not?"

In their comments, both Wilson and the participants highlighted how practices of state registration converged with practices of humanitarian recognition and concerns over accessing the transnational resources that NGOs were seen to bring. Wilson replied to Mavote affirmatively that "we are registering *all* the children." However, he continued:

> We will prioritize the children who have not benefitted from other programs to make sure that everyone benefits. What you should know is that you are always going to be contacted from now on. Because in a community, *this* committee is the most important. Whenever there is a program— for instance, INAS [the Instituto Nacional de Acção Social, the government social services agency—they are always going to contact you to find out about the children in the community. While the child sponsorship program [run by another organization] just chooses one child in a community and supports that child only, we are registering *everyone*.

In this description, volunteers were participants in state-making practices, sought out by state social service programs and concerned with "registering everyone," but they *also* laid the ground for intervention by transnational organizations. In both roles, volunteers were encouraged to see themselves as mediators between welfare agencies and the vulnerable community—in this case, a community of children—they represented.

That registration lent itself to both government control and possible humanitarian investment became particularly clear when Mavote sought additional clarification about the universality or selectivity of the registration program. He explained: "There are already activists from World Vision and Save the Children in this neighborhood and—they are really working in our community, but sometimes they say that they need only fifteen children or however many children for their groups.... They might subscribe fifteen children, and then another program comes and they don't want to support those children because they are already on another list." Wilson responded:

> You already have the strongest structure in the community. That's why the neighborhood leadership [like Sr. Mavote himself] has to be here, and has

to be part of this. Because when organizations that want to help children appear, they go to the house of the secretary, isn't that right? They say, "We want X children." So now when you have this list, you will start with the first X children and then when the next organization comes, you will start where you left off. In this way, you will reach everyone without repeating. When PSI [Population Services International, an NGO] comes to distribute mosquito nets and you already have the list, you will see that they have 1,000 nets and we don't have 1,000 children, so there is a mosquito net for everyone.

GCF trainers thus Wilson surely recognized that this was a common way that NGO goods were channeled into personal and political relationships. Yet in his reply, he moved between prioritizing the state (by describing neighborhood authorities as "the strongest structure," for instance) and prioritizing organizations (by suggesting that the aim of governance was to access nongovernmental benefits). In contrast to Violeta's assertion that GCF was "not forever" and "not for everyone," in this vision, the role of state authorities *was* to ensure that "everyone" had access to a donated mosquito net, to manage the population so that NGOs could extend their reach, by registering an always potentially vulnerable community.

Locating Institutional Multiplicity

What happens when government is organized around and sometimes realized through the activities and actions of NGOs? What happens when humanitarian categories, such as medical diagnoses or categories of "vulnerability," become the grounds for governmental action and care? What present and future possibilities inhere in debates over the benefits and limitations of community health programs? In the arguments over Paula's inclusion in the program, and in the mapping and registering of Morrumbala's varied communities, it is possible to see how public and nongovernmental individuals, programs, and practices were complexly entangled in Morrumbala, co-participants in the work of making individuals, populations, and communities "vulnerable" and therefore available for intervention. This overlapping of multiple institutions, as nongovernmental and governmental projects become resources (though unequally distributed) for one another, is what I mean by *multiplicity*. Amid a proliferation of critical and practice-based discourses aimed at distinguishing and delimiting the state and nonstate actors, institutional multiplicity provides insight into how singular practices—identifying the vulnerable, registering

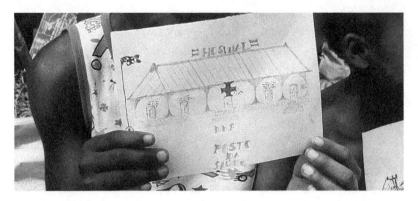

1.2 Drawing of a health post produced by GCF staff and children participants in a psychosocial support activity, Morrumbala Town.

populations, enrolling patients—are engaged in multiple ways, by multiple actors, to multiple ends. It makes visible how volunteers worked to identify individuals and populations in ways that were both governmental and nongovernmental. Institutional multiplicity captures how neighborhood residents, like Tomás and Mavote, worked, volunteered, and sought services in ways that crisscrossed public and nongovernmental authorities. And it reveals how Paula sought to articulate her claims to care across a variety of public and nongovernmental agencies.

By shedding light on how apparently singular practices, such as registration, or categories, like vulnerability, can be deployed toward diverse ends, however, governmental multiplicity also accounts for Paula's predicaments, as salient categories of governance and intervention are oriented through a relatively narrow, medically constrained lexicon of vulnerability. For GCF staff like Violeta, respecting the purview of the state in a self-critical discourse of restricted NGO intervention facilitated limited and discretionary care in a language of political solidarity. This political and institutional work of distinction, between state and NGO, between public services and private care, ignored how, in Morrumbala, recognition as a citizen often depended on recognition as a subject of nongovernmental and humanitarian action. As a result, the most vulnerable residents, such as Paula, were excluded from *both* public and nongovernmental forms of assistance as the relational and political work required to make claims entailed the same actors, the same notions of vulnerability, and similar processes of recognition.

Conclusion: Disentangling the State

Accounts of "transnational governmentality" (Ferguson and Gupta 2002) have described how NGOs may take on governmental practices. Such approaches highlight how, in Morrumbala, organizations like GCF have come play expansive and expanding roles in governance—for instance, as GCF comes to take on basic political work of registering and enumerating the population of Morrumbala through child registration campaigns. These forms of "humanitarian government," in which care is extended to the exceptional few, have been shown to be antipolitical, that is, to constrain political possibilities by framing questions of citizenship, rights, and belonging as moral and humanitarian, rather than political, questions (e.g., Ticktin 2011: 21; Fassin 2011). Here, for instance, GCF imagined the population as being constituted not by rights-bearing citizens or empowered voters but by children in need of governmental management, such as moving them from environmentally risky zones along the river, or humanitarian goods, such as mosquito nets.

In response to these processes, many accounts of health, medicine, and development in Africa have argued for the continuing importance of the state. Analyses of global health have shown how nongovernmental projects may rely on the very public infrastructures they are replacing (e.g., Biehl 2007). Scholars have noted that, in Africa, the state remains an important institutional and ideological force in the shaping of medical care despite the outsize impact of donors, organizations, "projects," and NGOs (Geissler 2015). Critics have highlighted the continued "struggle for a public sector" (Pfeiffer 2013), detailing how NGOs like GCF may undermine and complicate the provision of expansive and public care. In Morrumbala, too, it is clear that public systems and resources—including the networks of neighborhood authorities that GCF administrators engaged and deployed in their work, the INAS representatives to whom they referred difficult cases, the registration practices through which they enumerated neighborhood residents—were central to GCF's ability to carry out its projects. In a variety of ways, then, humanitarian categories and practices *and* governmental or public institutions and actors were frequently at work together, sometimes even enacted through the same people.

Recognizing the continued salience of the state, GCF staff like Violeta and Wilson frequently evoked the government as creating possibilities "forever" and for "everyone," thus making it "the strongest structure" and ultimate locus of care. While attention to the state incorporated critical discourses on the dangers of development, these discourses ultimately did little to furnish care to needy Morrumbalans like Paula. Instead, these explanations of "projects which might one day end" portrayed state services, like the patients GCF served, as momentarily vulnerable, institutions in need of "a hand." In so doing, they obscured how the very activities of NGOs may work to erode public capacities, invoking instead a distant temporal horizon at which NGOs were no longer necessary.

Yet GCF programs were profoundly entangled with public and governmental programs. They hired state-trained public health workers and relied on public authorities and practices to enact their projects. Governmental initiatives, meanwhile, relied on GCF to provide present and future services. These entanglements not only made care available, but also reinforced long-standing exclusions. It was the putative existence of state services that made possible GCF's circumscribed interventions, even as GCF volunteers and staff carried out both public and nongovernmental activities. Amid this political and institutional entanglement, attending to institutional multiplicity, rather than to the eventual disentanglement of diverse institutions, is necessary to understanding the resources and possibilities available to Paula, Tomás, and others as they work in the meantime between present realities and imagined public and humanitarian futures.

CHAPTER 2

Making Communities of Care

The city of Quelimane, the capital of Zambézia Province, lies a few hours' drive from Morrumbala, along a dirt road and then up the national highway to the north. Its modest downtown is marked by faded art deco buildings that hug the curves of the Rio dos Bons Sinais. Neighborhoods of mud, reed, and brick houses spread out across the low, flat landscape. During the time of my research, Zambézia Province was considered a key site for donor investment and development projects. In spite of fertile agricultural land and a long coastline, Zambézia had some of the worst development indicators in the country and few government services (UNICEF 2006), a fact that many residents attributed to the province's history of political opposition. It was also home to many development agencies, NGOs, and humanitarian aid organizations.

While these organizations targeted diverse topics, issues, problems, and approaches, they often relied on volunteers to do the work of implementation. For instance, GCF counted heavily on the knowledge and labor of community volunteers like Tomás. In Morrumbala, GCF recruited more than one hundred community volunteers across two dozen neighborhoods for health projects alone—in addition to those serving on children's committees or contributing to women's empowerment, emergency response, and agricultural efforts.[1] Moreover, it was not only GCF that mobilized volunteers in Morrumbala; two U.S.-funded transnational organizations coordinated similar health programs, while still others intervened in infrastructural rehabilitation, environmental risk management, hygiene and sanitation, and agriculture. All of these projects recruited volunteers, and most compensated participants through a hodgepodge of per diem payments, food baskets, and material goods such as pens, hats, or T-shirts. Such was the ubiquity of NGO T-shirts, in fact, that they did little to distinguish current volunteers.

I began to see the centrality of community labor to transnational medical projects early on in the research process, as I waited to get permission from the provincial health department to conduct research in Morrumbala. While I waited, one of my institutional workplaces was a tidy bungalow in Quelimane's town center, the provincial Office of the Program to Combat HIV/AIDS. With a wide, shady verandah and a few sparsely furnished offices, the bungalow was a busy place. There, at a spare desk with my laptop, I was able to conduct interviews, talk with the four permanent staff members, and occasionally accompany them on trips to nearby districts or to meetings and conferences in town. These routes and conversations helped me trace the institutional relationships through which NGO interventions were cultivated and coordinated, in state and nonstate spaces and "at the provincial level," in the spatializing descriptor often given to this small office (Ferguson and Gupta 2002).

Ana, a young lecturer at a local university who also worked part-time at the office, was particularly kind in letting me tag along with her. One morning we set off for a USAID-funded meeting on community-based care, held at the Hotel Chuabo, Quelimane's fanciest hotel. The hotel lobby oozed 1960s-era art deco glamour. But there was nothing old-fashioned about the top floor conference room, where bottled water was set up on a polished, U-shaped conference table. The workshop was led by Sandra, a stylish young woman from Maputo who worked for a USAID health policy program, and Reverend Francisco, a "health communication expert" whose pastoral background was evident in his confident and compelling rhetorical style. Representatives of about thirty community groups sat in attendance. Some had traveled from other provinces, while others were local activists and already knew one another; a majority of the participants were women, many in their fifties and sixties. The air-conditioning, beautiful riverfront view, and slickly packaged pens and notebooks seemed out of keeping with the mundane day-to-day tasks that we were there to discuss.

This chapter begins with the view from these offices and conference rooms, a "meso"-level or intermediary vantage point (Biehl 2007) well suited for teasing out how national policies and transnational agencies articulate and constitute their fields of knowledge and intervention. In a context where political belonging is mediated at once by relations, state structures, and NGOs, as shown in chapter 1, community was a key way that these relations were envisioned, represented, and enacted. It was also a historically rich and often contested site of political struggle and recognition. Although imagined as a preexisting "thing" into which NGOs could intervene, communities were in fact assembled through a variety of development, humanitarian, and government initiatives. Workshops were therefore not just opportunities for training volunteers; they were settings in which complex social spaces and relations were configured *as* "communities." In this context, community volunteer work did more than make practices of care available. It was also a process of assembling, labeling, deploying, and valuing knowledge and relations, a means by which volunteers struggled for political recognition and professional possibility, and a site in which moral and social solidarity was articulated (see also Prince 2015; Nading 2014). As a result, community labor provides a prime example of how the relations, practices, and knowledge through which global health projects are enacted are at once enabled by NGOs and rendered external to them. In the face of efforts to disentangle community work from the NGOs that mobilized it, health volunteers insisted on the inextricability of "projects" and the practices of work that made up community health. At the same time, they acknowledged the moral commitments (to friends, neighbors, or family members) that also motivated them.

Task Force

About sixty health volunteers sat around the table that morning at the Hotel Chuabo. They were affiliated with a variety of local and transnational NGOs, including GCF, that worked in four provinces. All the participants were active in care for chronically ill patients. Though their tasks differed from group to group and from patient to patient, most of the volunteers helped provide basic medical care and psychosocial support. They had gathered there for a two-day workshop aimed at soliciting volunteer perspectives on community health policies. The workshop began with an energetic presentation from Sandra, who explained that the meeting was part of a task force on community participation in health made up of Ministry of Health officials, donors, and staff of local and transnational organizations.[2] They would have liked to include more groups, Sandra acknowledged, "especially those of the base [or grassroots, like most of the participants here]." Unfortunately, she continued, "we knew that at this point it was simply impossible."[3] But, she hurried to add, there would be ongoing opportunities to participate in the future.

This opening, which spoke of inclusion even as it underscored the marginal place of the workshop participants, set an awkward tone. As Sandra described high-level meetings with ministry officials, it was hard to imagine that most participants would ever be or feel themselves included. Using jargon-inflected language, referencing meetings with ministers and department heads in Maputo, and dressed in stylish and expensive clothes, Sandra and Francisco put what seemed a gapingly large social and sartorial distance between themselves and their audience—many of whom were wearing NGO T-shirts. Even Ana's short hair and funky shirt and jeans were out of keeping with the staid appearance of the participants. When the facilitators spoke in rapid, English-inflected Portuguese ("You can lead a horse to water but you can't make him drink!" Francisco declared at one point), volunteers struggled to keep up. Only when Sandra suddenly described the meeting as a "task force" did the hum of whispered translation erupt into the conversation, as participants stubbornly requested a translation and insisted that "we don't know what it is we are being asked to participate in." Sandra offered "action group" and "workshop" as more familiar substitutes, and the meeting carried on. After this slightly antagonistic beginning, however, things got back on track as Sandra explained that the workshop was designed to "create a platform, a strategic document, that will allow us to provide better services to our clients," an activity in which everyone could participate.

In our first formal activity, community health volunteers were asked to speak about their current volunteer activities and the challenges they faced. Although Sandra had prefaced the activity with a concern for "service provision," it quickly became clear that most participants were preoccupied with questions of funding. Almost all described their desire for monthly salaries or subsidies. Some talked about how they had been trained to provide home-based care—learning how to give baths to the bedridden, how to dress or treat sores, how to help people in wheelchairs, and so on—but said they lacked the materials to perform these tasks: gloves, buckets, bandages, and the wheelchairs themselves. Many described problems of transportation and concerns with the time and effort required to visit patients in rural areas or to accompany rural patients to hospitals and health posts in town. Others suggested they needed more support for psychosocial care, such as additional training, access to food supports for patients, or resources to assist vulnerable children. A few groups spoke of broader structural issues. For instance, a participant from a neighboring province explained that his group struggled with the health assistants at the local hospital; they were afraid to talk to people about AIDS because their job training, part of an accelerated plan to rapidly increase the number of health workers in rural areas, had not taught them how to talk about illness. Throughout, Sandra listened impassively, taking notes and sometimes nodding slightly, but giving little indication of her opinion.

Because I had understood Sandra's instructions as emphasizing caregiving principles, I found myself frustrated by this immediate focus on material needs and the concerns with donor priorities that dominated the conversation. Yet I soon realized that the other participants had heard Sandra's instructions accurately, for our next activity was to find "a way to procure [donor] support" by brainstorming specific solutions with which donors could assist. For instance, if patients needed transportation to the hospital, we could ask for a bicycle-ambulance (a bicycle with a sling rigged up on wheels and suspended behind it). It would be easy to justify such a request, Sandra explained, because it was clearly necessary to medical care. But donors would also want to know more details about the request before they would fund it. Where would it be stored? Who would maintain it? By contrast, she continued, asking for a bicycle (as many participants suggested) would be more difficult since the purpose of a bicycle was only to help an individual and not a group. Even if it were used to visit patients who lived at a distance, it would be harder to secure donor support for this.[4]

By directly linking challenges and perceived needs to donor funding, workshop activities cultivated a vision of volunteer work as integrally connected to donor fashions and transnational resources. Emphasizing avenues to transnational nongovernmental funds, the task force highlighted how volunteer work and donor resources (including bicycles, medical supplies, and monthly subsidies) were connected, as volunteer work transformed the "needs of the community" into a potential resource through the intervention of transnational donors. For example, in response to the question of how to connect volunteer groups to "kits" of gloves, buckets, bandages, and other materials, one participant, who represented a well-established and well-connected local AIDS organization said, "You could develop a project [proposal] for the Ministry of Health and for donors. Or you can do negotiations, lobbying with [nongovernmental] partners, Social Welfare [Acção Social and INAS], and the Provincial Office for the Combat of AIDS. You can do a baseline study and find out what the needs are, then buy the materials—the problem is finding the funding." Other participants were less sophisticated about describing problems or the solutions they imagined. Nevertheless, the possibility of funding was a constant theme in the meeting, and, indeed, mastering the language of "donors," "projects," and "support" appeared to be a core, if unarticulated, aim of the workshop. As discussions progressed over the following hours and days, participants seemed to use the lingo of "sustainability," "capacity-building," and "proposals" with greater gusto. Even as Sandra articulated these potentials, however, the trappings of the workshop seemed to underscore how donor meetings, ministry offices, and USAID consultations were largely inaccessible to most of the participants there. The workshop thus illustrated how volunteers were taught to connect community labor to transnational funding flows—flows in which they were critically important actors but in which they were only partially included.

Genealogies of Community Volunteer Work

Why had I misunderstood Sandra's instructions when the aims and approaches of the workshop seemed so self-evident to other participants? My initial interpretation—that we were to focus on altruistic practices of care as opposed material resources—reflects particular definitions of voluntarism and community work. Many of these emphasize collective labor, mobilized for the common good, freely given, and rooted in emotional and affective attachments between the individual and the collective.[5] In this view, communities are assumed to be natural entities shaped by emotional affinities and a taken-for-granted sense of belonging, while volunteer work is often regarded as not just unpaid but antithetical to paid labor, motivated instead by the affective ties and affinities believed to underpin "communities."[6]

In Zambézia, these meanings and definitions have been shaped not only by nongovernmental and global health practice but also by long legacies of community rule and community labor deployed by the colonial and postcolonial state and by development initiatives. For instance, community-based interventions have been a central component of development projects over decades (Li 2007), but they were also mobilized by the colonial regime and by the socialist state. Although community volunteer work has become a central feature of contemporary global health initiatives across Africa, practices of both voluntary labor and community rule have been widespread in Africa since the colonial period.[7] In Mozambique, Portuguese administrative policies, especially in rural areas, installed and relied on "customary authorities" such as *mfumos* and *regulos* to enforce colonial rule (Vail and White 1980; Isaacman 1996).[8] These authorities were responsible for organizing workers to provide free labor to implement colonial projects (such as road construction), to work off tax debts, and as punishment. After independence, the socialist government banned traditional authorities, largely because of their association with the colonial regime, but community remained a salient political concept. Despite different terminology, rural areas in particular retained an emphasis on collective and community leadership. Later still, as socialist policies were abandoned amid the liberalization of the economy and political decentralization, traditional authorities were once again tasked with political representation at the local level in rural areas—a mode of political representation in which community was a central concept. This time, however, community authorities were incorporated into the apparatus of the state.

These changes produced a patchwork of political terminology, and new modes of citizenship and sovereignty emerged from this plurality of traditional, local, and national legal and political authorities.[9] In Morrumbala, for example, the rural villages where GCF worked were run by *mfumos* and *regulos*, while in Morrumbala Town administrative divisions were divided into "neighborhood cells" and GCF-mobilized "local secretaries." Despite the diverse projects that have relied on the terminology of community to mobilize local labor, however, community work has frequently meant work without pay. One GCF volunteer, for instance, recounted for me his frustration over many years of volunteering. "I [even] went to complain to the *mfumo* about this," he told me, "but he just said, 'Look at me! I too am here working for the community without receiving. If I could make them offer something, do you think I would be working here like this?" Thus, where GCF programs to target "the community" might evoke, in GCF's European offices or in presentations to donors, a vague notion of solidarity, belonging, or neighborliness, in Morrumbala community was a long-recognized political tool for governmental and nongovernmental projects alike.

Community is thus a boundary object or "traveling technology" (Laet and Mol 2000), traversing not only geographical space, but also logics of intervention (from development projects to medical interventions) and political institutions (from the state to NGOs) and acquiring a slippery "polyvalence" (Brown and Prince 2015) in the process. To put it another way, just as Tomás and Paula navigated multiple state and humanitarian structures, community labor more broadly was not a singular object but a multiple one, invested with many, partially overlapping, historical and technological meanings. For instance, in both public and nongovernmental programs, community was frequently invoked as a natural unit of social or political life and spatial organization to which interventions could be directed and through which claims could be mediated. But, as the workshop at the Hotel Chuabo made clear, community was also understood to be a specific, even technical mode of describing, mobilizing, and enumerating relationships between NGOs, volunteers, and patients. As a result, many volunteers were concerned *both* with caring for their communities and with accessing the resources that NGOs made available. And many of them saw "the community" not as a taken-for-granted site of emotional, social, and geographical proximity but rather as a way for NGOs, development agencies, and government programs to organize their interventions. Community was thus invested with a range of moral and political meanings including neighborly solidarity, party affiliation, political structure, and development practice.

Histories of Community Health

When I misheard Sandra's request on the opening day of the workshop, then, I overlooked how community care and material resources constitute one another. I also misread the long history through which questions of payment, remuneration, and resources have complicated and shaped aspirations to community work. Deploying health volunteers, GCF and other NGOs followed earlier efforts by government and international agencies to deliver medical care through local actors. As early as 1976, for instance, the Ministry of Health began organizing APES—Agentes Polivalentes Elementares, or Elementary Polyvalent Agents—to deliver first aid and basic medical care in communal villages and rural areas far from health posts. The tasks assigned to APES were more extensive than the activities of the volunteers assembled at Hotel Chuabo. They distributed malaria medication, monitored babies' weight and rate of growth, and referred severely ill patients to health posts. They were also intended to be agents of modernization, training rural villagers in principles of hygiene and sanitation, surveilling their neighbors' domestic arrangements, and representing the new state. These tactics reflected an international turn toward primary health care, as well as socialist principles. In many ways APES embodied the spirit of the Alma Ata declaration and attendant aspirations for "Health for All" promoted by the World Health Organization (Cueto 2004). Yet in the absence of substantive economic and material support, as international attention soon moved toward more selective approaches, and during a war in which affiliation with the state could be dangerous, the APE program quickly fell into disrepair. For a time, community health initiatives seemed to be relative afterthoughts among health programs. Through the late 1980s, for instance, GCF continued to organize small information campaigns on sanitation and hygiene, but most efforts were concentrated on building new health and social service infrastructures.

As global attention turned to the AIDS epidemic, however, the idea of using rapidly trained community workers to deliver basic modes of care was reinvigorated, and in the early 2000s, GCF began to focus more intently on care for the ill. Drawing on experiences in Malawi, Ethiopia, and Thailand, a number of national and transnational organizations—including GCF and the Mozambican Red Cross—began retooling existing community health projects, deploying volunteers who had previously focused on other issues, such as sanitation and hygiene, to provide home-based palliative care to people living with AIDS.[10] These programs became formalized, in the early 2000s, in the country's home-based care policy, which recognized and attempted to standardize the variety of nongovernmental entities that were providing care, most often through the work of volunteers.

Despite the formalization of these programs, their effects were mixed—standardizing and extending care, but also solidifying distinctions between NGOs and the public health system. In an interview at her home in one of Maputo's upscale neighborhoods, Judy, an American expatriate who had worked in health in Mozambique for more than a decade, recalled this period by reflecting on how NGO programs both sought to fill in and threatened to overwhelm public institutions: "In 2001 . . . [t]he Ministry [of Health] defined the programs as implemented by civil society because they didn't have the resources, the human resources to do it as a ministry program. We tried to design it so as not to overload [public] health personnel but, well, it causes problems. They both cause problems—overloading, I mean, sending everything through the public system, and not overloading; they both have pros and cons." On the one hand, promoting community volunteers as an alternative to the public health system alleviated the burden on overwhelmed public health facilities. On the other, this rerouting of care also contributed to the development of "parallel" systems that channeled resources away from public health. By 2004, when Mozambique's public AIDS treatment program began, NGO-sponsored volunteer and home-based care groups were providing medical care, food support, counseling, and psychosocial support to patients, especially outside major cities, and managing AIDS interventions beyond the clinics, offices, and hospitals of the public health system. In doing so, they both responded to and perpetuated the lack of public resources for community and rural health by channeling resources away from public institutions and into transnational NGOs and their local partners (Pfeiffer 2013).

By the end of the decade, volunteers were increasingly providing care to patients with a range of chronic diseases (from arthritis to asthma). For instance, the Mozambican supervisor for GCF's community health program told me that "home-based care came about when there weren't even anti-retrovirals, so it was designed to mitigate or treat opportunistic infections [associated with HIV]. Because there wasn't therapy, and there also weren't resources in the health centers. There weren't resources in terms of physical space, and also in terms of a lack of human resources. Now it's become a response to all chronic illnesses: to cancer, to TB, hypertension, epilepsy, and others, all diseases of long progression." As the program expanded in scope, it also expanded geographically. By the time I conducted my fieldwork, GCF volunteers were spread across two dozen sites in Morrumbala alone.

Between the early 1990s and the mid-2000s, then, GCF's community health program went from a small public health awareness campaign to a narrowly focused but more expansive effort to respond to AIDS as a public health emergency. Then it morphed again into a broadly focused engagement with "patients of chronic disease." (Eventually, as we will see, GCF switched its focus again to a concern with "health systems strengthening.") In the meantime, as community care became a response to this expansive category of chronic illness, volunteers took on social and therapeutic roles previously filled by paid health workers (and APEs)—providing health information, distributing water purification solution (sold by the international organization Population Services International at subsidized prices under the brand name Certeza), and directing neighbors, residents, and patients to receive help at the hospital or from social service authorities. By the time of my research GCF community workers in Morrumbala were engaged in an awkward "mélange" (Buse and Walt 1997) of activities—distributing goods and care, participating in trainings, maintaining or filling in for public infrastructures, and collecting and producing information required by NGOs.

Documenting Community Relations

Among this mélange of activities, generating and collecting data was key. While GCF programs tended to represent community as a "thing" that could be mobilized, empowered, and made use of, in fact the relationships on which GCF projects relied were often inseparable from the practices used to know, represent, and intervene in them (Barad 2007). Generating and packaging knowledge was central to the work of community participants, who not only were tasked with implementing many GCF programs but who also generated large amounts of data through which the NGO monitored interventions and maintained access to funding.

These data emerged from the relationships between volunteers and other residents, relations that included but were not restricted to GCF activities. Each month volunteers like Tomás and Artur recorded the number of visits they made and the activities they conducted, noting the name of the patient, the problems encountered (lack of food or medicine, problems in the family, health problems), and the type of help provided (referral to the hospital, to social services, to educational services). Each group of five to eight neighborhood volunteers then tallied the number of visits and submitted the totals as well as the original forms to Violeta or one of her colleagues. Although forms were supposed to be completed immediately after each visit, in practice, most volunteers waited until the end of the month, then filled them all out together, recalling or surmising the number of visits they had conducted. Knowing that I was always interested in the documentary practices that accompanied their work, volunteer groups would sometimes invite me to "come over and fill out forms." The resulting reports, a reconstructed guide to the volunteers' activities, were then compiled and submitted to the program staff at the central office (from where they were sent to donors) and reported to the NGO "focal point"—a Malawian nurse named William—in the local hospital. The original forms were kept in large three-ring binders in the GCF office.

The public circulation of these data via William and his supervisors was relatively new. For instance, Judy told me in 2008, "This is the first time that a civil society program is being monitored by the government and the information is even entered into SIS [the national Health Information System]." But, as the data produced by volunteers circulated unevenly through the Ministry of Health and donor reports, it became a point of bitter contention. GCF volunteers argued that that "we know that the information we give [our superiors] goes in the reports they give to the donors. They are making money from our work, but we see nothing." Some of the low-level (but nevertheless salaried) volunteer coordinators acknowledged this sentiment, saying that "all this information that we collect from them, the director puts in the reports; there would be no project if it weren't for the volunteers."

Data collection made clear that communities were not a priori things so much as compelling means of generating, labeling, and mobilizing relations and knowledge within particular economies of work and care.[11] It was also a site in which the value of volunteer work was articulated and contested. One group of disgruntled GCF volunteers went so far as to write a letter of complaint to GCF staff, noting:

> When is it that we will sign a contract with this program[?] [B]ecause the tasks are accelerating and the volunteer doesn't have time to do his or her work. Through our work there is satisfaction in the community. By way of your program we give social support and teach how to treat vulnerable children, the ill, how to protect children and even to know the rights of children. When we don't improve [our conditions of work] the volunteers will desist because *there never was work with forms* [fichas] *that didn't receive some profit* [rendimento]. *Imagine opening an agricultural field* [machamba] *without harvesting anything, would you continue plowing the same field or not?* [emphasis added]

On the one hand, by documenting and enumerating practices of care, data materialized what GCF understood to be the value of community interventions by producing metrics of care used to assess and manage the program. On the other hand, for volunteers, data and paperwork were seen as formalizing these activities as work, just like farming, and thus legitimating or reinforcing expectations of payment and reward.

Distinguishing Visits and Care: Disentangling Relational and Medical Labor

In addition to data, debate also centered on distinctions between "visits" and "care." National guidelines suggested (but did not require) that NGOs pay volunteers involved in home-based care a subsidy equivalent to 60 percent of the minimum wage in compensation for their time and efforts. Though a meager sum, this subsidy was an important source of income for participants in the projects for which it was available, and it signaled the role of volunteers as brokers between NGOs and the state (Swidler and Watkins 2009). Such subsidies, however, were restricted to *care*, defined in medical terms and encompassing the provision of medication, assistance with physical care such as bathing bedridden patients, and the facilitation of linkages between patients and health centers. Visits, by contrast, were understood to provide only social or moral support, and were not intended to be subsidized.

Even beyond the question of subsidies, the distinction between *visits* and *care* remained a salient one, and a central topic of Ministry of Health–run workshops. In Morrumbala, training sessions were usually held at a large guesthouse and restaurant in the town center; at other times, they were situated farther away, incorporating GCF volunteers from other districts. Short refresher courses or instructional meetings on specific topics took place in GCF facilities, including the yard outside the offices, in the hospital waiting room after hours, or in the community meeting spaces that GCF constructed in a number of neighborhoods.

Training sessions were arranged in a similar manner in Maputo as well. For instance, I attended a series of workshops in a small hotel and leisure complex at the edge of the city. A popular weekend spot for middle-class families, the complex had an air-conditioned conference room and a leafy garden surrounding a small, sparkling swimming pool. The community volunteers, who were collected by minibus from the peripheral neighborhoods where they lived and worked, would for the most part be unable to afford the US$4 fee to use the pool on weekends. This not uncommon discrepancy between volunteer work and the surroundings in which trainings were staged shaped both the tenor and the content of sessions.

Following a Ministry of Health–approved curriculum designed by participating NGOs, the training sessions instructed volunteers in basic aspects of medical care and treatment, including first aid, and familiarized them with treatment regimens for target illnesses (such as HIV, TB, and malaria), and psychosocial techniques for engaging patients and families. Paying particular attention to supporting, monitoring, and surveilling patients' adherence to medical treatment, the courses emphasized techniques by which to care for and evaluate patients' health but also to assess their adherence to a medication regimen. After completing their training, the volunteers were given a backpack of basic medical equipment to administer or use when necessary—including bandages, oral rehydration salts, and aspirin as well as water purification solution and latex gloves. Volunteers were supposed to carry these backpacks with them, along with a notebook to record each visit and the forms of care they provided. It was this medical equipment and the possibility of intervening to provide care that marked these volunteers as participants in a more technically sophisticated health regime, and transformed their status from *visitors* to *caregivers*, making them potentially eligible for the monthly subsidy. In practice, most volunteers left their backpacks at home, returning to fetch them if necessary. They did so not only because they rarely encountered situations requiring immediate care, but also because the formality that medical supplies conveyed lent an awkward air to the visits.

In addition to instructing volunteers in practical skills, trainings also sought to cultivate volunteers' sense of self in particular ways, emphasizing the importance of strong relationships between the volunteers and patients. For instance, many sessions began with pedagogical instruction on topics like "What is a volunteer?" or "What is an activist?" These questions served as a springboard to articulate competing and sometimes contentious understandings of the role of activists and volunteers. During one such session, participants suggested that an activist was the *"ultimo grau"*—the lowest grade—of the health service. Others agreed that they were "the person with the highest status of the lowest level, that is, the community level," while still others countered that, "no, we are just trash" and that "the activist is really nothing." The training facilitators earnestly explained that "an activist is a person who fights permanently for a determined cause, who agitates and moves with it, who has the cause in their skin." In telling volunteers about the history of access to pharmaceuticals, these lessons described treatment campaigns waged in Brazil and South Africa and emphasized the importance of access to medication. The picture they painted was one in which the volunteers sitting in a conference room in Quelimane were participants in the same struggle as Treatment Action Campaign protestors in Cape Town or Durban, or as Act Up protestors in New York.

An emphasis on the cosmopolitan nature and worldliness of volunteers was further reinforced by training them in everyday manners and mores that they would use to greet, engage, and communicate with patients. For instance, some sessions covered styles of appropriate dress (nothing too flashy or revealing); others addressed polite ways of approaching and entering a home, such as clapping loudly to signal one's presence before extending a greeting in the language of the patient or calling out, "Excuse me!" in Portuguese (*Da licença!*). This attention to everyday and even commonsense ways of being emphasized the potential distinction and social gap between volunteers or activists and the patients they served. These distinctions were further accentuated by comments that explicitly distinguished the volunteers' medical know-how from the lack of information the patients were assumed to have; one trainer, for instance, acknowledged that there are subtleties of care "that *we* know but that we don't share with the patient."

However, even as training sessions emphasized that participating in NGO projects facilitated transnational attachments between volunteers in Quelimane, Morrumbala, or Maputo and cosmopolitan cities and countries around the world, the volunteers were also exhorted to feel a sense of solidarity with the patients for whom they would care. Emphasis was placed on volunteers assumed implicit knowledge and understanding of community belonging and experiences. Through rhetorical questions such as "*Who* is the community?" facilitators explained that "*we* are the community. So when we say we are working for the community, we are working for ourselves." Volunteers were thus awkwardly and ambiguously positioned—at once separate from and simultaneously "of" the community. This formulation, written into the facilitator's manual, reflected a vision of community as a site of solidarity rooted in geographical and social proximity and served with an entrepreneurial twist. Such a view overlooked how "community" has long been a technology of rural governance in Mozambique. Since the colonial period, being governed as a member of the community has almost always meant that one is rural and poor (Burr and Kyed 2006). In this context, then, to work for the community has most often *not* implied working "for oneself" but rather serving as an instrument of governance linking objects of governmental programs to the state. To the extent that volunteers agitated to claim rights—as suggested by training in activism and volunteerism—it was not to claim a "right to health" and to demand pharmaceutical treatment from a recalcitrant state as suggested by analogies with South Africa and Brazil (Fassin 2007; Robins 2006).[12] Rather, they struggled to claim wages, benefits, and even food from humanitarian, development, and welfare organizations whose projects relied on their unpaid labor to distribute goods as well as to collect and generate data.

Who Are Community Volunteers?

From the perspective of GCF, communities were locally rooted *and* efficiently replicable across diverse project sites within and beyond Mozambique. Community volunteers were thus at once universal actors, who could be mobilized across a variety of projects, and locally situated, said to have special insight into the lives and needs of those around them. In keeping with this understanding, GCF aimed to recruit exemplary "community members" for work as volunteers. Some of this recruitment happened through public meetings in which information was distributed about GCF initiatives and attendees could nominate potential volunteers who met the criteria for participation. For instance, volunteers were required to be literate and to speak Portuguese. They were expected to master basic medical information and to demonstrate a commitment to biomedical principles over other forms of healing (a case in which a volunteer espoused and encouraged the use "traditional" medicine—

da Saúde" or part of the health establishment. Still others were nominated by neighborhood authorities on the basis of their social involvement in the neighborhood, their influential position, their connection to influential families, or simply their willingness to participate.

The therapeutic communities imagined (and partially constituted) by the community health program thus partly converged with participation in churches, political associations, and other governmental and nongovernmental groups. Rather than a diffuse sense of community as a site of belonging, many volunteers were successful precisely because of long institutional and organizational experience. Dona Carlota, for instance, was a short, plump, outspoken woman in her mid-forties. She had moved from the Maganja da Costa District on the Zambézian coast to dusty Morrumbala with her husband, an elementary school principal, when he had been assigned by the Department of Education to run a school there. Chatty and bossy, she was a wonderful guide through Morrumbala, and often on Sundays she and I would take long walks out of town, visiting friends of hers or viewing scenic spots nearby. In addition to working with GCF, Carlota was very involved in the Organization of Mozambican Women, and she was a remarkably dedicated volunteer, constantly on the go and committed to visiting and assisting neighbors. Violeta and her colleagues often assigned "difficult" or "critical" cases to Carlota, directing her to people who seemed especially in need of help or particularly resistant to intervention. Along with Tomás, Carlota was often asked by GCF staff to meet visiting supervisors, donors, or potential funders—to be the "face" of the Morrumbala volunteers. Her enthusiasm and evident competence was reassuring and inspiring to those responsible for these programs and their funding.

Watching Carlota at work, I was struck by her ability to help patients navigate not only GCF resources—for instance, the persistence with which she encouraged supervisors to enroll certain patients in the food program—but additional resources as well. She had an expansive working knowledge of other NGO programs in the district (and the kinds of benefits they might offer in response to an array of diagnoses and development categories) and a knack for directing people to INAS and other public services. This facility had little to do with localized community relations, however; it was rather the result of long-accumulated experience—not only as a GCF volunteer but also, previously, as an INAS representative, first in Maganja da Costa and then in Morrumbala. Eventually, Carlota left her position with government social service programs, which offered meager subsidies that were frequently delayed or diverted, for GCF—which, while offering no formal subsidies, nevertheless provided sometimes substantial benefits and perks. Volunteers received small subsidies during trainings and workshops, as well as access to medical supplies. Through these informal and intermittent benefits, volunteer work for nongovernmental organizations became more financially sustainable—or *potentially* so—than similar work in the public sector.

Carlota's success at GCF thus points to the complex relationship between volunteers and "the community" that they were expected to both represent and intervene in. On the one hand, it was as members of the community that volunteers were assumed to have the social relations and networks through which they could implement health projects. On the other hand, it was frequently proximity not to an abstractly imagined community but to networks of funding, possibilities for training, and previous nongovernmental, governmental, pastoral, and political experience that actually facilitated community labor and the distribution of care and goods. Carlota's experience also illustrates how a changing political, economic, and historical context shaped the way volunteers achieved recognition for their efforts. For Carlota, older and more experienced than many volunteers, work at GCF was a nongovernmental extension of commitments rooted in the church and in state and party structures, such as INAS and OMM.

By comparison, few of her younger colleagues shared this explicit involvement with Frelimo, and many were more involved in new evangelical churches than in the Catholic church that Carlota attended. Chatting with a group of young men who volunteered with GCF, for instance, I asked them what they hoped to get out of the experience. One of them, Jorge, had recently written a letter of complaint to his supervisor, arguing that the patients he counseled ignored his advice; his letter concluded concisely: "I am *sick* of counseling these people!" Another wrote a note complaining that he had been reprimanded by the health staff at the local hospital. "Meus chefes," his note began, "My bosses, please, if you do not come on the day that you have promised to take this patient to the hospital, I am not going there anymore. Because to come without the patient, I will not be given any more medications as the *técnico de medicina* [medical technician at the hospital] has already said."

Why, then, did volunteers persist? What did they hope to achieve? For some, especially younger volunteers and particularly young men, emotional commitments were inseparable from aspirations to professional advancement. "We do this for the community," Jorge explained. "My wife is one of the patients [served by the program]." Far from an abstract and impersonal set of relations, community was for Jorge inseparable from emotional ties and com-mitments. "But," he continued, "also because one day maybe we will receive [payment] for this. For instance, if they need people as *serventes* [maintenance staff] in the hospitals, they will see that this one has already had this ser-vice, is already familiar with the subject, and has some knowledge, so they will call us." His colleagues suggested that maybe the NGO itself would hire them. To my knowledge, with one exception, these aspirations were almost never fulfilled. To the contrary, it was more often experience within the public sector—as in the case of Carlota, Violeta, and many GCF staff—that enabled nongovernmental work. Yet within a humanitarian economy where NGOs and the state offered financial benefits and security, Jorge saw that volunteer work offered a step in the right direction. In the meantime, volunteers received free T-shirts, a notebook, and a backpack, and the possibility of spending one's time in pursuits more cosmopolitan than farming. In doing so, they also real-ized the wider neighborhood aims of GCF's interventions. Personal, financial, moral, and community commitments thus converged in the work of Jorge and others.

Incidental Incentives

It was not only Jorge who complained about volunteer work and the forms of recognition that volunteers struggled to achieve. As Tomás told me in a con-versation late one afternoon, as we watched Zimbabwean music videos with his kids, "Since last year we have been promised these incentives and they are not materializing." This was perhaps the most common topic of complaint among the volunteers. Chico, a young volunteer from the 21 de Julho neigh-borhood, and his wife, Bea, told me that "even our neighbors and friends don't believe us when we say we don't receive anything for this work. If they do [believe us], they make fun of us. They say, 'The war is over, man [*pá*]. No one works for free anymore.' Even when a rich man in the market asks someone to carry his packages for him, at the end, that person expects a little something. And we are working here for nothing?!"

As we spoke, Chico described the physically difficult, even repugnant, work that they were expected to perform: for instance, attending to patients who might vomit or have diarrhea, whose skin might be covered with sores, or who might need to be physically carried to the hospital. I was sympathetic with Chico's complaint—it was hard not to be—but I also knew that Chico was frus-trated with his lot in life. Sharp-witted and charismatic, he had received a fellowship to study in Quelimane and had been selected by the Department of Education to continue his studies abroad. Yet this opportunity had never materialized, and he had returned to Morrumbala. He was bored and frustrated at the prospect of a life of farming. Compounding this, Bea had yet to get pregnant, though they had been married for a few years by the time I met them, and the inability to have a child clearly troubled them. While they often joked and interacted affectionately, sharing a wry and critical sense of humor and lavishing attention on Bea's sweet four-year-old niece, they also fought frequently about Chico's heavy drinking. On a couple of occasions, Bea had thrown him out of the house they shared.

I therefore first heard Chico's complaint in the context of what I understood to be his broader financial and personal struggles. Yet only a few days later, Tomás, who seemed so exemplary of volunteer sentiment, repeated and extended this concern. "People are getting suspicious," he said. "They see that the patients are getting fatter, the staff at the organization are getting fatter. It is only us who are not getting anything. They are even promising to go on strike! They say, 'The war is over. No one works for free anymore.' That's why they're talking about a strike. They say, 'All the cars will have to stop out there on the road because we will be there with knives and machetes protesting against GCF.'" Tomás's comments not only drew on recent media images of riots and strikes that had rocked Mozambican cities (Bertelsen 2016). Through common idioms of "eating" and "getting fat," he alluded to the ways in which NGOs were seen as a common source of wealth, enriching the lucky few at the expense of others (see also Smith 2014), and showed how volunteers were excluded from accessing resources that they themselves "facilitated."[13] He also brought together how patients' recuperation, especially from medical crises associated with HIV, is evident as they regain weight, supported both by pills from the hospital—pills that volunteers help them to access—and by the food baskets that GCF provides. Meanwhile, GCF staff lived in conditions of (relative) comfort, with multiroom brick houses, motorbikes, televisions, and freezers. Volunteers alone seemed to work without reward.

As Tomás concluded his condemnation of these inequalities, he adopted a more conciliatory tone, adding, "It is not that the volunteers here really want to stop working, but these patients, they don't have a family, they don't have anything, and when they see the activist arrive, he is already their family, so we want this to be recognized." He thus contrasted the violent imagery of machete-wielding strikers with an affective language of kinship to underscore the value of volunteers' relational labor. In a context where much of the volunteers' work entailed making and maintaining social relations, Tomás both naturalized those relations in a language of family and asserted their value as the products of labor and as integral to GCF's aims.

The Politics of Lunch

Among the many critiques of GCF policies regarding reimbursement and compensation, perhaps the most pointed were reserved for complaints about workshops and seminars. In June, for instance, Carlota stood up at a monthly meeting to tell Violeta:

> The subject I want to discuss is this thing of subsidies for the training workshop. The volunteers are really complaining about this. Because we know that during the training, those who came from out of town received a per diem, or they received meals for free, and these things, and those of us who live in the town, we didn't receive this. But we were also not going to our fields; we were leaving our families at home too. And this difference was made very clear, *very* clear, at the end of the workshop when the trainers said: "Those who are from out of town come and talk to us afterward [to receive the subsidy]." That *hurt!* It would be better to hear about it afterward and not to see it in front of you like that. This is really the source of discontent among the volunteers.

In the training sessions to which Carlota referred, volunteers who had traveled for the training had been reimbursed a total of 250 MT a day (approximately US$10) for the initial ten-day workshop, while those who lived in town received only meals and snacks during the workshop and returned home at night. Subsequent sessions did not provide volunteers with per diems but covered all the costs of meals and hotel rooms for volunteers from out of town; again, those who were local returned home at the end of the day and therefore received only breakfast, lunch, and snacks. These disparities in the treatment of volunteers from different areas were the object of Carlota's complaint.

Carlota was far from alone in her concern with compensation during workshops. Participation in workshops, seminars, and training sessions—and the meals, snacks, and sodas and, often, per diems that came with them—constituted an important "incentive" for volunteer work. Seemingly "incidental" expenses were anything but, since they were often explicitly understood by staff and volunteers as a motivation for undertaking the work of community health and not only as compensation for travel expenses. Moreover, the supplement of a few dollars per day served as a crucial means of accessing cash for volunteers without regular sources of paid income. At many workshops and training sessions, volunteers also received material gifts, including pens and notebooks, and sometimes other markers of participation such as certificates of completion. Though these items were of little direct material value, in a context where establishing oneself as eligible and appropriate for volunteer work was one of few avenues to accessing the transnational economy of aid on which many incomes relied, such certificates and emblems of training and certification were important.

Even smaller benefits associated with workshops, such as the provision of meals and snacks, became both a resource to be redeployed and a site in which broader claims to salaries and subsidies could be articulated. During meals, for instance, many of the female volunteers discretely wrapped some portion of the ample lunch in a napkin. So concealed, half a chicken, a plate of French fries, or even a small salad might be secured in purses or plastic bags; sodas were decanted into empty screw-top water bottles and taken home. Marta, one of the most outgoing volunteers, turned to me as she put her lunch in a plastic bag she'd brought with her and said, pointedly, "I can't enjoy eating this when I know the kids are at home [without lunch]." I took this comment as both an explanation of her actions and an assertion, letting me know that many people depended on the unpaid labor she provided to GCF and to her household.

Contests over subsidies, reimbursement, and remuneration persisted, and were persistently complicated by the vision of volunteer work as a grass-roots expression of social solidarity. Thus, workshop participants sought to learn not how to *care*, but how to access the *resources* of care; community groups attempted to create "partnerships" that would bring new resource possibilities; volunteers wanted access to per diems and reimbursements. In all of these cases, assumptions about the taken-for-granted and natural bonds of community foreclosed demands for compensation articulated by unpaid workers. Yet by insisting on an economy of care in which voluntary work was essential and integral to global health, volunteers embedded their activities in transnational processes of exchange. Just as patients and volunteers relied on nongovernmental and public resources for health, so did nongovernmental actors rely on community labor to enact projects, realize interventions, gather data, and collect "names" and "faces." The politics of lunch were thus but a small instance in which the unequal relations of exchange that underpinned "community" labor came subtly to the fore.

Per Diem Economies

An emphasis on per diems was true not only of volunteer work but of the health sector more generally. Implemented in the wake of public restructuring that drastically cut health sector salaries, per diems became a means for NGOs and other health system partners to "top up" the untenably low salaries earned by public sector workers (Pfeiffer 2003). Analyses of "the per diem problem" in Mozambique (Pfeiffer 2004)[14] have shown how closely the emergence of a per diem economy tracked the restructuring of the health sector and how the proliferation of per diem–accompanied training sessions, seminars, and workshops—a proliferation jokingly referred to as *seminarite* or seminar-itis (Pfeiffer 2004)—disrupted the everyday work of the health system. Personnel sought to maximize their participation in training sessions and workshops at the expense of their regular tasks, and it became increasingly difficult to conduct workshops without resources for per diems, meals, and perks, even when training sessions were held in the regular place of work. Per diems, as seen at GCF and in the view of critics, became a precondition for recruiting local partners.

Yet workshops proliferated not only because of the demand for per diems on the part of participants; they also reflected larger trends in how transnational medical interventions were structured in Mozambique (Pfeiffer 2003) and in the financial flows that accompanied these interventions (Conteh and Kingori 2010). In many ways, workshops and training sessions were a "supply-driven" phenomenon, meeting the needs of donors and NGOs. As anthropologist Vinh-Kim Nguyen has shown, amid economistic health regimes that valued efficiency, efficacy, and quantifiability, it was not only public institutions that were expected to demonstrate lean financial practices. Rather, with the "advent of a flexible model of NGO-driven development," workshops met the needs of NGOs that had to dedicate expenditures to program activities rather than overhead, infrastructure, salary support, or social programs. They were frequently "required to rely on paid consultants because precarious funding made it impossible to hire local paid staff" (Nguyen 2010: 41).[15] While per diems became a means of survival for public servants in the wake of economic restructuring wrought by structural adjustment, similar dynamics impacted NGO employees and consultants as donors and aid regimes increasingly emphasized organizational adaptability and low overhead costs (including salaries). In this context, volunteers' expectations regarding compensation through perks and per diems were very much in keeping with the conditions of medical and nongovernmental labor more broadly.

Workshops therefore met the needs and expectations of local participants while also accommodating the desires of organizations such as GCF. As Daniel Jordan Smith notes, workshops are compelling development practices precisely because they allow diverse actors to accomplish their own aims, even when they may be at odds with one another. For NGO staff, for instance, workshops provide an opportunity to engage in concrete and reportable "capacity building" activities and to count "outputs" in quantifiable and standardized ways (Smith 2003). These have become increasingly important markers of the success of NGO activities in an era of metric-driven and quantitative analyses (Erikson 2012). Yet workshops also facilitate the redistribution of resources, social connections, and markers of knowledge and expertise, and may allow local participants to build up social and patronage networks as they accumulate per diems, bags, T-shirts, and other goods that they can distribute through their social ties and networks. Smith notes that "because workshops accommodate both Western and [local] priorities, different as they are, training is something that donors and host country partners readily agree on" (2003: 713).

In Morrumbala, complaints about trainings and seminars speak to their central role in NGO practices of compensation, making visible the material inequalities through which nongovernmental practices of unequal "partnership" are enacted between NGOs, communities, and the health system (Crane 2013). Though they also provided useful skills and information, participation in NGO-sponsored trainings, meetings, seminars, supervisory visits and workshops was sought after by both volunteers and health staff for a variety of reasons.[16] Complaints—for instance, that certificates of participation promised during previous workshops were slow to materialize—indexed the importance of workshop participation for volunteers even beyond the material benefits they brought, since certificates of training were essential objects in the construction of a professional portfolio that might facilitate *future* participation in NGO programs and thus further access to the forms of work and compensation that NGOs made available. That volunteer work was not only about providing care but also achieving recognition was clear in how workshops, per diems, seminars, and training sessions became consistent, recurrent, and highly prized.

Looking for Partners "in the Field"

On the final day of the "task force" back in Quelimane, after closing remarks at the Hotel Chuabo, I accompanied Ana, Sandra, Francisco, a visiting USAID supervisor, and a medical doctor working for an American NGO on a "field visit" with Albertina, an active and lively participant in the task-force meetings. A funny and outgoing woman in her thirties, Albertina had been one of the first community health activists I had met in Quelimane and was a core member of a small patients' association at a local clinic. I attended their meetings whenever I was able to do so, and I had occasional opportunities to conduct home visits with Albertina and her colleagues. I often ran into her as she zipped around on her blue scooter, and she always had a funny story, cheerful greeting, or amusing predicament to share. Today, she had agreed to host a visit to the association's offices, which were housed in a small building that nestled at the foot of a Catholic cathedral on the western edge of the city. We set off in a shiny white van bearing the logo of one of USAID's American partner organizations. On the way, Albertina regaled us with stories of her life. Although many of her stories alluded to a difficult marriage, she told them with a disarming and often uproarious humor.

As we arrived at the association, Albertina introduced the director, Sr. Eugenio. An older man dressed in a suit jacket and tie, the charismatic Sr. Eugenio rarely attended group meetings or dealt with the day-to-day workings of the group, but his presence nevertheless loomed large in the association and his name was frequently invoked at weekly meetings. Today, he greeted us graciously before turning to Albertina, who explained the details of the association as she led us around the diminutive, slightly rickety building. We wandered through the president's limited office area, a larger meeting room, and "Albertina's room," a cramped space in which two sewing machines were stashed. We were also shown the storeroom where materials such as gloves, buckets, Certeza water purification solution, and condoms were kept. It was currently empty except for a small mattress and a pile of personal belongings. Albertina explained to the visitors that it was being used as "the guard's room" by Antonio, an association member who had lost his house several months ago when he could no longer pay rent. The association had offered him a place to sleep in exchange for his working as its security guard, which entailed fetching water, sweeping the yard, and generally keeping an eye on things.

As we took our seats on the expansive covered verandah where the group held weekly meetings, Sr. Eugenio and Albertina explained that the association paid about 1,500 MT (US$60) in monthly rent and an additional 500 MT (US$20) for electricity. To cover its costs, the association relied on assistance from the Italian nuns who sponsored the local HIV clinic, and who also covered the association's administrative costs, including small subsidies for the president, Eugenio, and core members, primarily Albertina. In addition, Albertina explained, a development organization had given them the sewing machines, which they used for projects such as making school uniforms and creating and embroidering curtains, tablecloths, napkins and towels to sell. They also had an agricultural project—shared communal fields, where we would later visit glowing green rice paddies—and the association's work included mechanics, baking pastries, selling sodas, projects related to the "environment," and "administration and finance." As Albertina rattled off this diverse and surprisingly long list of activities, the visitors shifted somewhat uneasily. Sandra, notebook and pen in hand, did not take notes but asked a series of pointed questions about the activity levels and potential success of these projects.

In response to Sandra's inquiries, Albertina acknowledged that the bakery project had in fact ended since the people involved got personal contracts to cook for the Department of Education, and, she noted ruefully, the mechanics project hadn't started yet. Also, she conceded, the home-based care that the association provided really amounted to "home visits," because of the lack of money for the gloves, buckets, soap, aspirin and other first-aid supplies that transform social support (or home visits) into medicine (home-based care). Still, association staff continued to visit patients referred by the hospital and to offer "moral support and guidance." The distinction between visits and care was crucial to accessing donor support, which was provided only for "care." Government guidelines suggested that once an organization like the association registered as a donor-supported volunteer group, each volunteer should receive a monthly subsidy of at least 60 percent of the minimum wage. In addition, volunteers would often receive bicycles and other supplies that were useful in daily life as well as in visits. In a catch-22, however, without financial support, the materials that marked home-based care *as care* (such as gloves and medicines) were impossible to obtain. As a result, groups like the patients' association were anxious that their activities be recognized as (medicalized) care rather than (social) visits for financial as well as medical reasons. Still, as they listened to Albertina's litany, the visitors appeared disappointed, if not entirely surprised by the ad hoc and largely entrepreneurial nature of the association's activities.

When the conversation turned to membership statistics, however, Albertina recovered her footing. In response to questions, Albertina told the visitors that the association had eighty-nine members in all, two-thirds of whom were women; they conducted regular visits to forty-two orphans, of whom twenty-six were girls, as well as to the homes of fourteen HIV-positive children, of whom nine were girls and five were boys. Albertina's facility with these numbers was impressive, and Sandra and the NGO representative, till now relatively impassive, began to take rapid and admiring notes, nodding all the while. When Albertina paused, Sandra looked up from her notebook and asked whether the association had applied for funding. Albertina explained that they had applied to the National Office for the Prevention of AIDS (notorious for awarding grants only to those with "connections"), to the British NGOs Concern and ActionAid, to a community development association, "and to the nuns." (Later I learned that they had also met with the provincial governor and his wife.) Yet this had all been to little avail. The association had received hardly anything, and—though Albertina didn't share this with the visitors—what it had received (enough to purchase a small number of goats) had led to bitter internal fights and struggles. Growing animated even by her exuberant standards, Albertina declared, "We even asked [a U.K. NGO] whether they could just offer us some pamphlets so at least we would have information here. But they said there weren't any pamphlets, and that they are only helping with the floods. . . . Foreign organizations never want to give us any money or support us—but they use our names and lists and photos when they need to justify their expenses!" In reply, Sandra simply nodded and said, "What's important is that you can't get discouraged. It's important to continue your work, knowing that one day you *will* have partners." At this point, the NGO-affiliated doctor spoke up: "You have to do this work and show how you are doing it, because the biggest fear that donors have is putting money in the wrong place. Now, my organization already has [local] partners; we are already working with CASA, Hope, and Network for Health, but perhaps you could link to the health department to distribute mosquito nets or something like that." Albertina responded politely but unenthusiastically to this suggestion. Though it was possible that partnering with the health department might help to legitimate the association and to assuage the fears of potential donors, it was evident that the doctor was also making clear his organization's unwillingness or inability to partner with the association.

Referring to the "fear that donors have," the doctor alluded to possibilities for corruption—for instance, that groups might not distribute funds appropriately, or might not visit those they claim to enroll, or might not assist those they do visit (see, e.g., Johnson 2009). More importantly, he conveyed how making oneself the "right" place for donor money entailed participating in the economies of audit, transparency, and sympathy that are composed of "lists," "names," and "faces" and are validated by certificates and participation in training that not only generated data but also helped organizations assure *their* donors of the suitability of their projects.

As the meeting concluded, Sandra asked Albertina how she would describe the association's priorities. Albertina replied that they wanted to focus on "making bricks and sewing—income-generating activities—because in this way, we can generate funds for the association, and also for the person who does the work." But at this, the visitors became visibly agitated, frowning and making disapproving noises. Finally, Sandra said, "I want to caution you here. Instead of just thinking about how to generate an income, you should realize that the time you invest in visiting people is indirect profit, because *it is as a result of the visits that you can get funding from partners.* But if you start, let's say, making bricks, and you pay the people who make them, then *everyone* will want to make bricks. And if you don't pay them, no one will. Do you see?" Albertina and Sr. Eugenio nodded, and Albertina said, as if in clarification, "Well . . . we are working for charity, because that is the idea of [the religious organization that funds the hospital], but it is also different than an association that does visits with a partner, because then you must pass [by the office] twice a week and bring the information to the partner. That's why you have supervisors, to make sure you are really going." As Albertina clearly saw, the association's work was used by "partners" who needed "information"— names, lists, faces, and visits. The importance of these humanistic data points was evident in the eagerness with which the visitors wrote down the statistics of women assisted, orphans visited, and children supported, even as they demurred when it came to the financial assistance that Albertina, Eugenio, and others were seeking. If information was the raw material of a transnational visual and narrative economy through which GCF raised funds, it was unevenly extracted and distributed.

The language of partnership is used to describe a multitude of institutional arrangements, from the promotion of community health to large-scale structures of transnational investment and administration to practices of knowledge production and extraction. Yet the interaction between Albertina and Sandra showed how difficult and contingent these relations could be and how, as anthropologist Johanna Crane (2013) has shown, notions of partnership obscure unequal power relations. Albertina and Eugenio sought partnerships not only to expand caregiving activities but also to provide material support for members of the association, most of whom lived in precarious circumstances. NGOs relied on "partners" to realize their interventions yet feared "putting their money in the wrong place." This fear drove the economy in "completion certificates," emblems of nongovernmental trainings, and other trappings of global health participation and nongovernmental legitimacy, as diverse participants sought to fashion themselves into trusted sites of humanitarian investment. The language of volunteerism and partnership in fact described complex and contingent negotiations on the parts of both volunteers and NGOs, even as the inequalities between them were familiar aspects of nongovernmental intervention.

Community Data and the Ethnographic Field

While humanistic accounts are composed of names and narratives that are often central to NGO fund-raising, they are also the materials through which much global health ethnography is forged. As this suggests, anthropological accounts of NGOs are not separate from these processes. In fact, ethnographic work may participate directly in these economies of documentation, and I too was interpolated into these processes. At times, the link between ethnography and the humanitarian economy may be direct. For instance, I was occasionally asked to take photographs or craft brief narratives describing GCF projects and recipients. Like Sandra, my ethnography relied on the mediation of actors such as Albertina, and like Albertina, my ethnographic accounts helped generate the names, faces, and numbers that underpinned GCF interventions. At other times, ethnographic accounts of medical work and medical experience in Africa may participate more obliquely. By generating ethnographic accounts of health disparities, often through rich, detailed, and poignant portraits of patients and caregivers, medical anthropologists may criticize existing structures of care and inequalities of health and well-being while also helping to shore up the urgent need for intervention or to legitimate the sense that there is a "right place" or "right way" to distribute funds and deliver care.[17]

Moreover, just as NGOs have come to rely on local volunteers, so too have medical anthropologists taken volunteers as key subjects in accounting for global health. In fact, activists, volunteers, and community members sometimes seem to be ubiquitous and self-evident objects of ethnographic observation and analysis. At the offices of GCF, in conversations with the District and Provincial Health Directorates, and at other NGOs where I conducted interviews, community health work was consistently presented as an obvious location for ethnographic investigation. This enthusiasm was matched by a flood of publications by consultants, anthropologists, and development practitioners,

Mozambican and expatriate, on the work of community health activists. Volunteers were thus a means of understanding not only how transnational programs articulated with particular places, patients, and workers but also how located forms of knowledge, relation, expertise, and distribution helped to constitute global health through engagements with "communities."

Finally, it is not only African health systems that are prone to seminar-itis, I suggest, but ethnographies as well. In anthropological portrayals of development projects in Africa (for example, Bornstein 2005; Englund 2006; Nguyen 2010), workshops seem to be almost a core or classic site of ethnographic analysis in which the social dramas and moral economies of transnational intervention are performed. They make clear that many projects and interventions are guided by self-serving logics and proceed with global replicability, deploying models and social dynamics that are easily transferrable from one part of the globe to another.[18]

What is it about workshops and volunteers that make them such central sites of ethnographic analysis? In an essay on "AIDS derivatives in Africa," historian Nancy Rose Hunt (1997) suggests that the workshops, seminars, group exercises, acronyms, and role-playing games that have accompanied AIDS interventions in Africa reflect the "tedium" of institutionalized responses to the disease. She suggests that such spaces reduce complex experiences to formulaic, stereotyped, and hierarchical encounters. This description is evocative, capturing how Sandra skillfully repackaged the complicated stories relayed by volunteers into the bullet points of funding proposals and the numbers of "community data." It also captures how the format, roles, and even the language of the GCF training sessions appeared to be already familiar, tediously so, to the many participants who had experienced comparable sessions in similar venues, sometimes even with the same trainers yet hosted by different organizations or organized around a slightly different topic. Workshops are therefore important sites in which to observe and analyze the circulation and stabilization of policies and technologies of intervention.

Yet I wonder whether the centrality of workshops to ethnographic studies of humanitarianism, aid, and global health may also reflect changes in ethnographic practice. While anthropological locations have diversified in important and dramatic ways in recent decades, the discipline's connection to area studies and to "local" as opposed to "global" places has also been renewed by the explosion of "global health" projects and by the role of anthropologists in defining and constituting the field (Cohen 2012). Even as anthropologists have tried to move away from old-fashioned yet somehow commonsensical understandings of fieldwork, such as locality, marginality, and even exoticism many of these concepts remain built into and even invigorated by global health practices.[19] For anthropologists who sit in uneasy relation to global health as a discipline, both helping to constitute and looking critically askance at such interventions, perhaps workshops are sites in which the awkward "embrace" (Ferguson 1997) of anthropology and global health is ethnographically worked out. Workshops and seminars, then, are spaces in which important conceptual work is performed *both* by the objects of study—the participants and conveners—and by ethnographers themselves. By simultaneously presenting "the field" and showing how it is constructed by global health and development practices, perhaps workshops allow ethnographers to have our "local" cake and our critical distance from it, too.

CHAPTER 3

Afterlives

Food, Time, and History

It was a Saturday afternoon, and Renato, Mucavele, and I were driving along a dirt road near the southern edge of Morrumbala District. We were headed back to the office after dropping off food baskets in a rural neighborhood supported by GCF, for which Renato worked as a driver and Mucavele as a logistician. A few years older than me, Renato had an enthusiastic interest (and half-finished university degree) in political history. I always looked forward to driving with him and Mucavele, knowing our trip would be full of commentaries on Morrumbala history and Mozambican politics.

It was late in the day by the time we had dropped off the food, checked the names of the recipients against our list, and stopped at a small kiosk to buy ourselves Fantas and cookies for the ride back. Although dropping off food was an ostensibly simple act, it was frequently fraught, as patients appeared whose names were not "on the list" or as patients who were on the list but who had tired of waiting for us, almost always hours late, had to be fetched from their homes or fields. Sometimes arguments broke out, as residents demanded recognition from Renato and Mucavele. "I'm just the driver," Renato repeated again and again, "you need to take it up with Violeta," who controlled entry into the food program. I often found the uncertainty and antagonism that accompanied food drop-offs upsetting, but today the distribution seemed quick and efficient: the people assembled in the shade matched the distribution list exactly, and the packets, known as the *cesta básica*, were in well-organized bundles, easily unloaded from the back of the old converted ambulance used for deliveries. In less than an hour, we were back in the van, bumping back toward the NGO offices in Morrumbala Town, about twenty kilometers away.

Renato was driving quickly, eager to salvage what was left of his day, when he gestured out the window and, half turning back toward me on my fold-out seat in the back, called out: "During the war, this area was really *mato* [bush]! Just bush! This road we're driving on now, you couldn't drive like this, alone, just one car. You could only drive in convoys." Describing the convoys, and the attacks on them, Renato referred casually to events of the mid-1980s and to fighting between the FRELIMO government (now the ruling Frelimo party) and RENAMO (now Renamo, the major opposition party). Yet Renato had been only a small child at the time, and while material traces of the conflict were still evident in some of the ruined structures that dotted the *zona baixa* (the low-lying flood plains), the vividness with which Renato spoke contrasted with the warm peace of that afternoon.

"[This] was all controlled by RENAMO," Renato continued, speculating about the villages we had visited earlier. "All those *regulos* [community leaders] we just visited? They were all *comandantes*. . . . And a truck like this delivering food? They would just attack you!" Relishing the story, Renato chuckled as he recounted the opportunism that had accompanied the food provided by Calamidades Naturais, the government disaster response agency that had coordinated humanitarian relief during the war. Fighting was particularly fierce in Morrumbala. In the mid-1980s, representations of the extreme violence that marked Morrumbala circulated not only across Mozambique but in international media as well (Finnegan 1993). This afternoon, however, Renato gave his story a more comic spin. "It wasn't only RENAMO [that attacked food trucks], man!" he said, amused. "Maybe they attacked three or four trucks. Then the next *ten* trucks were assaulted by everyone else. The drivers! Those same guys from Calamidades! And it was *only* the food they wanted. Everything else, they just left it there on the road."

Renato's historical enthusiasm was contagious, and Mucavele soon joined the conversation. Mucavele recalled that, in contrast to the food aid delivered to communal villages in rural areas, in FRELIMO-controlled cities where they had each grown up, residents were organized in neighborhood cells with strict control of the food they had on hand. "Each house belonged to a group of ten," Mucavele recalled, "with a boss, a *chefe*, in charge of each one. And he *knew* what was in your house. If you had so much as a bag of rice, he'd want to know where it came from, how you bought it. Everything was like this, controlled. For example, sneakers? There were two brands. If you wore a different brand, you'd be questioned too."

"It was like that," agreed Renato. "All your food you got through ration cards. It's not that there weren't stores, there were—*lojas do povo* [people's stores]. But everything already belonged to someone. It was divided according to quotas, so they would say this family has five people so they get this much. Family X has X people, and so on. . . . Then when the time came, you would go to the store with your card and pick up your quota of food—corn, oil, whatever. At Christmas—well, let's say Day of the Family [as December 25 was formally known]—on the *Dia da Família,* each family would get two liters of wine and two eggs!" Renato laughed at the scene he had conjured up.

Trying to reconcile it with what I knew of present-day Quelimane, Renato's hometown, I asked, "But couldn't you just keep chickens and get eggs that way?"

"OK . . ." Mucavele considered, "but you really couldn't. It was difficult. Because your neighbors would see [the chickens], the *chefe* would see."

"You couldn't," Renato reiterated. "You just had your ration card to take what you were given at the store. It was like the cesta básica!"

Cheerful and chatty, Renato was in his early thirties when we had these conversations, and had been only a teenager when peace accords were signed in 1992—an event he celebrated by traveling to a neighboring town for a dance party. Much of what he recalled was embellished by his enthusiasm for a dramatic story. His analogy between socialist rations and the food baskets we had just delivered overlooked important differences in the design and distribution of food as it shifted from government ration to humanitarian good. Yet if he sacrificed historical accuracy for narrative effect, Renato's account also captured in important ways how contemporary NGO interventions—in this case, the food baskets that we had dropped off—were situated in relation to other governmental interventions, past and present. In drawing these continuities between wartime aid, socialist rations, and contemporary nongovernmental projects, Renato and Mucavele spoke to one of the central questions of this book: how are contemporary practices of medical assistance articulated within a broader set of current and historical governmental practices?

It was not only Renato and Mucavele who drew connections between present and past in the distribution of food. I was chatting with Susana, a friend, interlocutor, and GCF food recipient one afternoon as she lamented the conflict and misfortune that seemed to characterize life in her neighborhood. Sighing, Susana suddenly said, "Xi, Malawi is not like this." She was describing the conflict and problems that had followed on the heels of a child-sponsorship program run by one of GCF's children's rights projects. Because NGOs and "programs" provided so many medical and child-related services in Morrumbala, Susana and her neighbors were keenly attuned to the projects that were implemented in each neighborhood. Though Susana had earlier speculated that one of her own children might have been signed up for benefits, now that enrollment had closed she expressed a lack of interest. She commented disdainfully on neighbors who harbored grudges against families whose children had been selected. Nevertheless, she was frustrated by the apparent fickleness with which programs arrived and departed in particular neighborhoods, enrolling or excluding participants seemingly at will.

Susana had grown up in the *zona baixa*, close the Malawian border, but I had never heard her mention Malawi. Yet when I asked if she had been there, she looked surprised and responded: "Me?! I lived there for ten years during the war."

It soon became clear to me that Susana's experience was far from unique. After fleeing the village of Megaza with her parents in 1982, when she was thirteen years old, she lived in Malawian refugee centers for the remainder of the conflict, marrying and having her first children there. "Some people worked in the fields [kulimavam]," she recalled, "but I didn't. We lived off the food that was offered."

"Who offered the food?" I asked. "The World Food Programme [PMA]?"

"Yes . . . programs like that. They gave us *farinha* [flour]—I was there with three children so we got a sack of farinha; they did it on the basis of your agregado [aggregate household]. If you had five children—ei! You got a lot. We got a sack of farinha, soap, oil, salt. We used to sell farinha because it would rot there in the house, they would come every week. . . . Peas. . . . The only thing that was missing," she concluded with a laugh, "was a man—that's the *only* thing they didn't give you."

Drawing connections between past and present, between food (farinha, peas) and relations (a husband), and between politics and aid, Susana, Renato, and Mucavele made clear how humanitarian goods and practices, like food distribution, are embedded in historically informed practices of consumption, distribution, politics, and care. As I have argued in previous chapters, unfolding entanglements of markets, politics, and NGOs have come to shape public health and development in Morrumbala, enacting new forms of governance and enabling new forms of work and precariousness. Yet while these entanglements are in important ways newly salient, I have also suggested that, in Mozambique, humanitarian projects have unfolded over decades.

As the comments by Renato and Susana make clear, the programs that Morrumbala residents observed were simultaneously new and familiar. In addition to socialist projects like the ones Renato and Mucavele recalled, emergency feeding programs for malnutrition have long been a part of Mozambican hospitals. Pharmacies at some, if not all, hospitals and clinics are stocked with cans of enriched infant formula and fortified milk powders with names like F75 and F100, and with packages of PlumpyNut, a high-calorie peanut-based food supplement developed for use in emergencies. Doctors write prescriptions for multivitamins, also distributed at subsidized cost through pharmacies, and emergency food aid has been a core component of development programs since the 1980s. For those who had once been refugees in Malawi, food aid was a central aspect to life during the war, but it was important, too, for those who had stayed in Morrumbala. Food baskets and food assistance thus have long and contested political histories in the district—within hospitals, through public and nongovernmental networks of distribution, and in the everyday experiences of district residents.

Despite this longevity, food aid, like the baskets provided by GCF, has been a relatively small (and shrinking) component of international development assistance (Barrett and Maxwell 2005). Yet even as development initiatives have turned away from food support, food has become an increasingly common component of AIDS and global health programs. Food assistance thus mirrors larger paradoxes in global health and development projects, as increases in funding for transnational medical interventions have proceeded together with a decrease in "pro-poor" interventions (UNICEF 2006). Thus, even as programs targeting poverty and providing food for the poor have lost funding, funding for global health (including the provision of food) has increased. Global health programs have therefore enabled forms of distribution and care that have become progressively less available to those who do not meet medical criteria of eligibility. Moreover, such initiatives have had little to say about the global dynamics that produce poverty to begin with. As a result, food baskets have crystallized tensions in contemporary models of assistance. Tailored to help patients "get back on their feet" or to "lend patients a hand," as GCF supervisors often put it, food baskets were experienced by some recipients as both insufficient and temporary, providing too little food over too short a period in the absence of broader possibilities for work.[1]

To shed light on how Morrumbala's histories of aid, work, and displacement shape global health practices in the district, this chapter first explores how Susana and her neighbors recalled and experienced life in Mozambique and Malawi. Pointing to the longevity of humanitarian action in the district, Susana and others contested narratives of NGO ephemerality, highlighting their long-standing experiences with organizations and the enduring dynamics of exploitation and extraction through which poverty is produced in Morrumbala. Where NGO staff like Violeta, and NGO consultants like Sandra, worked to disentangle the state and humanitarian claims, Susana and others emphasized the durability of their experiences. In the second part of the chapter, I show that, through these historical discourses, Susana and others articulated expectations of future NGO responsibility and sought a more inclusive mode of assistance, one that might give rise to ongoing relations of care and support. For recipients like Susana, transnational assistance was not only a material resource but also a relational one, constituted through experience with NGOs over time. As a result, attention to how past humanitarian experiences were recalled offers insight into practices of relation and distribution in the present and into the futures that Susana and others sought to construct in Morrumbala.

Zambézian Circuits

When I met her, Susana was renting a small adobe house in a neighborhood just off the main road into Morrumbala. Tucked behind a small market, the house was cool and pleasant, with three interior rooms and a wide, shady verandah. Home to Susana, her three children, and her elderly but lively mother, the house was also situated a short distance from the house where Susana's sister lived with her husband. Proximity to her sister was not incidental; despite growing up in the district's rural flood plains, Susana had long lived outside the district and had returned precisely to be closer to family. In the course of our conversations, I had heard much about her years in the large, central Mozambican town of Mocuba, the relative ease of life there, her journeys to the larger cities of Quelimane and Nampula, and the difficulty of her return home. My surprise at hearing about "Malawi" was thus not that Susana had left Morrumbala but that, in all the discussion of her travels, Malawi had not previously come up.[2]

Although Susana had roots in Morrumbala District, she had not lived long in town when we first spoke. Susana had met her first husband when both were living in the refugee "zones" in Malawi in the early 1990s. Returning to Mozambique with their children, they settled in the large town of Mocuba, just north of Morrumbala. Neither had family there, but the size of the town and its busy commercial sector offered more opportunities than Morrumbala. Susana's husband worked as a bricklayer, and Susana sold clothing with a friend who owned a small store. Her memories of this time evoked relative economic success, a comfortable house, and possibilities for travel to the northern province of Nampula and to other towns in Zambézia. When her son was about three years old, however, Susana's husband married again, and he and Susana split up soon afterward. Less than a year after their divorce, her ex-husband had fallen ill. He returned to his family's home near the Zambezi River tributaries that mark the district's southern border, where he died some months later, without visiting a hospital or receiving biomedical treatment. In the meantime, Susana too remarried. She became pregnant and was told during a prenatal visit that she had tested positive for HIV. Frightened and unconvinced by the diagnosis, Susana left the hospital and refused treatment that would have helped prevent the transmission of the virus to her baby.

In her sensitive ethnography of pregnancy in central Mozambique, anthropologist Rachel Chapman (2010) has found many reasons for women to refuse medical care as they seek to navigate the social and physical risks that accompany pregnancy. Accepting treatment, for instance, might have threatened Susana's marriage at a time when she and her three older children were deeply dependent on the support of her new husband. It would have introduced dramatic new social risks, to herself and her children, even as it mitigated potential physical harm. Despite her refusal of treatment, her son appeared healthy at birth and, for a time, Susana's life seemed to have found new possibilities for stability. When her son was about eighteen months old, however, he became ill with a series of health crises, each increasingly severe. Repeated hospitalizations failed to help, and he died before his second birthday, leaving Susana distraught and bereft. In the wake of his death, Susana's marriage deteriorated, and Susana herself became ill. Still grieving, she returned to Morrumbala where she had family to care for her and for her three older children. (A fifth child, her eldest daughter, was already married and living in the *zona baixa* near Susana's mother and close to where Susana herself had grown up.)

Susana recounted to me that, in planning her own return to Morrumbala, she had assumed that her fate would follow that of her first husband—if she were going to die, she thought, at least she would be close to her family who, she hoped, would care for her children. Instead, events took a surprising and hopeful twist, one made possible by the rapid expansion of HIV services that had occurred between her first husband's return home in 2002 and Susana's, four years later. With the involvement of her sister and Sr. Artur, she was enrolled in medical treatment through GCF and the district hospital. Artur visited her daily, encouraging her to take her medication. "He really pushed me," Susana later recalled. "He was here every day pushing, pushing, pushing."

Artur also advocated for Susana's inclusion in the food program. By the time I met her, she had been receiving a *cesta básica* from GCF for several months. This provided her with a monthly allotment of rice, oil, beans, sugar, and soap. Once a month, Susana and other GCF recipients assembled in the shady cover of the neighborhood *paiol* where they would wait, often with growing and understandable impatience, for the GCF materials manager, Gilberto, along with Violeta or another supervisor, and a driver, usually Renato, to arrive. Bouncing up in the old ambulance or a newer Toyota HiLux, stuffed with bundles of cornmeal or rice, beans or split peas, sugar, oil, soap, Certeza, and mosquito nets, the staff would hurriedly distribute food baskets while checking off patients from the master list.

On the one hand, with assistance from GCF volunteers, her sister and brother-in-law, and her mother, who had moved from her rural home to live with and care for her, Susana was recovering quickly. On the other, she was grappling with the stringent limitations of medicalized food support. After six months, program guidelines recommended that each patient be "cut off" from assistance to make room for others. It was this deadline that Susana thought might have been less inflexible had her older son, age seven, been enrolled in one of GCF's children's programs. The limitation seemed all the more egregious when contrasted with food aid she had received in the past. The support that Susana received from GCF was thus at once unexpected, much needed, deeply familiar, and (compared with past experience) newly constrained.

The contrast between present restrictions and recollections of past abundance was heightened by historical continuities. Susana was supported by an organization, GCF, that had provided much of the food aid in the Malawian camps. Moreover, just as she had sold extra flour in Malawi, she had in recent months turned her therapeutic food aid into extra income: the cooking oil and sugar in her food basket were used to fry cakes that her daughter sold in the local market. While Susana was particularly entrepreneurial, selling or redistributing portions of the food basket was not uncommon. A group of GCF volunteers from Mponha, near Susana's home village, for instance, noted vehemently in a monthly report that they had "counseled people that you *can't* sell the food basket!"

Yet short of selling the goods she received from GCF, Susana had little opportunity in Morrumbala for commercial work of the kind she had relied on in her earlier life. Although Violeta and her colleagues frequently exhorted patients to plant "some small thing" in their *machamba* (fields), the "return to farming" that GCF envisioned for patients such as Susana went largely unrealized.[3] Susana's mother, now in her late sixties, frequently walked two kilometers to cultivate a small and not very productive plot, but Susana herself preferred market work to long hours raising cassava, maize, or sorghum—activities on which she had rarely relied prior to returning to Morrumbala. Not only were her fields small and hard to access, but back pain (much later diagnosed as extra-pulmonary tuberculosis) also made farming painful and difficult.

Despite similarities to past experiences of aid, then, the assistance Susana now received was not distributed along the same lines of collective need that she recalled as having governed assistance in the camps. Instead, it was calculated in diagnostic terms of CD4 counts, tuberculosis treatment, and low body mass index that governed GCF's food program. It was distributed according to medical, individual, and time-limited understandings of need and vulnerability that left little room for considering the relations on which she relied, and it was governed by a strict temporal reckoning. Six months seemed just long enough to recuperate before being thrown back on one's own devices. For Susana, then, the end of food aid seemed to mark not a return to health but to old predicaments and no clear prospects of support. It was from this precarious vantage point that life in Malawi allowed, perversely, for a critique of present constraint.

Community Critique

Susana's critical perspective on the politics of assistance was not uncommon. Many recipients (and aspiring recipients) of food baskets also compared life in Malawi with their present circumstances, often in spontaneous response to the frustrations of food aid limited by time and diagnosis. For instance, during home visits with health activists, I heard "Malawi" invoked to express the irritation of an HIV-positive woman whose eligibility for food support had expired the previous year and whose work as a healer provided insufficient income. In response to a routine visit, the ostensible purpose of which (providing moral support) remained unsatisfactory, she exclaimed bitterly, "At least in Malawi they gave us something. Not like this 'help' you are offering now!" When I asked what she meant, she commented that she had spent more than a decade in Malawi before returning with her children. There, she had received "more adequate" help for supporting the household. Likewise, an elderly disabled woman who received food support referred to "Malawi" to express her frustration with biannual evaluations of eligibility. "In Malawi," she asserted, "they did not make you show up [just] to ask the same questions every time." Sarcastically recounting a previous social work visit, she indicated her one-room house and simple woven sleeping mat as she mimicked the social welfare officer's questions about the number of rooms in her house and the kind of mattress she slept on. In her recollection, "Malawi" was a space in which social support was not hinged to such governmental indignities.

In addition to complaints about the amount, duration, and composition of food aid that beneficiaries received, "Malawi" was also invoked to critique the emphasis that contemporary programs placed on diagnostic criteria to regulate inclusion in the program. In this regard, community health volunteers were particularly sensitive to complaints made by people who were excluded from the program. For instance, one recently trained health volunteer, Sr. Vasco, explained his interest in community work by drawing on and contrasting it with his work as a volunteer in the refugee camps in the mid-1980s: "While I was there, the Malawian government said, 'We want volunteers, we want ten volunteers for each zone.' There was each zone, big, like this neighborhood, and we would walk knocking on doors. We had forms that we would fill out when we found someone whose legs didn't work or they needed a wheelchair." In Vasco's retrospective view, tensions and resentments associated with resettlement were glossed over in recollections of refugee "zones" ruled by responsive and caring authorities.

Vasco's memories offered a critical point of comparison with the "programs" that structure social benefits in the district today. He contrasted the institutions and agencies that responded to the problems his clients faced. He now experienced long delays and many difficulties when he tried to arrange wheelchairs from the government social services office. He compared this to the responsiveness of wartime relief, noting that "we would take the form to the office there, and the people in the office would look for whatever kind of help was necessary, if it was a hand bicycle or something else. For example, I had five patients who needed hand bicycles and they all received them."

Ultimately, Vasco recalled assistance in Malawi as more organized, generous, and compassionate than the goods he now distributed:

For those who were patients, it was better there [in Malawi]. In terms of food, it was better. They received food every fifteen days and it was food *for* fifteen days. Also a blanket, a bucket, things like that that they needed. The patients didn't suffer. But now the patients are suffering. They are suffering and they begin to gossip and complain. They receive food for six months and then are cut off because they have recuperated. They have recuperated—that is, they look healthy again. But they have no strength. Without strength, how are they supposed to live? It doesn't mean that they have strength to go in the *machamba* and work.

Vasco's experiences in Malawi gave him grounds for a critique of the selectivity with which contemporary aid programs defined eligibility, their capacity to respond, and the social aggravations this posed for volunteers and beneficiaries. Whereas, in Malawi, refugees had once received support on the basis of a shared predicament, goods were now distributed along medical, individual, and time-limited diagnoses of vulnerability, and were explicitly tied to efforts at moral instruction or exhortations to productivity. As he remembered walking around refugee neighborhoods "knocking on doors," Vasco described a form of assistance that was directed not to the exceptional but to the everyday, and not to the select few but to all who needed it.[4] Vasco and others pointed, too, to how mobility, whether between Mozambique and Malawi or Morrumbala and Mocuba, has long been a frequent life and livelihood strategy for residents of Morrumbala (see also Lubkemann 2008). In contrast to imaginaries of patients as rooted in long-standing and localized communities, patients like Susana, community volunteers like Carlota and Tomás, and staff like Violeta and Mucavele had all constituted lives and profits in circulation.

Nevertheless, it was surprising to me that GCF volunteers and patients emphasized the relative dignity of refugee assistance.[5] Certainly, many Morrumbala residents who had gone to Malawi and returned expressed sorrow and revulsion with regard to their experiences (see also Macamo 2006). Refugees had little choice in how they lived, recalling that "it was a war: we accepted what we were given." The high rates of malnutrition that many experienced indicate the harsh difficulties of life in the camps, particularly in the early 1980s, when the region suffered severe drought. For most, humanitarian support was only reliably forthcoming in the years after 1984, a point noted by some, but not all, Morrumbala residents with whom I spoke.

As a result, descriptions of "Malawi" as an alternative, even more adequate, way of life were not just surprising but also pointed and partial. Nevertheless, even NGO workers and local volunteers drew on this notion of a generous past. For instance, one of GCF's volunteer supervisors, Dona Adelia, commented that in Malawi

> . . . people received. They *received*. Not just patients, *every person* received. And received well! Peanuts, sugar, they received well. But who gave this was not the government of Malawi. What happened was that the government here [in Mozambique] arranged with other countries to say: "We have all these people there because of the war." So they helped them. When even the Malawians were badly off, they didn't receive anything. . . . But they didn't get angry because they saw that "our brothers are suffering because of the war," so there was no envy between us.

In contrast to contemporary "programs" limited to narrowly circumscribed patient populations, residents such as Dona Adelia asserted an alternative vision of assistance in which nongovernmental practice was more inclusive, even productive of solidarities across categories of need and belonging.

"Ways of Living" in Nsanje

The ways in which some residents recalled Malawi were also shaped by the political context of the war itself, and the ambivalence with which socialist policies were received in Morrumbala. Although some residents—including health workers—enthusiastically recalled the socialist era as one in which their work was better organized and more fully recognized (Pitcher and Askew 2006), I did not hear such histories evoked among families who now relied on GCF support.[6] Instead, while flight *to* Malawi was presented as a moment of chaotic disruption ("You just wanted to save your soul!"), life *in* Malawi was described as relatively saturated with governmental practices and formative of ongoing modes of live. Life in Malawi was, for instance, the moment at which many residents first experienced "improved" brick houses organized in the gridlike neighborhoods that would later be associated with postwar development in Morrumbala.

Significantly, the same resettlement practices that were described as benefits of life in Malawi had been objects of conflict in socialist Morrumbala. The communal villages run under FRELIMO's aegis, for instance, promised social services but also aimed to "rewrite the landscape of power" in rural Mozambique (West 2005: 167; Borges Coelho 1998). Resettlement practices that disrupted familial residence patterns and relations of power were fiercely resented (West 1998). In Morrumbala, efforts to construct communal villages were met without enthusiasm. Political scientist Sergio Chichava, for instance, quotes an elder in the *zona baixa* as responding to efforts at villagization by saying:

> "We won't agree to go live in the communal village. . . . They can kill us but we will not go to communal villages. . . . You say that our government is a people's government, and that the people are in control . . . why do they continue to insist to build communal villages if we don't want them . . . ?" (2013)

Similar attitudes were commonly recalled elsewhere in Morrumbala. For instance, in response to a question about communal villages, local authorities in one neighborhood told me: "No! No, we didn't want to [live there]! We just wanted to live each one on his plot, wherever he wants in the rural areas. We lived far away from one another." Overhearing this, the neighborhood secretary, Sr. Carlos, interjected. As he pointed to the orderly rows of houses organized on small, adjacent plots, he said,

> When this ended was in the camps. When we fled to Malawi, we went to live in the neighborhoods, and we got used to living together like that. We forgot another way of living. We forgot that we wanted to live there [a long way from one another]. The government there also liked that we lived in common because it was easier. If something happened it was easier if everyone was close together. Then when we came back here, the government saw that you can live in a neighborhood, so now we have these neighborhoods here but before there was nothing like this.

"It was only after you got used to it in Malawi?" I asked. "It was like that," Sr. Carlos answered. "In Malawi, we forgot the other way of living. The idea of bricks also came from Malawi. There they have houses like this. So those who lived there saw that that is how they make houses there. We didn't do this here before we went, we just had traditional houses." If the planned village was a place in which no one wanted to live, it was also a form of spatial life that was relearned in the refugee camps of Malawi as "other way[s] of living" were forgotten.

These partial recollections of a humanitarian past were therefore shaped by a remembered forgetting of other "ways of living" as transnational projects were tangled up—intentionally or in unanticipated ways—by ongoing efforts to remake authority and politics in Morrumbala. These processes show

how organizing the delivery of care through spatialized communities failed to reckon with gendered histories of displacement, migration, and movement. While Susana was able to mobilize community relationships in order to be recognized as a patient and food recipient, her experiences of flight, migration, and circulation were not so different from Paula's, described in chapter 1. Indeed, the primary difference seemed to be that Susana could call on the help of her mother and sister, both to provide assistance and to mediate her entry into GCF's community health program, in ways that Paula, orphaned as a child and estranged from her in-laws, could not.

In addition, postwar life was shaped by a transformation of economic activities and aspirations. These transformations not only posed individual challenges for district residents but also underscored the problem with GCF's assumption that all rural residents were able and content to make a living through farming. "There [in Malawi] we lived as we do here, in neighborhoods, but to open agricultural fields was difficult. We just had the food that the government gave us," a group of GCF volunteers told me. "Like this one," they commented, pointing to Emilia, a shy eighteen-year-old volunteer: "When she came back, she didn't know what it was to use a hoe." Experiences of the camp remained visible, therefore, not only in the spatial organization of neighborhoods but in the livelihood strategies and skills of young people who had grown up without opportunities for (or interest in) the agricultural practices that had been part of life in prewar Morrumbala.

Postwar Developments

Given the poverty that marks life for many in Morrumbala, do retrospective views of "Malawi" tell of a golden age of aid that never was? Although humanitarian memories were selective, they were not just nostalgic fabrications. UN reports show that during the final years of the war, these recollections were amply supported (Crisp and Mayne 1996). More importantly, however, these memories show how Morrumbala's humanitarian histories are situated in relation to political economic changes that have shaped life in the district in the postwar period.

When peace accords were signed in 1992, refugees began returning to Morrumbala with assistance from the United Nations High Commission on Refugees (UNHCR), international NGOs, and the Mozambican government. Though the repatriation effort provided transportation (in trucks, boats, and even planes) to facilitate the refugees' return, a majority of those who returned to Mor-rumbala participated in an early trial of what became known as "Spontaneous Assisted Repatriation." UNHCR documents define this form of repatriation as "the provision of facilities aimed at helping those who are moving of their own accord to do so in dignity and safety." Because free transportation was provided for those who were living at a distance, however, cynical character-izations of the repatriation process described it as "dumping at the border" (Crisp and Mayne 1996).

Returned refugees, moreover, found their conditions and possibilities for living significantly transformed by the war. Although GCF encouraged resi-dents to "return to farming," Morrumbala had ceased to be a district of small-scale farmers long before the war broke out, and few district families survived on farming alone (Isaacman 1996). Rather, the district had been a center of colonial agricultural production, home to European-owned plantations pro-ducing rice, cotton, and sisal, and profiting from the extraction of barely compensated labor from district residents (Vail and White 1980). Throughout the nineteenth and early twentieth centuries, district residents were required to give six months labor per year to the colonial government or to a company or landowner (Mondlane 1969). Because these labor demands took families away from food production and subsistence farming, while offering them next to nothing for the cotton they grew, colonial economies produced intense poverty in Morrumbala, along with profits for the metropole (Isaacman 1996).[7]

While independence brought political change, economic conditions re-mained difficult. Residents were required to work on state-owned farms to meet labor and production requirements—requirements that continued to limit possibilities for food production and subsistence farming, and that compromised possibilities for food security. As resentment over the socialist remaking of agricultural and social life combined with anger over continued dynamics of compulsory labor, collective agricultural production foundered (Pitcher 1998). With the advent of the war, even these economic opportu-nities were undermined, compounding the risks faced by district residents and further constraining possibilities for life in the district. By the end of the war, the industrial and commercial possibilities that existed in Morrumbala through the early 1980s had been destroyed, even as humanitarian support was increasingly restricted.

By the mid-1990s, amid rising world cotton prices, agricultural production increased in Morrumbala once again but economic possibilities remained somewhat grim. Instead of contracting labor to work on industrialized plantations, for instance, cotton production was subcontracted to individual farmers who purchased seed from extension officers. At the time of my research most extension officers were employees of Memphis, Tennessee–based Dunavant Enterprises, which cultivated and processed cotton in the district until 2010.[8] With seed they purchased on credit, farmers planted a portion of their own fields, and then sold the cotton back to Dunavant at the end of the harvest. Until they sold their cotton operation in 2010, Dunavant also owned a ginning factory and processing plant on the outskirts of Morrumbala, and a number of GCF volunteers, including Artur, had permanent or seasonal employment there. Nevertheless, cotton production remained a difficult and labor intensive way to make a living, often requiring the labor not only of two healthy adults but also most often of children as well.

Such labor intensive ventures were difficult for patients who were ill, disabled, or elderly, and few of the families I knew had persisted in cotton production for much time. Mozambican social scientist Manuel Araujo, who has analyzed the Mozambican cotton sector, quotes one area resident describing an average day:

> I wake up early in the morning to fetch water for my kids to wash before going to school. Then, I go to work in the fields where I work till it gets too hot at around 9:00 or 10:00 A.M. Then, I go back home to prepare lunch for the children to eat when they get back from school. In the afternoon, when it is less hot, I go back to the field where I grow food, with my kids. It is hard work and, apart from my children, there is no one to help me in the fields. (2009)

In addition to the hard work of cotton production, prices were low during the time of my research. Local residents received US$0.22–0.55 per pound in the mid-2000s, less than a third of what they received during the 1990s and reportedly less than farmers across the border in Malawi received (Araujo 2009). Thus farmers commented that "we are not happy with the prices [Dunavant] pays us, which do not compensate for our hard labor. [But] we will continue to produce because we have no other source of income" and "there are no other jobs here so, in reality, we have no other choice . . ." (quoted in Araujo 2009). Amid these hard "choices," residents also grappled with an assemblage of incongruent and inconsistent humanitarian practices that evoked wartime governance as much as postwar life. These practices were now configured around new and selective criteria of evaluation even as economic life remained hard.

Historical connections between Portuguese colonial rule, American capitalism, and contemporary cotton production speak to how longstanding and transnational dynamics of work, race, and capital are recapitulated across diverse historical moments and political regimes (Robinson 2000). Describing the longevity of these dynamics, Allen Isaacman has argued that relying on "crops like cotton that displace labor from food production, damage the ecosystem, and satisfy foreign, rather than domestic demands, has long-term economic and social consequences. In the minds of most Mozambicans, cotton will always be the mother of poverty" (Isaacman 1996: 243). In this context, the comments of Susana and her neighbors reflect not only historical experiences in Malawi but also critical perspectives on the limited and brutal economic possibilities available to them at home. They suggest how transnational aid works alongside rather than challenging the market forces that contribute to their predicaments.

Reflecting on the manifold ways that aid regimes reinforce rather than challenge the exclusions of global capital, scholars and activists have called for conceptualizing aid as reparations rather than donations (e.g., Honest Accounts 2017). More broadly, scholars have argued for reparations as a "framework for thinking" about the politics of inequality (Thomas 2011: 4). As anthropologist Deborah Thomas argues, reparations thinking makes visible "the historical rootedness of contemporary inequalities . . . throughout the black world" through the resurrection of shared and collective memory (Thomas 2011: 174).

Neither Susana nor her neighbors articulated demands for reparations, yet Thomas' perspective is salient for understanding the perspectives they voiced. Rooting memories like Susana's in structural accounts of historical inequality shows how experiences with contemporary forms of assistance are situated amid broader processes of extraction. In postwar Morrumbala, district residents who had been the exploited but essential backbone of a corporate colonial system for more than a century were presented with humanitarian practices aimed at helping discrete groups deemed "vulnerable." Others were left to float on Mozambique's ostensibly rising economic tide, even as global and national economic policies sharply increased disparity. In this context, memories of Malawi not only drew on past experience, but also served to critique and demand political economic possibilities in the present. They offered a means of engaging with the devastating transformations wrought in the district, not only by the war but also by the economies that followed in its wake.

The Politics of *Tambira*

That racial or ethnicized imaginaries and economies shaped the dynamics of food aid in Morrumbala was clear from broader debates about assistance. Indeed, it was not only recipients who situated contemporary politics in relation to the district's past. Debates over the harmful effects of food aid were frequent, and fears of aid "habituation" and aid "dependency" were commonly articulated by aid workers and policy-makers as well as recipients. As I show below, notions of "aid awareness," "dependence," and "habituation" resulting from past experience continue to circulate among aid workers, government officers, and project staff, who attribute the difficulties of contemporary aid delivery to Morrumbala's history. Narratives of a generous Malawian past have therefore shaped and continue to shape material configurations of aid, state, and support in diverse ways and to far-reaching effect. However, by showing how historical humanitarian experiences shape present politics, humanitarian memories challenge simplistic narratives of rural dependency on relief. Instead, they highlight how global health projects are enacted in relation to the past, to adjacent modes of care (emergency relief or socialist rations), and to racialized global economies.

Frustrations with contemporary aid practices were not only expressed by recipients of food baskets. Aid organizations and government teams that distribute food and other supports complain that years of intervention have bred a peculiarly intractable form of dependency in Morrumbala's rural localities (Foley 2007). Perceptions that "lazy" residents take advantage of a humanitarian system established for their benefit reflect broader stereotypes and perceptions of rural people. During the time of this research, for instance, President Armando Guebuza commented at a public rally that rural hunger was due to "the lack of a habit of hard work.... There are many lazybones in Mozambique" (Buur 2010: 47).

Similarly, among workers charged with distributing aid, the frustrations of identifying and demarcating the "most vulnerable" have given rise to folk ethnologies regarding the poor work ethic of Morrumbala residents (see also Vail and White 1980). Notions of unseemly aid dependence were colloquially expressed by aid workers, including GCF staff, and town residents using the Sena term *tambira*—to receive—often the only Sena word that foreign aid workers or Portuguese-speaking officers might know. Listening to these complaints, it seemed that "this thing of *tambira*" was everywhere: rumors that people had signed up for benefits in multiple villages in the hopes of receiving double benefits were breathlessly reported. These perceptions also impacted the practices through which aid was delivered; food aid was sometimes delivered as late as 1:00 A.M. with the intention of restricting claims to only the neediest or most desperate.

Not only aid workers but also town residents shared this view. Though most town residents enjoyed a higher standard of living than rural families, it was not uncommonly asserted that "they [who live in the *zona baixa*] receive help every year so they become accustomed to this thing of *tambira*. They receive when there's a drought, when there's a flood. In spite of suffering a lot, they also benefit from these things." Distinctions between town residents and their rural neighbors, and between aid distributors (Mozambican or expatriate) and ethnicized recipients also evoked political differences, as rural communities continued to be associated with the Renamo opposition. Such affiliations and assumptions extended to Morrumbala as a whole. In 2015, armed conflict between Renamo fighters, the Frelimo-controlled national military, and reported paramilitary groups again emerged in Morrumbala amid reports of disappearances, attacks on vehicles, and human rights abuses. Health posts in Morrumbala were targeted and medicines stolen from dispensaries in villages and towns in Zambézia (Human Rights Watch 2016). Aid discourses have thus not only echoed but potentially reinforced exclusionary and violent political alignments. Health thus continues to be centrally located amid political struggle. As a result, humanitarian legacies are not remnants of a distant past but remain linked to ongoing political tensions and inequalities. Humanitarian suspicions meanwhile reflect enduring imaginations of Morrumbala residents, long considered dangerously anti-modern, as demonstrating an unseemly and suspicious reliance on transnational humanitarian goods. Yet such accusations have paid relatively little attention to the extractive economies in which rural residents are enmeshed

From *Tambira* to Dependent Relations

As economic inequality increases, and as long-standing if also difficult patterns of migration, work, and care are transformed, anthropologists have attended to relations of dependence and distribution in contexts of sharply curtailed economic possibility (Scherz 2014). James Ferguson, for instance, has argued that working to access distributive streams, such as remittances, pensions, grants, and other forms of welfare assistance, become an increasingly important means widespread in any case—attracted concern and outrage from Violeta and other supervisors). They were to be people held in "good esteem" by their neighbors and relations. (In some organizations, including many of the groups that attended the task force, volunteers were selected specifically because they were living with the conditions—most often HIV—in which they intervened; this was not an important selection criteria at GCF, though some volunteers also happened to have HIV or another medical condition.) And volunteers were instructed that they were expected to embody exemplary attributes, such as good health, sobriety, and respectfulness. Although these principles were not always observed, discourses about "good volunteers" intersected with a long-standing dynamic in which agents of medical work were also to be agents of modernization and to embody and exemplify principles of modern living (Lubkemann 2008).

Most often, however, volunteers were nominated directly by neighborhood secretaries, or were recruited by way of other volunteers, or were selected on the basis of their participation in other community programs, including health interventions. As Tomás described it, "GCF, when they came and entered into contact with the neighborhood, [they mostly chose] neighborhood leaders, OMM [members of the Organization of Mozambican Women], these [kinds of] people. Then [in my case], I'm a pastor, it's part of our work—it recommends this very thing, that you should have charity and look to the needy." Even when volunteers were nominated through processes of public participation, suggested nominees were often already involved in voluntary work with other organizations. As a result, volunteers who worked with GCF often worked with two or three additional organizations as well.

Although GCF supervisors were sometimes skeptical of volunteers who combined work for GCF with other projects sponsored by other programs, they also sought out volunteers who already participated in community-minded work. Tomás, for instance, not only volunteered for two NGOs, but also worked as a pastor, which allowed for the cultivation of social relations and ties through his congregation. In addition, he served in a province-wide "pastor's network" and volunteered with District Health Department campaigns, including the intermittently mobilized mosquito-spraying brigades. In this way, his "appropriateness" for and "commitment" to the work was confirmed by other activities and organizations. Other volunteers participated in political organizations such as the Frelimo-affiliated Organization of Mozambican Women (OMM) and the Organization of Mozambican Youth (OJM). Others had worked in the hospital, even if only as cleaners, and were thus seen as "dentro of survival in southern Africa (2013). As Ferguson notes, distributive labor (2013: 25) is not itself new. Over centuries, for instance, migrants have distributed wages and goods in ways that sought to ensure their families' well-being and the possibility of their return. What is new, this literature suggests, is the acuteness with which people have come to depend on distribution as opportunities for wage labor decline amid racialized extractive and humanitarian economies. In such a context, cultivating relations of dependency—on family, social networks, state or political parties, NGOs or other expert institutions— becomes increasingly crucial.[9]

Such perspectives on the relational work of distribution are particularly helpful in considering how Susana and others made use of medical goods. It suggests how Susana and Renato came to see food baskets as recent iterations of distributive streams that had long made politics, family life, economic productivity, and physical health possible in the district. Such distributive possibilities were tenuous and rarely taken for granted—hence, the critical interest with which Susana and her neighbors kept track of nongovernmental programs in the district—but the longevity of institutions such as GCF also belied a description of aid as something merely short-term and temporary. Where Violeta claimed that aid was "not forever and not for everyone," Susana and others drew on personal experience and political history to suggest that aid, if not forever, could nevertheless be durable, and if not for *everyone*, then nevertheless distributed along more inclusive lines.

Feminist anthropologists, too, have explored how gendered practices of care and self-making in Africa may entail not the avoidance but the cultivation of dependent relations. Jennifer Cole and Lynn Thomas, for instance, have shown how romantic relations may entangle affect, exchange, dependence, and care in mutually constitutive ways (2009). Focusing on the gendered relations that shaped Susana's consumption and distribution of food and other GCF goods, then, helps to make clear how the incorporation of transnational goods into ongoing projects of livelihood and survival, as well as into critical political subjectivities, entailed the complex negotiation of relations. These relational practices contradict notions of short-term "recovery" or ongoing "dependence," making clear that recovery and recuperation are also processes that extend over time, that draw on past experience and entail expectations for the future.

Such relational practices were evident in how food baskets were consumed. Mealtimes at Susana's house included her three children and her mother, well within the bounds of the "average household"—five adults—used by GCF (and many other organizations) to calculate the basket's contents. Yet the relations of care that influenced Susana's recuperation extended much further than her household alone. Many meals included her close friend and neighbor, Hortencia, who spent much of each day at Susana's house and to whose radio Susana listened whenever there was money for batteries. (Recalling her illness, Susana once told me that "if it wasn't for this radio, I wouldn't be alive.") Most months, Susana also shared a portion of the food she received from GCF with her sister, who had provided her with assistance on her return and whose husband helped to maintain Susana's house, fetch firewood, and do other odd jobs. These practices of redistribution were considered by GCF to be a violation of food support rules, according to which aid was primarily intended for the patient and immediate members of a household envisioned as finite and fixed. In theory, had Violeta known how Susana used her food, she could have removed her from the list of recipients. Yet Susana's practices were common to many recipients and were tacitly accepted. As Tomás summarized it, "Yes, they [recipients and their families] know the food is for the patient. But [the patients] also think, 'If I don't share now, who will rescue me when I fall sick again?'"

Most importantly, food helped Susana create and maintain social ties—not just with Hortencia, but also with many other neighbors who stopped by to chat in the afternoons—in a town where she had only recently arrived. As she recuperated, she bought flour in the market and used the sugar and oil she was given by GCF to make and fry small *bolos* (or cakes, similar to "fried dough") that her eldest daughter sold in the market. In doing so, she turned her food basket into cash, just as she had done in Malawi. This allowed for the purchase of household necessities or preferred foods, and Susana hoped to eventually save a small amount for the future. Individualized aid was turned to new social purposes as Susana invested in relations with family and friends and in market activities in ways that both acknowledged past distributions of care and assistance and opened future possibilities. Food support enabled physical health by providing needed nutrients and facilitating medical treatment. Just as significantly, it fostered relations of care among family and friends—whether providing assistance to her sister, sharing food with Hortencia, or helping to support her elderly mother, who assisted Susana in turn. NGO assistance therefore allowed for relations of solidarity that extended in important ways beyond the boundaries of the household to include friends and family, mostly women, who had sustained Susana in the past and who might do so again in the future.

Close attention to how Susana and others deployed and made use of food assistance suggests how historical legacies, entangled relations of dependence

and care, racialized transnational economies, and future aspirations come together in the experiences of program recipients. In Morrumbala, organizations
such as GCF emerged as central to the provision of social services through the
combined effects of state restructuring and reform alongside legacies of violent conflict and the interventions that accompanied them. Yet the organization insisted that the care it provided was merely a supplement to more
enduring forms of care. By contrast, through their experiences in and out of
the district, residents like Susana and Vasco pointed to how NGO interventions
were not only ephemeral but also durable. In the face of GCF assertions that it
aimed only to "lend a hand" in moments of need, insisting that its assistance
was "not forever" and "not for everyone," recipients recalled aid organizations
providing assistance over decades and in ways more inclusive than the narrowly restrictive assistance of the present. Complaints that Malawi was "not
like this" reflected on historical processes by which residents came to constitute humanitarian populations even as these processes became more exclusive.
And they spoke to the distributional practices through which humanitarian
goods enabled biophysical and relational futures.

Yet such complaints were not merely straightforward demands for public
systems of health and social services.[10] Governmental practice in Morrumbala
has been sporadic and often contradictory. Some residents recall histories of
state intervention with ambivalence or distaste. Moreover, many nongovernmental and community interventions—such as the use of volunteers—have
echoed both colonial rule *and* humanitarian action; practices of governance,
enacted by national government and NGOs alike, have straddled the geographical and institutional borders of the state. Instead, as they critically assessed the
predicaments of restrictive and medically oriented assistance, the experiences
of Susana and others in like circumstances highlighted the discursive work
required to make projects temporary in a context of enduring or "perennial"
intervention.

Conclusion

What difference does it make to realize medical projects and food support
within a global health rather than a socialist, developmentalist, or public
health frame? How do diverse historical modes of (or aspirations to) providing care differ from and articulate with one another? Recent public health
scholarship (in Mozambique and beyond) has located interventions like the
ones implemented by GCF in the aftermath of nationalist aspirations to public

health—what anthropologist Lawrence Cohen has described as "the dream of the clinic" (2012). The emergence of global health and humanitarian interventions as primary modes of administering life in much of Africa, such accounts have shown, has enabled new structural, institutional, and clinical practices of care. It has also enacted new temporalities of care and labor. Cohen notes that as medicine has come to be provided as "humanitarian gift" rather than developmental good, it is "increasingly organized less around a future promising access to basic clinical and preventive care and more around a present demanding the urgent supply of lifesaving medication or emergency supplies" (2012: 87). Drawing on Jane Guyer's discussion of punctuated time, he suggests that this new temporal organization evacuates the near future in favor of the urgencies of the present and the timelessness of moral values (Guyer 2007). "Near futures," he shows, are emptied out of global health practices, much as public health spaces are said to have been emptied of resources, expertise, and even politics (see also Masquelier 2001, Adams, Murphy, and Clarke 2009).

Analyses of humanitarian action, too, have emphasized how notions of "emergency" and "crisis" orient interventions around short-term temporalities and responses that ignore unfolding or long-term needs, conditions, or projects (see, for example, Fassin and Pandolfi 2010; Calhoun 2010). Critiques of nongovernmental intervention (such as Pfeiffer 2013: 167, n. 10) have observed that these approaches are often "unsustainable," where sustainability refers to the gradual unfolding and near-future possibilities for continued care, treatment, or intervention, and are thus opposed to the kind of "punctuated" (Guyer 2007) and temporally discrete modes of project management that have accompanied global health.

These temporalities are distinct from earlier temporal models of development, care, and growth. In the wake of colonial projects, the macroeconomic theories encoded in national development plans asserted that impoverished postcolonial countries would inexorably and incrementally "develop," gradually resolving the problem of global poverty since "history—the passage of developmental time—would in the nature of things raise poor countries up to the level of the rich ones" (Ferguson 2006: 178; also Escobar 1995).[11] By linking historical time and economic, political, and even cultural development, these narratives made the near future into a site of intense political and technological action.

The progressive temporality of modernist development was not only implicit in development theory but also discursively produced through development technologies (Ferguson 1994; Mitchell 2002) and national political practices, such as the "Five-Year Plans."[12] By contrast, as transnational intervention in medicine in Mozambique intensified over the 2000s, catalyzed by efforts to address HIV/AIDS, it brought with it new actors, agencies, and notions of medical emergencies, and produced new and often entangled public and nongovernmental medical spaces. In this context, looking to how past experiences of public and humanitarian care and labor shaped the experiences of GCF staff and recipients offers an opportunity for understanding how the resources such interventions make available are worked into practices of care.

Did food baskets echo socialist rations or wartime assistance? Was wartime assistance the purview of Calamidades, the World Food Programme, or GCF? Rather than locating historical continuities, the comparisons raised by Renato, Susana, and their neighbors show that the materials of humanitarian assistance are constituted in relation to many, sometimes competing historical legacies and oriented towards many future political horizons. For some, histories of socialism contextualized the *cesta básica* as a biopolitical good; for others, legacies of humanitarian assistance pointed to possibilities for a more robust politics of aid. The longevity of aid and the political complexity of food made the *cesta básica* simultaneously rich in meaning and politically ambiguous. As a result, it articulated a future that included but was not limited to the entangled field of care that state and nongovernmental agencies make available.

Food baskets (and recollections of them) show how materials of assistance are redeployed into the fashioning of life projects—whether the violence of appropriation or the cultivation of care. In Morrumbala, where a humanitarian history shaped the past distribution of medical goods, patients like Susana incorporated food into relations of care shaped by their own historical experiences. In the aftermath of war, flight, or diagnosis, and as support "forever" or "for everyone" remains elusive, humanitarian goods became grounds for temporary, changing, but meaningful relations in the meantime. In Maputo, too, food support nourished not only bodies but also relations. In the following chapter, I turn to a small Maputo health center, Clínica 2, where I first met Dr. Luísa and where I have conducted research since 2007. Here I saw that not only patients but also clinicians and NGO staff sought to enable more enduring and encompassing forms of care through critical engagements with the resources of global health.

CHAPTER 4

Nourishing Relations

Located in an innermost suburb of the city, just a few kilometers from the cafés and restaurants of Maputo's *cidade de cimento* (or downtown), the proximity of Clínica 2 to transnational resources and national authority was evident. Though clinic resources were sometimes scarce, it was a much busier and more energetic place than the hospital in Morrumbala. An ambulance pulled in and out of a paved parking area in front. Patients walked up from the nearby *chapa* stand on the corner. The front gate bore the logos of recent nongovernmental partners. In the middle of three low-slung buildings, patients waited in a pleasant courtyard. Others sat on rows of benches that filled the open-air waiting room, a cement roof providing shade and the open walls allowing a small breeze. To one side, a new building was under construction. This was sponsored by the International Center for Health Care (or ICHC), an AIDS care and treatment program and one of the consortium NGOs whose work I followed, but it was not the only nongovernmental project in evidence at Clínica 2. From UN agencies to development organizations to global health projects, transnational actors were easily visible at the clinic. Even the Sisters of Charity in their blue and white habits were a biweekly presence, bringing patients from their hospice to be treated.

It was here at Clínica 2 that I met Sr. Francisco, sitting under the awning outside the office while he waited to check in with Emília and Raquel, staff members who managed the front office. A tall, slender man in his early forties, he stood out among the mostly female patients sitting alongside him. Later, after Emília saw us chatting while he waited outside the office, she mentioned that she was happy I'd met him. "His story is important," she added. Indeed, when Sr. Francisco first recounted his experience to me, he began with narrative flair. "To know about me," he said, "you have to know that I used to work in South Africa. I was a miner for eleven years . . . But in these last years, I was sick all the time." Finally, he explained, a colleague had insisted he see a doctor. Diagnosed with tuberculosis, he was sent back to Mozambique with a small pension and instructions to continue treatment at home. It was only when he arrived here that he was diagnosed with HIV as well. Now, after beginning treatment, he was receiving food support from the United Nation's World Food Programme, medical care from clinic- and NGO-employed doctors, and even homeopathic treatments from a clinic volunteer. Yet even as he recovered, he seemed to feel that his future was grim. He would never return to work, he told me. He received no disability benefits, and though he collected a small monthly pension, it was hardly enough to live on. He seemed to feel he was stuck, depending on clinic support and recovering slowly.

Unemployment and food insecurity were high during the time of my research. In 2009, the year I met Sr. Francisco, almost 300,000 Mozambicans experienced seasonal food insecurity despite an exceptionally good harvest, and the GDP per capita of approximately $900 put the country near the bottom of the Human Development Index (United Nations 2009). Moreover, while donor funding for health increased over recent decades, poverty alleviation programs stagnated. While rapid economic growth has resulted in concentrated and highly visible pockets of wealth, many Mozambicans have become poorer in recent years (Hanlon 2007). Even as the discovery of natural gas and coal deposits have created more millionaires than ever before, many Mozambicans are struggling (Kew 2015). It was the predicaments of poverty and inequality as much as the need for care that kept Sr. Francisco in line for food at Clínica 2.

This chapter explores whether and how patients and healthworkers sought to distinguish between poverty and illness, poverty relief and medical assistance. The previous chapter illustrated how historical experience and contemporary economies give rise to relational practices of claiming resources and care. This chapter extends this approach geographically, by bringing new clinical spaces into the story, and analytically, by focusing on the material circulations of therapeutic food. As food moves between warehouses, clinics, kitchens, households, neighborhoods, and markets, it makes clear how care is fashioned not only through medical relations and practices but also through complex social and nutritional relations. Therapeutic food was seen by patients and staff alike to be valuable not only as a source of calories but also as means of ensuring and "shoring up" sources of care. Such work was distributive, gendered, and temporal, as well as nutritive, and it was recognized as important by (some) medical staff as well as by patients and program recipients. As a result, the movement of food offers an important opportunity for understanding the deeply gendered relations of distribution that accompany global health resources and that make caregiving and recuperation possible. It demonstrates how relational and biological forms of care are entangled in the provision and politics of global health.

Locating Food in the Medical Archipelago

To understand the paradoxes of therapeutic food aid, this chapter draws from fieldwork conducted in and around two food support programs. I focus first on the food program at Clínica 2 in Maputo. Though the clinic received support from the U.S. government, the food program was administered by the United Nations' World Food Programme (WFP), one of the largest distributors of food support in Mozambique. Though WFP emerged and works primarily in response to emergency situations such as violent conflict or environmental disaster, it also intervenes in situations of ongoing need. In Mozambique, WFP supported relief efforts in areas of drought, famine, or environmental disaster. It also provided food to schoolchildren through a school feeding program and to patients, especially AIDS patients, through a number of clinic partnerships. Later in the chapter I draw from and contrast these efforts with the program run by GCF and managed by Violeta and her colleagues, which we encountered in the previous chapter.

Drawing from two sites of food distribution—similar in their emphasis on feeding the ill and diverse in how they sourced and delivered food—offers certain analytical advantages. First, it affords us a "multi-sited" (Marcus 1995) perspective on a food distribution effort driven by transnational interventions in HIV/AIDS cases and coordinated through Mozambique's National Health Service. In this way, thinking across two sites provides a view into how the forms of care enabled by global health initiatives—including the provision of food support—are situated in relation to diverse and partially articulated modes of intervention. Transnational funds, materials, and policies are important resources for medical staff, patients, community members and households because of the large historical role that aid has played in Mozambique's national health budget (Pfeiffer 2013). Critical scholars of global health have described these processes of "projectification" (Whyte et al. 2013; Whyte, Whyte, and Kyaddondo 2010) as producing "archipelago[s]" of medicine and care (Geissler 2013). While the archipelagic character of global health provides the context in which food support programs are situated, it also shaped how recipients made use of food, given that such assistance could be simultaneously widespread and repetitious *and* short-term and tenuous. In such a context, knitting together various kinds of care becomes a key means through which short-term resources are given durability. In the programs I followed, food support was restricted to relatively small numbers of patients (approximately 120 in GCF programs in Morrumbala and 60 at Clínica 2). Yet it provides an important example of how gendered social relations are essential to transforming material goods into practices of care.

In addition, the multi-sited perspective of this chapter reflects the different locations and positions that were available to me within my field sites. In Morrumbala, the structure of the food program was such that accompanying food entailed working closely with the GCF staff that delivered it, but I also conducted fieldwork with patients and community volunteers outside of GCF spaces and encountered foodstuffs and other nongovernmental materials serendipitously in houses and markets. Nevertheless, as is already evident, developing a broader understanding of the food program often entailed the view from back of the old ambulance. In Maputo, though I observed the delivery of food to (and distribution of it from) the Clínica 2 warehouse, the more centralized nature of the program paradoxically made it easier to encounter and follow food through patients' houses, lives, and relations in ways that were relatively separate from clinic staff and spaces. My perspective here enabled me to observe a greater a greater variety of relations and practices. Ultimately, however, I conceive of these diverse therapeutic and nutritional spaces less as points of comparison than as illuminating nodes within a patchy and partially articulated regime of health.

Distributing Food in Two Global Health Locations

That food support was common across the programs I studied reflects how global health programs have been shaped around treatment for HIV/AIDS, in particular by the provision of antiretroviral therapy. Antiretrovirals, especially when patients first begin to take them, often increase "metabolic demands," causing patients to eat more, to feel hungrier, and to require more nutrient-rich and calorically dense foods. Patients enrolling in HIV treatment often feel intense sensations of hunger, which were described to me in phrases like "the hunger that I feel [when taking ARVs] is not like any hunger you know" or "these pills are the worst—they really gnaw at you." Hunger also exacerbates other side effects such as dizziness, sensations of weakness or fatigue, nausea, and fuzzy thinking. These sensations are a common and uncomfortable dimension of HIV treatment in Mozambique, as anthropologist Ippolytos Kalofonos has thoughtfully explored (2010). The metabolic demands of treatment were a problem in households where illness accompanied or was precipitated by poverty or unemployment. In some cases, patients or families resisted treatment, anticipating new nutritional needs that they were ill equipped to meet. Lack of food was cited by patients as a reason for delaying or ceasing medication, and by global health programs as a barrier to the success of their initiatives. In a context of widespread malnutrition, providing access to medication to patients who lacked food came to be seen as counterproductive, a potential waste of resources, and even cruel.

Responding to these predicaments, in 2006, a coalition of NGOs together with Mozambique's National AIDS Council, the Nutrition Department at the Ministry of Health, and the National Health Service adopted national guidelines for the provision of food support to patients. At first focused on HIV patients, these projects were expanded at GCF to incorporate patients with any one of a number of chronic diseases. As we saw in the previous chapter, food aid has become increasingly prominent in global health interventions even as its distribution has become narrower. As a result, food assistance makes visible some of the most pressing contradictions of humanitarian aid and global health. Compared with the forms of emergency nutrition distributed by hospitals, for instance, GCF's food baskets and similar food aid programs offered more robust nutritional support—they were composed not only of nutritional supplements such as fortified milk powder or peanut butter but also of staple foods such as grains, beans, and oil, and were designed to provide the majority of the daily calories needed by an "average household" of five adults. At the same time, because food was tied to medical treatment, and because it was time-limited, it was provided in ways that some experienced as newly restrictive.

On the Border of Economy and Care: Gendered Circuits

Amid restrictive clinic practices, relations of care between family members, neighbors, and friends assumed great importance. This was evident, for instance, in the story that Sr. Francisco told me. By enrolling at Clínica 2, Sr. Francisco was able to access important forms of medical treatment, including ARVs, and supports related to treatment, including food. Yet when I asked him to tell me about his experiences, neither medications nor food packets were at the

4.1 Food, including lentils and rice, and soap for distribution, Morrumbala District.

center of his narrative. Instead, Sr. Francisco singled out his wife as the source of care that kept him alive, noting that

> when I came back here, I was so sick that people didn't recognize me. I used to be fat and strong. Suddenly I was so weak. . . . My wife had to put me on a chair in a tub and washed me sitting like that. That's how I took a bath. Like a child. That's why I say that I was a child to my mother first and now I am a child to my second mother, to my wife. When I went to South Africa to get my final pay packet, she came with me. She had all the money—she could have taken it and left me, but she didn't.

His comments described a world inverted: in a gendered economy of labor, he had become a child to his own wife, cut off from the robust working life that he envisioned across the border. A former laborer, he now accessed support through illness, not employment. He yearned for work, which had allowed him to build a pleasant and spacious house, to educate his three children (now in their late teens and twenties), to provide his wife with a comfortable material life. But he also saw the circulations entailed by his employment as central to his illness and to the poverty that followed it. He felt exploited by the mine where he had worked for so many years, even as he blamed his own lack of understanding for the extent of his debilitation. He described his predicament as rooted in and reinforced by poverty, and the relations of care that sustained him—and that his labor had sustained—as deeply gendered.

In some ways, the story of Sr. Francisco (and the importance that clinic staff placed on it) seemed historically overdetermined.[1] Since the nineteenth century, many Mozambican families have relied on labor migration to South Africa and the salaries it makes available.[2] In colonial Mozambique, migration was encouraged by the South African and Portuguese governments, which coordinated practices of labor recruitment by South African corporations. High rates of migration were also shaped by the higher wages available in South Africa and by the reliance of the colonial state on coercive programs of forced labor. Despite the dangers of work in South Africa, migration offered an important alternative to unpaid and abusive working conditions at home. At the height of labor recruiting in the late 1920s, over 100,000 Mozambicans were recruited to work in South African gold mines (Lubkemann 2008).

While these jobs paid relatively higher wages, they were also precarious. Working conditions in the mines were dangerous. Falling rocks and accidents could lead to disability or death. Even above ground, mine work was risky and living conditions in the hostels where workers slept were crowded. When workers became physically unwell, whether from physical debility or from illness, there were relatively few protections available to them. For instance, describing the history of tuberculosis in South Africa, medical historian Randall Packard writes that before World War I "African workers who became ill were repatriated without regard to the consequence this would have on the rural populations from which the mines drew their labor. . . . Mining authorities adopted the somewhat self-serving argument that Africans disliked being placed in a hospital and preferred returning to their own homes when they became ill" (Packard 1999: 95). Despite these risks, rates of migration to South Africa remained high through most of the early and mid-twentieth century.[3]

Mozambican independence in 1975 and the violent fighting that followed dramatically transformed experiences of labor and everyday life on both sides of the border (Lubkemann 2008). However, South African livelihood opportunities remained an important resource for Mozambican workers and families even as transformations in the mining industry and in the South African economy made work harder to obtain.[4] Thus although Sr. Francisco's HIV diagnosis was somewhat new at the time, his predicament was deeply familiar. His words evoked national histories and economies developed over decades as migrants who have lived and worked in South Africa later return to Mozambique—to retire or to seek whatever forms of care might be available (Lubkemann 2008). What was different was that these forms of care now included global health infrastructures in the making.

Gender, Labor, and Historical Erasures

In keeping with these histories of labor migration, the figure of the male migrant has long haunted public health in southern Africa (Hunter 2010). Depictions of male migrants as potential vectors of disease, transmitting illness from work to home and across national and urban borders, have characterized public health initiatives in the region over decades. Such images were reproduced, for instance, on billboards around Maputo that depicted stereotypical images of men crossing the border laden with goods and declared, "Stop! Don't compromise the health of your family," urging those returning from South Africa to seek HIV testing. In such renderings, acts of masculine care—epitomized in the miner whose physical labor and long absences make possible their family's life in Maputo (Moodie 1994; Moodie, Ndatshe, and Sibuyi 1988)—are transformed into domestic threats. In fact, Sr. Francisco's comments seemed to suggest that he sometimes saw himself as both vector and victim. That such circulations were long encouraged and exploited by the colonial regime, which channeled the earnings of Mozambican miners in South Africa into foreign exchange reserves, or that many lives, male and female, are now constituted in circulations across Mozambique's borders, goes unmentioned in these discourses of moving bodies as menace.

These representations also obscured how the steady employment that Sr. Francisco enjoyed has become ever harder to access and erased the extent to which women's livelihoods in Maputo, as well as men's, depend on entrepreneurial migration.[5] In fact, the historical continuities evoked by Sr. Francisco's story actually distinguished him from many of his (mostly female) companions waiting in line at the hospital food warehouse. His anxieties over pension benefits were uncommon; few of the patients I talked with had ever known this kind of formal labor. For most, even informal work in South Africa was hard to secure, and life for many Mozambican migrants in South Africa was characterized by intense insecurity. The very historical resonance of Sr. Francisco's story also made it somewhat anachronistic within the broader setting of the clinic.

More typical than Sr. Francisco's were stories of husbands, parents, or children working informally across the border while loved ones remained and sought care in Maputo. My neighbor, for example, cared for her young granddaughter whose parents were in South Africa; the pediatric AIDS program at Maputo Central Hospital, she explained, was better than the treatment her granddaughter might receive in South Africa. In this way, families combined the economic possibilities available on one side of the border with the humanitarian medical supports available on the others.

Strategies to combine work and care, however, also caused problems in the clinic. Doctors sometimes rejected claims of employment in South Africa as "stories" told to excuse missed appointments or poor test results. Women whose husbands were absent from consultations because they were working on "that side" of the border were often dismissed by skeptical doctors. When one young woman, for instance, told a psychologist that her husband was working in South Africa, the clinician responded:

> One thing you have to do here is tell us the truth, *mãe* [mother], because what happens a lot is people come here with stories and they say, "Oh, my husband is in South Africa" and I don't know what what what what what [*e não sei que que que que que*]. And later when there are problems with treatment, we find out that everything they told us was not true at all! But when you ask them, when they first come here for consultations they tell us, "No, he is coming . . ." and it turns out not to be true at all!

Sr. Francisco's experiences were thus at once historically "typical" and unusual. Steady employment, the emphasis on masculine labor and migration, the concern with salary and pension, even his return to a long-standing, geographically stable household were out-of-keeping with many experiences of the mostly women patients who frequented the clinic.

These features threw into sharp relief the disjunctures that existed between patient experience and the Clínica communities imagined by GCF. They highlighted a divergence between stories deemed "important" for visiting social scientists and the more common and deeply gendered ways that patients engaged with medical care. For this very reason, while Sr. Francisco was described to me as an ideal patient, his experience obscured as much as it revealed. Yet his story remains instructive, because it exemplified how both clinic and WFP staff envisioned the patients they served and how they idealized the contributions of food support to patient recovery.

Distributing Food in Morrumbala and Maputo

Clínica 2 received funding from the European Union and the UN as well as from the American AIDS relief program, PEPFAR (President's Emergency Plan for AIDS Relief), but food at the clinic was distributed via WFP. It was WFP that had built the zinc-roofed, cement-walled warehouse at the far edge of the clinic courtyard, where sacks of grains and beans were stored and canisters of oil were delivered each month by truck. The food, distributed monthly to the approximately sixty people enrolled in the program, was stacked inside in mountainous piles. The iconic white and blue sacks of corn-soy blend—a powder that could be cooked into a cardboard-colored porridge—maize, or split peas were emblazoned with national flags, linking each nation's agricultural surplus to the pluralistic and market-mediated institutional landscape that underpins WFP. (The historical dependence of WFP on surpluses is frequently the basis for critical views of the organization, which point to how the agency relies on the same globalized market forces that contribute to poverty in Mozambique.)

Food from WFP was intended for patients with chronic diseases, and in particular those who were beginning antiretroviral therapy and whose body-mass index (BMI, a ratio of height to weight) was less than 18.5, a cut off determining "underweight" status. Each month, patients enrolled in the food program arrived on a designated afternoon. After checking in with the clinic administrator, a young woman named Raquel, and having their weight checked and recorded on their green food cards, patients lined up to wait outside the warehouse. It was here that I had first met Sr. Francisco. Eventually, Raquel and a clinic staff member named Mateus would call names one by one. As each was called, the person would hold out his or her sack while Mateus scooped up the monthly allotment of beans and grains and decanted cooking oil into yellow two-liter containers. Patients were responsible for bringing their own sacks and containers, and as time went on, many families made do with repurposed bags, sometimes scooping up spilled maize when a previously unnoticed weak spot gave way. It was also the responsibility of families and patients to carry the food home from the clinic. For those unable to carry the heavy load, a group of young men with large hand carts waited outside the clinic gates where they charged about US$0.80 (20 MT) to trundle the food to patients' homes.

Food was most often distributed in the afternoons, beginning about 2:00 P.M. and continuing on until 4:00 P.M. or so. Although food distribution at Clínica 2 was not subject to the logistical complications and delays that characterized the program at GCF, it nevertheless had its challenges. The warehouse was stuffy and frequently hot, and the sun was often strong on patients waiting outside. Short tempers were not uncommon, and staff members like Mateus complained about the hours of lifting heavy sacks in the heat and the dust. In this regard, Mateus, Raquel, and others were in good company: I was frequently told that "*no one* want[ed] the headache of food support." It was, I was informed, a hassle to transport, deliver, store, and distribute food while ensuring that it did not become infested with bugs or get too old to be edible. Despite the attention of the clinic and WFP to quality-control issues (WFP conducted periodic checks of the storage conditions and the clinic had constructed a dedicated space entirely for food), patients complained about bugs in the corn and about the hard dried beans that were edible only after hours of cooking, requiring families to spend more on charcoal than the beans were worth (Kalofonos 2010). Some of these problems were avoided by the GCF program in Morrumbala, which bought food from local merchants, distributed a wider range of goods, and was not responsible for storing food between deliveries. However, the underlying dilemmas of distributing food to the ill in a context of generalized poverty were not only logistical; they were built into the structure of food baskets themselves.

Food and Social Justice

Proponents of food support programs have importantly argued for food as a means of incorporating social justice principles or human rights principles into public health care (Drèze and Sen 1991). Yet rights to livelihood or to food were rarely discussed at the clinic. Instead, guidelines for eligibility emphasized metabolic and therapeutic parameters, which were determined by the medical and metabolic effects of AIDS treatment. As a result, practices through which food support was provided reflected a view of the recipient not as the subject of social or economic rights but as a body whose well-being could be broken down into measurable factors—access to medicines, psychological care and motivation, and physical support including food. For instance, the WFP website at the time described the program as providing "a nutritional supplement for clients of care and treatment programs for greater wellbeing and drug tolerance and also represent[ing] an incentive for regular attendance and participation in care and treatment services. . . . The food ration aims to encourage household involvement in the care of the clients by providing a contribution to the household resources." The vision described a body that, with the right attention and inputs, will return to normal, stable levels within a discrete time period (six months).[6]

Specifying that beneficiaries were to be "the most vulnerable clients enrolled in and attending selected programs," this vision of the patient also saw vulnerability as something that could be similarly measured and ranked: "The program focuses on the individual clients and their respective health improvements but acknowledges the role of the family and immediate care and support environment. . . . Thus selection of the *most vulnerable* clients takes into consideration both the individual wellbeing and the household vulnerability" (emphasis added). For patients on treatment for HIV, the food support was to be "provided to selected clients during the first six months of antiretroviral therapy so as to facilitate the stabilization of the client on the treatment." The rationale for this was both physical and psychological, even financial: "It is believed that food support will improve physical and psychological well-being and thus contribute to improved drug tolerance. . . . After six months the majority of patients are observed to be less affected by the treatment side effects and *are expected to be physically recovered to the extent that economically productive activity* is possible" (emphasis added). In this view of the body and its potential, the question of what "economically productive activity is possible" might mean—or whether physical debility was the only barrier to such productivity—was left aside.

Compared with the vagueness of evaluating "individual wellbeing and the household vulnerability" or the possibility of economic productivity, body-mass index (BMI) promised a more straightforward means of measuring and comparing vulnerability, precisely because it measured the patient's body. Yet this approach left little room for recognizing how food was consumed, deployed, and exchanged within and across households and neighborhoods. As a result, sticky evaluative dilemmas were built into the *cesta básica* itself. Each basket—or bundle—was expected to feed not only a patient but an "average household" of five adults. At clinics supported by WFP, the "baskets" included approximately 40 kilograms of cereals (like maize), 6 kilograms of beans or lentils, 1–2 liters of cooking oil, and 10 kilograms of corn-soy blend, portions calculated to provide a majority of the daily caloric needs of a household of five. (The GCF basket supplemented this with small portions of sugar and a long bar of soap, but in most other respects it and the WPF's—and the imagined household to which they were directed—were the same. In fact, the WPF basket served as a model or baseline for a number of programs, including GCF.)

Despite the standardization of the baskets, however, recipients lived and ate not in "average households" but in complex sets of relations. In Morrumbala, as we have seen, Susana deployed her basket to feed her family and her close friend and to generate income. Another GCF recipient, Beatrice, shared her food basket with eight nieces and nephews as well as her own two children. Antonio, by contrast, used the food basket to support himself and his wife, as well as their three children, yet he also offered some portion of the food to GCF volunteers who had helped when he was ill and unable to work. At Sr. Francisco's house in Maputo, by contrast, the food was "controlled" by his wife, but it was primarily directed to Sr. Francisco along with assistance from his adult children. In this way, too, Sr. Francisco's experience was somewhat unusual. Yet another Clínica 2 patient fed her niece and her niece's children, with whom she lived.

Household Distributions

The diversity of uses to which food was put highlights how, as food baskets entered into differently composed households, they were distributed and consumed in a variety of ways. In many homes, notions of the "average household" failed to account for the fluctuating number of people who ate together or for the ways that food was shared across and beyond the limits of a single household. As a result, despite the techniques through which medicalized vulnerabilities were established, patients, volunteers, and even staff worked to reconcile notions of vulnerability that were calculated through formulas of weight and height with relational understandings that shaped how need was lived and support deployed. Though body mass index was the primary measure used to determine eligibility for food support, calculations of need were based not exclusively on body mass index but also on assessments of the relations that a patient supported and that, in turn, offered care for him or her.

A clinic patient named Anita, for instance, distributed her food among her husband's family, with whom she lived while her husband worked in South Africa. In his absence, her food basket contributed to the household and shored up a position she felt was precarious. Though her eligibility for support was established on the basis of a medical diagnosis and low body weight, in practice she (and the health volunteers who assisted her) understood her vulnerability as fundamentally social in nature. It was not simply ill health, but also the fragile nature of the relations on which she relied that made her an object of concern. A clinic volunteer commented sympathetically that "*nora é nora*"—a daughter-in-law is a daughter-in-law (*not* a daughter), less bound to the family by ties of affection and obligation. By providing Anita with food, the staff aimed to build up her physiological capacity and to support her difficult position of dependence on her husband's family.

As Anita's experience shows, Clínica 2 staff determined eligibility for food support by means of both bodily measures and social estimations, and the assessments of community volunteers were especially important in this regard. Volunteers told me that "principally, I look for those who are most isolated" or "I see that we are to choose those who are totally bad—who have a totally bad aspect." Even Raquel, the clinic administrator, described biophysical criteria like body mass indexes or assessments of metabolic processes as crude tools that ignored important differences in social position across patients and community members. A wealthy patient whose poor appetite had resulted in rapid weight loss might qualify for food, she noted, while a poor patient whose family sacrificed their own food to sustain her weight would be excluded. As a result, Raquel said, "I try to give [food] to people who I know really need help, but the criteria they give us are clinical. Even if someone shows up nicely dressed, and comes in a car to pick up their food, if they are on TARV [ARV treatment]—especially if they are just starting and they meet the weight criteria, they can be included [according to program guidelines]." It was dilemmas such as this one, in which a single measure was used to determine the multiple needs of different patients, that caused Raquel to "wonder whether this program is doing more harm than good." Although most patients who met the criteria and asked to be enrolled eventually were, Raquel tried to dissuade patients who "didn't really need it," cautioning them instead to "wait for a rainy day." Even as poverty was a rationale for food support (it was because so many patients are poor that a policy of providing food in clinics came under consideration), poverty alone could not justify intervention. Instead, food support for patients was always justified on clinical grounds, despite broader debates over the morality of providing food to the sick in a context of general hunger.

Feeding the Sick

Complicated relationships between poverty, economic productivity, and medical vulnerability were particularly evident in patient complaints over food support. For instance, many patients disliked the contents of the *cesta básica*. Food supplies reflected donor availability and priorities, and in 2007 WFP itself faced shortages of food. In this context, they began encouraging food support partners to emphasize (or "push" in Raquel's words) soy flour or corn-soy blend, which were more widely available than corn and which, because many people didn't like the taste of soy flour, were regarded as more likely to be eaten by hungry patients rather than other members of the household. "The idea is that you can make it into porridge [*papas*], but people don't like to eat soy papas all the time, and they are not used to it," explained Veronica, the community staff coordinator. When this issue was raised at meetings of WFP partners, Raquel later recounted, "they basically say that if people are complaining it's because we are not selecting the right people—hungry people would not complain about the soy. Also some people eat it intermittently with other things, so at the end of the month they still have some left and will ask if they can put off collecting the new package until the old one is finished. But WFP also responds that these people are not 'needy' enough, since needy people would want to eat it all." Body mass index promised a single measure through which "the most vulnerable" could be determined, but questions of taste, practice, and familiarity shaped how people used the food they were given.

An additional point of contention were guidelines based on the idea that a period of six months was sufficient time for people to "get back on their feet" and resume "economic productivity." Inherent in this vision were twin assumptions: that people were food secure prior to falling ill, and that hunger caused by or related to medication was different from other forms of hunger. In this view, once patients had recuperated and were successfully enrolled in treatment, therapeutic food support was no longer necessary. Yet these assumptions were not borne out by the experience of patients and workers in the clinic, and patients frequently complained when their six months came to an end, just as Susana had complained to GCF. For some patients (pregnant women, for instance), food support could be extended until patients had regained and maintained a healthy weight for at least two months. Most, however, were limited to six months of support. Raquel followed a standard practice of preparing recipients at each monthly distribution, announcing that "this is your second month, you have four left" or "this is your fifth month. After this, you have one more and then in February you won't receive anything, OK? You understand?"

When I asked Raquel about this practice, she first explained that she was concerned that people be prepared when they arrive at month six. After reflecting for a minute, she added that she found it hard to stop giving people food and she wanted them to be clear that food support "is not going to be forever." "The WFP guidelines really only give them six months," she said. "I can sometimes stretch it to nine months, or even a year, if people are not getting better, but in principal it should be six months only. And anyway, I don't like to break the rules too much. I have to go to the [WFP] monthly meetings and report on how things are going, and I don't like to feel like I'm lying." I asked whether she thought that by sticking to the guidelines and reporting on the problems she might encourage WFP to change the program parameters. "Well . . . but they are not changing the guidelines," Raquel asserted. "Their attitude is, 'This is not feeding the poor, this is feeding the sick.' When I raise these issues, anyway, they're like, well, refer them to UNICEF, they're orphans or whatever . . . whatever way they can find for passing on the issue. And when I complain to the hospital, they say call Acção Social [Social Welfare]. Everybody knows Acção Social isn't going to do anything."

Not only did WFP not respond to Raquel's complaints, but Raquel also worried about antagonizing WFP. They had recently cut the numbers of partners they supported, disproportionately ending contracts with groups that were not directly involved with medical treatment. In this context, Raquel worried about extending support beyond six months except in the direst cases. Lying to WFP not only "felt wrong" to Raquel; it also jeopardized the program, since feeding "the poor" rather than "the sick" was grounds for termination. Under pressure from WFP, which in turn was under pressure to stretch resources as far as possible, Raquel had to manage the distinction between illness and poverty in everyday interactions with patients. Thus, she acknowledged, "sometimes I really have to be fierce, really repeat that it's only six months, and . . . I have to use a fierce voice, almost an angry voice. Because, you know . . . I kind of don't want to hear how it is for you at home, because there is nothing I can do." Far from looking fierce, however, Raquel looked sad as she sat at her desk. "Sometimes I just have to tell people, you know, we are not a social services program; we're a health clinic."

Aiming to feed the sick but not the poor, clinical nutrition programs sought to constitute food as a therapeutic input, targeted at physical recovery, and not as a social safety net, supporting impoverished patients. By focusing on *medical* hunger, these programs worked to inscribe what has become familiar to anthropologists as a form of humanitarian exception (Ticktin 2011), by which urgent or emergency circumstances and recognition of bodily suffering make possible forms of government and care that were otherwise legally or institutionally proscribed. As critics have noted, these zones of exception often ignore how hierarchies of race and gender constitute understandings of the human that lie at the heart of such efforts (Weheliye 2014). Yet in practice patients and staff recognized that bodily and medical experience were inextricable from racialized and gendered social relations. In this setting, medical hunger was socially as well as physiologically pressing, and responses to hunger were at once caloric and relational.

Food and the Conditions of Care

Lived experiences of food support challenged distinctions between food as medicine and food as an economic, material, and relational resource. In a context of both illness and poverty, sympathetic providers sometimes tried to work within the constraints of the food program to care for their patients. At the same time, food also became the grounds for scrutiny and evaluation, as providers also tried to distinguish between more and less deserving patients in a context where physiological measures (such as body mass index) failed to capture both the demand for food and the nuances of food, health, and illness.

This was clear for instance, when Marta, a woman in her early forties, brought four-year-old Esme in for a consultation. Like many patients anxious about being seen at the clinic, Marta and Esme had dressed up for the consultation, as if heading to church. Wearing a cream-colored blouse, a skirt covered by a *capulana* (a length of patterned cotton cloth) with a pretty flower design, a handkerchief on her head, and the black, rubber-soled, canvas shoes worn by many older women in Maputo, Marta looked neat and respectable. She carried a bright blue handbag, the color flaking off around the corners. Her daughter Esme was prettily dressed, too, in a pink sweatshirt and stretchy leggings.

They were here, they explained to the staff member who joined them in the consultation room, because Esme, who had HIV, was being considered for a more expensive, complicated, and physically demanding treatment regime. The switch in medications had been recommended by the clinic director,

Dr. Joana, after the more commonly prescribed "first-line" medications that Esme was taking ceased to be efficacious. This was frequently interpreted as a sign that patients have not been taking the medications correctly. A switch to "second-line" drugs—difficult to take, more expensive, and less widely available—was often viewed with suspicion by clinic staff. In Esme's case, Dr. Joana had requested a series of counseling appointments to evaluate the family's ability to manage the new pharmaceutical regimen.

The medications used in "second-line treatments" were widely seen in the clinic to be more complex: a greater number of pills are taken at more complicated time intervals, and the medications are stronger. Because side effects are frequently more severe, it is particularly important that patients eat regularly to offset the strong medications. In a context where drug supplies are limited, and where no alternative treatments exist should second-line treatments fail, doctors were also reluctant to enroll patients who might be unable to follow the treatment properly. In fact, second-line treatment had to be approved by a special Ministry of Health committee. Nurses and psychologists at the clinic frequently expressed a sense of futility around second-line treatment, reasoning that those who had not followed simpler regimens would be even less likely to comply with more complicated dosing schedules and arduous treatments. Indeed, these patients were often seen as already having failed. In Marta and Esme's case, the psychologists on duty that day, Dr. Luísa and Dr. Felícia, as well as the medical intern who was helping conduct the consultation, tried to evaluate what to do about this—"whether," as Dr. Felícia put it, "it's worth it to switch the medicines or whether it's just going to cause a new set of problems."

In response to Dr. Felícia's questions, Marta said she had seven children at home, including one granddaughter. Her eldest daughter was twenty-seven, and had just left her job working in a neighbor's fields because of conflicts with the neighbor. Marta's husband was too ill to work, so they were surviving on money she earned selling peanuts on the street. Hearing this, Dr. Luísa asked how much food they had in the house—what, for instance, had Esme had to eat today? Marta explained that they had left home early to find room on the bus ("You can see when we come here we are always first because we have to leave at 5 [A.M.]") so Esme had only taken her pills, and when they arrived at the hospital, Marta bought her a piece of bread. "Did she have tea this morning?" Dr. Luísa asked. "It's important to give the child something, even if it's just tea. Do you have tea for her? Do you have sugar at home, in the house?" "Yes, I have sugar [at home]. It's just that we left early," Marta answered, though she seemed anxious and spoke abruptly. Dr. Luísa nodded, then left the room to consult with Dr. Joana. When she came back, she said that they would wait for a month to see how the little girl progressed. In the meantime, the mother could begin to think about what would happen if the doctors wanted to switch to second-line therapy. In addition, Nurse Elsa would visit the family's home "to see who is there, or near there, who can help you and what are the conditions in which Esme is living." Although this visit was presented as an effort to help, it was also aimed at evaluating the truthfulness of Marta's claims. The vagueness with which Marta described the location of her house suggested that she was likely aware of this double intention.

The staff's concern with evaluation was made particularly clear after Marta and Esme left. As Dr. Luísa finished writing up her consultation report, I asked, "Do you think it is possible for nine people to survive on the money she earns selling peanuts?" Dr. Felícia, who had been observing throughout the consultation, suddenly interjected, "Yeah, that's very difficult—that's why we want to go to the house, to see if it really is as she says it is." An attending intern, a medical student from the nearby university, added, "Because she was wearing nice clothes, and she gave the child bread, and she said she had sugar in the house," rather than less expensive food like cassava or *xima* (cornmeal). For the psychologists, the possibility that things were not "as she says" raised the prospect that Esme's struggles were due not to financial constraints but to parental "choices," such as failing to follow the medication schedule or relying on traditional therapies rather than ARVs.

For patients, however, the line between constraints and choices was ambiguous, since the very conditions that made them reliant on clinic assistance also threatened their eligibility for care. Although Marta had made manifest the disjuncture between the neatness of her clothing in the clinic and the conditions in which she lived, an alternative interpretation—that things were not "as she said," because she was *over*stating the conditions in which they lived— was not explored. Just as many patients dressed in their "Sunday best" in an effort to be treated respectfully by clinic staff, so too might Marta overemphasize her ability to provide Esme with tea and bread precisely in order to convey her care for her daughter and her recognition of what were sometimes seen as "more modern" norms of consumption and care. Where transparency and openness were assumed to guide care practices and relations, the mere hint of untruthfulness seemed to discredit patient "stories." Patient narratives were heard as "lies" rather than reflections of the complex social relations through which patients and providers assembled their lives.

Nodding in agreement with the intern's assessment of Marta's contradictory appearance, for instance, Dr. Luísa asserted,

> Yes, because they don't always tell you the truth . . . you should see some of the mothers that come in here saying they don't have this, they don't have that, they don't have material conditions [condições]. The young ones are the worst, they come in here with the child crying because it hasn't eaten since yesterday and they are wearing the fanciest jeans, brand-name clothes and their hair . . . They come in with extensions and then when I say, "If you have nothing to feed your baby why are you spending your money on this?" Ha! One said to me, "These? No, these were a gift. My cousin gave them to me," and I said [sarcastically], "Ohhhh, thank you very much for explaining that to me."

In her characterization of young patients, a characterization I found rather unfair, Dr. Luísa referred to condições, the material conditions of life, and to patient claims that they lacked the material resources or conditions necessary for life in the city. In practice, many patients benefitted from relations of exchange and gift-giving between friends and family, practices that facilitated relationships and expressed affection. Yet despite the apparent attention to "social relations" in clinic practice, mention of friendly and familial exchanges elicited skepticism from the staff. In these encounters, assessments of patients as truthful or dishonest were frequently made and articulated via judgments about gender, class, education, and disposition.

Concern with the imbrications of money and medicine, with the relation between "conditions" and care, was not restricted Clínica 2 staff. Medical anthropological and global health approaches to the imbrications of economy and care have often emphasized how financial need and economic inequality produce and exacerbate ill health. Anthropologists and scholars of global and public health have shown, for instance, how even small financial constraints may impede care—for example, when the costs of public transportation leave patients to choose between a meal and bus fare for a trip to the clinic, or when conditions of financial precarity drive patients to high-risk occupations that negatively impact their health (e.g., Farmer 2004). These biosocial accounts of gender and health have emphasized that the economic determinants of care can be a matter of survival, and in this way they capture the high stakes of Esme's situation.

Yet for Marta, Esme, and others, financial need, social relations, and medical necessity were complexly entangled. Accessing care at the clinic required a subtle navigation of competing expectations: that patients would be neatly presentable but not too well dressed, that they would exert themselves to earn a living, but not be too concerned with money. Care required *condições*, but also enabled them, as enrollment at Clínica 2 facilitated proximity to new sources of support. Precarious livelihoods rendered patients vulnerable and therefore deserving of support but also opened them up to judgment about the legitimacy of their claims. Amid these competing dynamics of evaluation and encouragement, food—what and when one ate and with whom—was central.

Feeding the Poor, Feeding the Sick

On the one hand, distinctions between feeding the poor and feeding the sick obscured how *condições* and the capacity for giving and accessing care were complexly entangled. On the other, the notion of the food basket as an incentive for care quietly illustrated how practices of care are embedded in relations. The nuances of these relations, however, were not captured by clinic imaginings of care as constituting a neatly bounded domestic sphere, often envisioned along heteronormative and deeply gendered lines. One nurse, for instance, told me that she felt more "at ease" when men fell sick rather than women because "we [women] stand by them, but a man will just leave her." In practice, however, relations were not circumscribed by the bounds of the household nor by gendered assumptions. Instead, both patients and staff distributed food in ways that brought a variety of gendered political and temporal relations into view. While Raquel, Violeta, and others used diagnoses, body mass indexes, and metabolic criteria to calculate inclusion in the food program, they also drew on gendered understandings of need in choosing whom to include and when.

Although the food basket was designed to be shared among an average of five people, community workers and volunteers were also instructed to emphasize that the food was "*really* for the patient" and to underscore the importance of good nutrition. Following the training they received, they explained to caregivers how to make *papas* or porridge if the patient was unable to eat solid foods. For the very ill, especially, the extra food was important in itself, but it was also important to the household as a whole. For many beneficiaries, the prolonged illness of an adult had affected everyone in the household—from eating less to missing school or work. Thus food was important not only to the patient but to the others who relied on or supported the patient. While in some cases this behavior was disparaged by the volunteers as "taking advantage" of the patient, it was most often seen as understandable or even appropriate. As described in chapter 3, patients appreciated a chance to reciprocate support they had received while ill, or even to repay food or money they had borrowed. For some, opportunities for reciprocity were as important as the nutritional benefits of the food they consumed.[7]

Practices of exchange not only characterized how people used food within the household; they also extended into encounters with clinic staff. Although Raquel lamented that social criteria were not taken seriously in the enrollment of patients into the program, social considerations did shape how some patients accessed clinic resources.

The work of the community staff was particularly important in this regard; for instance, it was by way of the community staff that the clinic learned of and became concerned about Anita's situation. In many instances, recognizing the difficult circumstances in which patients found themselves, the community staff struggled, in their words, to "close their eyes" to patients' needs. As a volunteer named Adelina told me, "The main thing the patients need is food. Sometimes, if I have food of my own, then I will give it. I'll bring some *papinhas* [porridge] to give to them. This is how we practice our charity. But if I don't have it at home, then there is nothing I can do." For Adelina, a devout Catholic in her sixties, serving as a community health worker and occasionally sharing food with those in need offered an opportunity to deepen her faith and live out its tenets along with her community and political commitments. Yet the exchanges of food worked both ways. Not infrequently, patients who were enrolled in the food program might also pass some portion of it to the staff member who visited them or who they felt had helped to facilitate their enrollment. This was not, strictly speaking, allowed, but many accepted it as normal practice. Adelina, for instance, also said, "Yes, I'll accept it. But only afterwards, once they have recovered. If it is to thank me for assisting them, and they are well enough to spare it, why should I refuse?"

Contesting Food Support in Morrumbala

Unlike Clínica 2, the food support that GCF provided to patients in Morrumbala was not provided by WFP. Instead, GCF bought the food from local merchants, providing beneficiaries each month with rice (20 kilos), beans, oil, sugar, soap, and salt. Yet many similar tensions surrounded the distribution of food. As was the case for clinic staff, GCF program staff found food distribution to be a source of headaches and complaints, and, as at the clinic, these tensions centered on the criteria and evaluative strategies for inclusion in the food program. For GCF program staff and volunteers, access to the food basket was equally determined by a combination of need and enrollment in the HIV/AIDS or TB programs at the local hospital. While hospital documentation of malnutrition (like BMI) was taken into account, the staff in charge of enrollment in the program also relied on clinical indicators, reports by the home-based care volunteers, and their own judgment. Although, like Raquel, they were aware that enrolling one patient meant excluding another, GCF staff did not have to be as concerned about donor funding and partner program constraints; GCF criteria for inclusion were more flexible. Violeta, in charge of enrollment, cited various factors in explaining her decisions about entry into the program, including perceived need in the form of clinical malnutrition or visible poverty. Nevertheless, "papers from the hospital" remained the most important factor. They not only provided a diagnosis but also served as evidence of patients' efforts to improve their health. Patients who were ill but refused medical treatment were considered to be "just running after food" and were excluded.

The efforts made by clinic staff like Violeta to distinguish food as a therapeutic technology from food as a response to poverty were reinforced by lectures on nutrition delivered regularly at food drop-off points and in community meetings. These focused on the need for a varied and balanced diet, discouraged the consumption of alcohol and fatty foods, and emphasized the management of nutrition as central to the management of the patient self—a good patient was one who cared about and monitored what he or she consumed. This neat formulation of therapeutic food and of a body that could be measured and managed quickly broke down in practice. Nutritional lectures left aside the restrictions that poverty placed on most people's diet. Community volunteers who themselves had little to eat half-heartedly encouraged patients to consume a wide range of unavailable fruits and vegetables.

Distinguishing between food as therapy and food as poverty alleviation was also a source of tension and contradiction, the weight of which was borne particularly by volunteers who felt themselves the target of complaints. For instance, one volunteer, Vasco, said in annoyance, "The problem is that [the patients] come here and Violeta sends them away. Then they are already against us, the volunteers. And they are right! They say, 'why did you tell me to come here to be treated in this way?'" Medical food support in Morrumbala, moreover, was situated in relation to a wide variety of food support initiatives.

As Sr. Chico, a community volunteer in a small village in the southern part of Morrumbala district, commented,

> Now, there is Oikos [a European development agency], they are giving food to the elderly and the handicapped. But there are a lot of elderly and handicapped people who aren't included although they could be. And there is the food for work program, but that is only for some. There are fourteen *mfumos* [traditional authorities], and they were each allowed to put twelve people in the program. Twelve people! Out of maybe one hundred! And the others? They are going to be enrolled in what?! It's a shame. And the people are starting to complain.

Similarly, in discussing the insults and complaints they received from "people who want to be in the program, or who don't get the food basket, or who get food and then it's stopped," Pastor Tomás and two fellow volunteers made these comments:

> They say, oh, why don't you enroll me? Or: why can't you renew my food card? Then we go to their houses to visit and they almost don't receive you. Whereas before they received you well.
> And you try to say "there is Certeza [water purification solution] here that I am offering you." And they say, "Certeza?! I am asking for food and you are offering me *this*? Do you think I will eat this Certeza? All my life since I was born and was a child I have never used this. Go away [*vai lá*] with your Certeza!"

The contestations of food support were therefore not only difficult for patients and program staff but also for community health workers and volunteers.

Food and Gendered Relations of Care

Much like Morrumbala residents who complained about and contested the use and limits of therapeutic food, patients in Maputo argued with Raquel about the disenrollment process. Some patients drew on the understanding that the food was provided "for their greater well-being and drug tolerance" and as "an incentive for regular attendance" at the clinic by using medication as a bargaining tool. For instance, an elderly woman with glaucoma said heatedly to Raquel, "They are giving us this food so that we can take our pills. So when they stop giving us our food, how are we supposed to take them?!" She threatened to "quit!" In this case, food support *was* extended, the precarious conditions of the woman's life having been documented by the clinic's community volunteers, who sent the case to Acção Social. More frequently, though, patients were sent away, after being told many times that their eligibility was going to expire.

Other patients deployed gendered understandings of illness and vulnerability. When I accompanied Clínica 2 community staff to visit Ruth, who had just finished her last month of food support, she complained that in addition to being involved in a protracted fight with her ex-husband, she was struggling to make ends meet, subsisting off the money she earned selling charcoal. "Tell Raquel," she told me as we sat next to her small kiosk, "that I don't have anything to eat. If I don't have food, I'm going to stop taking my medicine. Not altogether, but I'm not going to comply the way I have been . . . Or maybe I'll just arrange a man," she concluded pointedly. When I joked that this might be a problematic solution, she laughed and said: "Well, they [men] give you something to nibble on."

Anthropologists have variously accepted and disputed the assumption that entanglements of romantic and sexual relations with economic necessity can put women at risk. For instance, scholars have demonstrated how poverty may constrain women's choices in ways that put their health and well-being in danger—for instance, by making it more difficult to leave abusive relationships or to negotiate safer sex practices (e.g., Farmer 2004). Anthropologists have also shown, however, that emotional, sexual, and financial dependence can be "entangled" and "mutually constitutive" in ways that are positive as well as risk-promoting (Cole and Thomas 2009; see also Archambault 2013). Yet the perception that romantic relationships were threats to women's well-being importantly shaped clinic policies and practices. At Clínica 2, one of the key justifications for providing food was to discourage reliance on sexual partners for economic survival, and clinic patients were subject to frequent, often haranguing, lectures regarding the dangers of relationships. Ruth's words thus spoke to public health discourses that emphasized personal behavior but ignored how relationships were situated in relation to the broader conditions in which urban residents worked to make ends meet. (Other recipients took an opposite approach, hiding relationships from clinic or program staff in the belief that single women or single mothers appeared more deserving than others of extended support.)[8] Ruth also, like the elderly woman with glaucoma, played one understanding of vulnerability—that of the medicated patient—against a more gendered view of women as vulnerable to dangerous relationships.

Ruth was not the only one who spoke to these clinic assumptions about the need to disentangle relations, care, and food. Sometimes in earnest and sometimes jokingly, women often spoke about men as a source of support in the absence of other forms of care—as "something to nibble on." In these comments, women showed how claims to the resources of global health, and deployments of those resources, were shaped not only by interactions with Raquel or with medicalized definitions of vulnerability but also by their own shifting circumstances, relations, and possibilities. As Sr. Francisco's experience shows, relationships were central to practices of care and possibilities for recuperation for women and men alike. The difference between the appreciation with which clinic staff responded to his story (as important) and the criticism they often offered women reflected gendered and heteronormative assumptions about reliable or dangerous sources of support.

Such assumptions were held by both the public health staff who managed much of the day-to-day work of food support at the clinic and the NGO staff who enabled these programs. Clinic practices made some forms of support appear more legitimate and reliable than others. Thus the generous financial, physical, and emotional care offered by Sr. Francisco's wife was distinguished from the forms of emotional and material support or practices of exchange referenced by female patients in the clinic. However, despite the emphasis by the clinic and scholars alike on "boyfriends" as a source of both danger and care, a boyfriend was only one, and perhaps the least important, of many relations that shaped women's engagements with food support. For example, although Susana joked that "the only thing they didn't give you in Malawi was a man," she was *not* in actuality sustained by boyfriends and husbands; rather, she relied on female friends, like Hortencia, and female kin, including her mother and sister, to care for her and her children.

Distributing the Metabolic Body

What kinds of relations were nourished, then, through and beyond medicalized food support and the adjacent forms of care made available at Clínica 2? On the one hand, to suggest that global health resources gave rise to and were entangled with social relations is not to suggest that these were always positive entanglements. Hunger and eating are long-standing and meaningful idioms—in Mozambique as elsewhere—for expressing how political power mediates access to economic or material resources, how the powerful consume at the expense of the poor, and how moral obligations to redistribution are imposed on those with access to resources (see especially Bayart 2009; with regard to food support in Mozambique, this topic has been particularly taken up in Kalofonos 2010).

To talk about food, eating, and care, then, is somewhat inevitably to talk about power in ways that capture both dangers and possibilities. Just as common as moments of familial generosity were conflicts over the division and distribution of real or imagined resources that global health projects brought with them. The perception that global health projects made illness a perverse source of wealth was the basis of ambivalence, skepticism, or cynicism about how some—whether patients, aid workers, or government ministers—seemed to benefit from the misfortune of others, as when Tomás observed bitterly that "everyone is getting fat from these programs but us." A patient at Clínica 2 asserted that "[the government] wants us to be sick" because "the more the numbers [of patients] go up, the more money they receive." Similarly, in an interview, a staff member at the Ministry of Social Welfare compared AIDS organizations and drug traffickers, noting that both enriched people at the highest levels. These examples show how the resources of transnational interventions not only facilitated solidarity but also anger, cynicism, or resentment.

Alongside gestures of donor largesse, then, were suspicions of how some were enriched, perhaps illicitly, even as others suffered. The possibilities for well-being enabled by health interventions were at once sustaining and fraught. In addition to facilitating short-term survival and, sometimes, longer-term well-being, they also produced new predicaments and frailties including, sometimes, the very vulnerabilities (like familial conflict or patient non-adherence) that they aimed to prevent.[9] As a result, many anthropologists have demonstrated continuities between therapeutic food programs and neoliberal projects of care and public reform (e.g., Foley 2009). They have shown how new practices and rationalities of government—for instance, the market— have replaced concerns with society and the social that were once seen to animate efforts to promote public health (Joyce 2002). Anthropologists have emphasized how therapeutic food programs imagine health and well-being in asocial terms of physiological recuperation and metabolic stabilization, focused on the individual body and ignoring the rich social and political meanings that also attend to food and its distribution. For this reason, such programs have been described as enacting a neoliberal and antisocial vision of care.

Attention to how food, material support, and modes of livelihood are brought together, however, makes clear how ongoing possibilities for care are nevertheless fashioned through gendered relations. The food programs I followed understood food as contributing to a return to health, where health was defined by individual, biomedical measures of well-being and in relation to metabolic understandings of the body. Yet patients, and even staff members, involved with these programs were not only concerned with medicalized notions of health. They were also concerned with strength, well-being, and relations of care that extended from the clinic into cooking spaces, markets, and social interactions that traversed geographical locations and temporal bounds. By distributing the resources of care into diverse spaces, relations, and practices— the family, the neighborhood, the market—food recipients reworked the time-limited nature of contemporary interventions into longer-term forms of care. As a consequence, gendered expectations regarding care, well-being, and financial support came to define how patients accessed and used food itself.

Yet if the relational dimensions of food caused "headaches," they were also what made food so central to patient experience. As metabolic experiences and gendered relations came together in new ways, the limited possibilities of food support—both aimed at a household and never enough—became a resource through which physiological *and* relational health was cultivated.

Nourishing Relations

What emerges, then, when we attend to bodily experiences, such as hunger, and to the material specificity of food and pharmaceuticals that enable distributive practices and that are enabled by them? In a context of shifting regimes of development and health, and where families struggled to meet the nutritional needs of patients, the metabolic demands of medication were socially and physiologically pressing.[10] At the same time, responses to such demands, such as food support, became resources through which to forge new and old distributive connections. Alongside clinical concerns with time-limited metabolic change, patients navigated temporalities in which relations, just like bodies, require nourishment. Bringing global health resources into relations with friends, kin, and the market, women in particular sought to construct more robust forms of well-being despite the temporary nature of these interventions. In this way, patients sought to cultivate health not as a moment of full recuperation but as a future capacity.

As suggested by philosopher Georges Canguilhem, who has defined health as "the luxury to fall ill and recover," this future capacity for health was a *bodily* capacity, vested in the physiology of the patient (Petryna 2013).

4.2 A street side stall near Clínica 2.

4.3 In the neighbor-hood near Clínica 2.

At Clínica 2, however, it was *also* a relational capacity, located and cultivated in the relations between women who cared for one another, as mother and daughter, sisters, neighbors, friends, and market colleagues. These caring relations were central to the efficacy of global health programs, and were tacitly and sometimes explicitly recognized as such by clinic staff, but they were seen as a potential threat to program logics that sought to deliver narrowly defined and time-bound inputs to discrete patient bodies.

Embedding health in the body and in time and relations helps to make sense of how women were concerned not only with gaining weight or strength but also with nourishing the relations on which they had relied in the past and on which they would rely again—the relations that would allow them, or their loved ones, to fall ill and recover and that would facilitate entry points into spaces (including social, kin, and market spaces). Concerned with more robust conceptions of well-being, nourishing relations as well as bodies, patients worked between the limits of food support and the luxurious horizon of future health.

CHAPTER 5

The Work of Health in the Public Sector

One morning, soon after I began my research at Clínica 2, I knocked on the door of the Psychology Office. When I entered, Dr. Carolina, the clinic's head psychologist, was sitting with a staff counselor and a middle-aged patient introduced to me as Dona Emilia, who was describing her house and her activities selling a few things, mostly food and drinks, and discussing a plan to buy land in the suburb in which she lived. As Dona Emilia concluded, she handed 1,500 MT (approximately US$55) to Dr. Carolina, who thanked her and said, "I am so happy—really, this is so wonderful." Then she paused, and recalled, "Remember how low you were when you last came here? And now look at you! You look great, this is great." Both were smiling as Dona Emilia got up to leave, and she promised to stop in to say hello when she came back in a month's time. As Dr. Carolina sat back down, she looked thrilled and commented that "cases like this make everything worth it!"

Turning to me, Dr. Carolina explained that Dona Emilia's son was being treated there, as was she. But Dona Emilia's problems were not only medical: her husband had left her, she had no family to support her, and when she first came for counseling sessions, she had been too depressed to work, struggling even to leave the house. "And now, doesn't she look great?" Dr. Carolina asked. I agreed; she did look great. Dr. Carolina explained that Dona Emilia had been raised by her uncle following the death of her parents. Her uncle was not wealthy, and he had stopped supporting her as soon as she was old enough to get married. Now her husband, and his family, had left her alone and sick with the children. "So this woman has always been abandoned," Dr. Carolina said,

> Everyone who comes in here has challenges, but for her, this situation is just bringing back all the other instances in which she's been abandoned. Now, normally with a depressed patient, you start psychotherapy. But for

her, I felt that the most important thing was to make her feel that there was somebody in her life who would not abandon her, who was supporting her. Instead of psychotherapy, I lent her some money so that she could have somewhere stable to live and figure out how to support herself. And now she is talking about the land she wants to buy, starting a little business— and she paid back a third of the money!

Described this way, money was both a financial help in a moment of crisis and a symbolic support that provided emotional rescue. If Dr. Carolina's enthusiasm was evident, it was also surprising, an unexpected moment of empathy and trust that seemed to depart from the rushed routines and scripted encounters that frequently characterized consultations at the clinic.

Later that week, Dr. Carolina asked to hear my impressions of the counseling I had observed so far. Caught off guard, I blurted out, "I'd expected that there would be more talking about feelings." Dr. Carolina nodded sympathetically and said, "You know, the people who come here are really struggling with basic needs—food, support, these things. There is not a lot of time for feelings." She referred back to the incident I've just described, saying, "Emilia, the woman who was in here on Monday, remember her? She had *no energy* for talking about feelings. Sometimes [patients] will get there, but sometimes what they need is more immediate." Then she laughed and said, "Ramah, this is *African* psychology!"

Tall and stylish, Dr. Carolina supervised the psychology program with a warmly animated demeanor and an evident sense of humor. She delivered her comment on "African psychology" with smile, but her remark was wry, too. Dr. Carolina's use of the term *African psychology* connoted not just a departure from clinic norms but a *loaded* departure, one that I might see as not only different from but less than "talking about feelings." Her humor poked at what an American anthropologist might assume about psychology "in Africa" and "by Africans" in a context where clinical excellence meant adhering to foreign standards of care and where local specificity was minimized—as, for example, when the paintings that adorned the clinic's walls portrayed a childish but generic landscape that had more in common with the suburban United States than with Maputo.[1]

By provincializing what I described as "feelings-talk" and distinguishing it from "African" psychology, Dr. Carolina's comments engaged a presumed tension between material support and affective care, as anthropological accounts of the global circulation of psychology, psychotherapy, counseling, and other "psy" disciplines have suggested (for instance, Fassin 2011; Carr 2010; Matza 2012). Her joke brought to the fore the unequal stakes of professional practice in this context, where glossing her practice as "African" made it distinct from and possibly less than the "global" and "humanitarian" endeavors that were also staged in the clinic (Brada 2016). Yet her encounter with Dona Emilia also showed a deeply empathetic moment between clinician and patient, even as Dr. Carolina deferred attention to "feelings" to an indeterminate future.

This chapter returns to consider the multiplicity of medical labor. Who cares, I ask, and how? In earlier chapters, I explored how therapeutic and professional resources mark certain entanglements of material support, affective relations, and professional practice *as* care within a globalizing therapeutic economy. I showed how NGO staff, community volunteers, and patients navigated competing conceptualizations of care as medical, nutritional, economic, relational, and even historical, and as they are shaped by diverse institutions, politics, and temporalities. In this chapter, I explore these entanglements as they shaped more elite professional activities. How did loans, listening practices, affection, or disapproval become visible or excluded as measures of care at Clínica 2? What are the professional, economic, and dispositional stakes of caring, for Clínica 2 patients and for the staff who worked there?

Care in the Global Clinic

Despite its relatively small size, Clínica 2 was a bustling place deeply imbricated in transnational relations. With support from the International Center for Health Care (ICHC), the staff sometimes included four or five physicians (up from the usual two), along with three full-time nurses, two pharmacists, health technicians, and custodial and archival staff. In addition, NGOs provided food, purchased and supplied HIV-testing technologies, facilitated the purchase of medications, and hired counselors, a community coordinator/ clinic supervisor, and six community outreach workers. This extra support was necessary, since in some months the clinic received up to four times the recommended patient load. In the course of my fieldwork, I circulated through main areas of clinic activity, from the nurse's station to the pharmacy, talking with patients, health workers, and staff, and observing everyday clinic practices. I also spent time at other clinics in the city, and with patients and health workers outside the clinic—in homes, restaurants, and churches, and on social occasions—because the institutional setting both facilitated and constrained possibilities for ethnographic engagement (Manuel 2009).

Transnational interventions at Clínica 2 were supported by a variety of nongovernmental actors; primary among these was the ICHC, the U.S.-based global health organization that supported the clinic's HIV-related activities, as well as pediatric and family care. An additional agency supported social development initiatives in the surrounding Maputo neighborhoods. Still other activities were paid for by UN agencies like UNICEF and WFP. Thus, despite the clinic's small setting and public mandate, Clínica 2 was also a site of diversely articulated transnational connections—from the expatriate and local staff that provided services to the patients they attended, whose lives circulated across national borders.

As a result of these connections, I thought of the clinic as a site in which caregiving and clinical practices were deeply informed and even driven by the presence of transnational funds and humanitarian commitments. This was particularly true of the Psychology Office. A small cheerful room full of toys and decorated with childlike paintings—a sun and a butterfly hovering over a blue, dolphin-filled sea; a house next to a river with trees reaching up to the stars and silhouettes crossing the water—the office contrasted with the stark examination rooms elsewhere in the clinic and the minimalist forms of childhood intervention I had witnessed in Morrumbala (Redfield 2005). In fact, the very existence of the Psychology Office—not to mention its toys, amply filled cabinets, and large, flat-screen television broadcasting the Cartoon Network—seemed to evidence how work at Clínica 2 was conducted with global connections; it was this office, after all, that Ena described as "like Holland."[2] Over time, though, I saw the glossy amplitude give way. By 2013, Clínica 2 was no longer supported by the ICHC, and a single psychologist—Dr. Luísa—worked alone to manage an ever-increasing caseload.

Talking with Clínica 2 staff, and observing the changes that marked the clinic over time, I came to see that imbrications of public authority and humanitarian practice were as contested in Maputo as they were in Morrumbala. Much like the GCF volunteers who sought to "invest" in relations in ways legible to NGOs, Clínica 2 nurses, psychologists, and doctors worked creatively with public and nongovernmental resources in order to fashion new forms of care and to cultivate professional possibilities. They sought to manage the entanglements of health work, relations, and material resources in ways that made possible the provision of care but also reflected and enabled their own career trajectories. Focusing on the work of the clinic's psychology staff, this chapter reflects on how the multiplicity of humanitarian and public medical efforts in Mozambique have transformed not only community labor and patient experience but also elite and professional practice, opportunity, and aspiration. As transnational interventions opened up professional opportunities for Mozambican health workers, they also reformulated and reinforced moral and professional hierarchies between staff and patients and among workers themselves.

Learning to Listen

I was not only the only one who expected to observe feelings-talk at the Psychology Office. About six weeks earlier, I had spoken with Laura, a clinical adviser at the ICHC. Clinical advisers were core members of the ICHC team in Mozambique and were responsible for supervising care and treatment programs across a range of areas. Laura, who was originally from Brazil, coordinated psychosocial activities in all ICHC-supported sites—that is, all the clinics that received ICHC funding and logistical support (including materials), hosted ICHC staff (as supervisors and medical practitioners), or participated in ICHC programs such as community interventions. At Clínica 2, the ICHC funded most of the Psychology Office's needs and supported a number of additional medical staff at the clinic.

When we met at the ICHC office in Maputo, Laura explained that she had come to work in Mozambique through an exchange program that brought doctors, nurses, psychologists, and other experts experienced in the treatment of HIV to provide clinical support for Mozambique's rapidly expanding AIDS treatment program. Now in her early thirties, she had worked with AIDS patients and their partners and families in Latin America for about four years before taking this job in Mozambique. These experiences informed her understanding that all patients need strong psychological support and gave rise to current efforts to "maximize entry points" for patients into psychosocial support programs. For instance, she promoted group therapy and information sessions held in clinic waiting rooms and coordinated monthly coffee hours, where patients could ask questions or share concerns. She promoted art therapy activities for children and emphasized the need for family counseling in the care of HIV-positive patients.

Although her primary task was to improve adherence to HIV treatment— that is, to ensure that patients were taking their medicine faithfully and correctly—Laura explained to me that she saw adherence as both a crucial measure of well-being and an opening into the broader welfare of patients and families. Drawing on medical anthropological as well as public health definitions of adherence, Laura characterized it as "biosocial," shaped by both social and clinical dimensions of AIDS treatment (see, e.g., Castro 2005; Farmer et al. 2013). Laura understood adherence as a regimen determined by multiple factors beyond medical treatment itself—including economic factors, cultural ideas about health and well-being, and the personal and psychological specifics of each patient, family, or household—and suggested that this complexity required open and supportive therapeutic relationships. Psychologists were particularly important, Laura believed, in a context where many strategies for monitoring and measuring adherence—for instance, blood tests to measure viral load in HIV patients—were unavailable. Relationships between patients and clinicians assumed special importance in light of medical information that often appeared uncertain, partial, or incomplete in comparison with what Laura had come to expect. As a result, the program made a special effort to recruit and train well-educated staff. Even a designated "Psychology Office" conveyed a level of expertise and professionalism distinct from more usual counseling practices. Even so, Laura told me, all too often "counselors just don't listen." This was, she suggested, the major impediment to her work.

The practices of "not listening" that Laura mentioned were not hard to identify at Clínica 2. For instance, following one consultation, Dr. Felícia commented that she thought the family would do well, "even if they are still a bit confused," because they had a "strong social network, primarily," and seemed "open." By contrast, the psychologists evaluated the next patient harshly when they realized that she had attended three consultations without bringing the documents she had been asked to provide. As the door closed, Dr. Luísa turned to me and said, "You see, this woman is a *malandra* [trouble-maker]. She is *always* telling lies." The doctors marked her file as "resistant." When I asked why patients like this woman would go to the effort of lying, I was given a variety of explanations. "Sometimes they think they have strategies of their own, and they think these strategies will work better than what we tell them. Usually they don't resolve anything and even make it worse," Dr. Luísa noted. And, Dr. Felícia added, "some people just tell premeditated lies." In this view, lying reflected both patients' genuine difficulty in accommodating clinic requirements and the staff's perceptions of patients as ignorant of, opposed to, or subverting medical norms and medical authority.

For Laura, however, the presumption that patients were lying, without an exploration of the emotional, psychological, or social stakes involved in telling stories, was yet one more example of "not listening." From her perspective, it was psychologists such as Dr. Luísa who had trouble acclimating to new

ICHC and clinic norms, rather than patients. "I've tried explaining and doing trainings to show that you have to *listen*," Laura noted, "but it's very difficult." When I asked why she thought that might be, she linked it to a professional habitus rooted in (a misreading of) Mozambican history. "It really starts with the whole educational system," she replied, "and the health care system. They are set up on the model of 'I am talking. You, the patient, are listening.' I don't know if it comes from the communist period, you know, a kind of communist model of pedagogy, but it is really something that is built up all the way, even from early education."

The view that a lack of listening was a significant barrier to successful interventions and that it was limiting the number of patients who were thriving in treatment was widespread among staff members at the ICHC and other NGOS, many of who pointed to legacies of "communism" or, more accurately, socialism, to explain this. I was surprised by this recourse to history and puzzled that these historical narratives were often inaccurate. More significantly, however, these explanations overlooked how many clinic practices derived not from Mozambican history but from the history of AIDS care. Many early AIDS projects brought with them a disciplinary form of counseling in which patients were expected to conform to clinical standards or risk losing their access to treatment and care.[3] The often interrogative and disciplinary therapeutic style of Dr. Luísa and Dr. Felícia was more likely to be an artifact of global HIV/AIDS responses than of a more distant and tangential socialist past.

Misguided historical explanations also obscured a more immediate hiccup in the therapeutic landscape imagined by Laura and others: funded by AIDS projects, and tied to the measurement of adherence outcomes, psychological practice at Clínica 2 was not an open-ended endeavor. Counselors were not only called upon to facilitate empathetic relations; they were also charged with surveilling and evaluating how patients conducted themselves.[4] Although Laura understood her role as one of designing and supervising psychosocial support programs and of fostering relations of empathy and solidarity between therapists and their clients, funding for the project was tied to efforts to ensure that patients were appropriately monitored and that they returned for regular clinic visits. Clinic staff such as Dr. Carolina and her colleagues—Dr. Luísa and Dr. Felícia—thus navigated between two tricky imperatives: a disciplinary effort to improve clinic attendance and a therapeutic effort to listen. As a result, it was not easy to learn how to listen.

In fact, I soon discovered just how difficult learning to listen could be. Because listening was so frequently tied to practices of evaluation and possibilities for dispensing resources and care, as well as to therapeutic and empathetic engagement, listening to patients required subtly or explicitly clarifying the stakes and expectations that attached to listening of various sorts. Distinguishing ethnographic from therapeutic listening, open-ended engagement from evaluative strategy, and emotional support from access to material resources could be difficult. Competing imperatives were thus a sticking point not only for therapeutic counseling but also for ethnographic practice; I too had to learn how to listen in the clinic—learning, for instance, to listen around and beyond my expectation of "feelings-talk." I had to become attuned to how patients, who brought diverse expectations to clinic encounters, anticipated being heard, or not, in ethnographic and therapeutic ways. As a researcher, I separated my ethnographic listening from the therapeutic context by conducting very few patient interviews in clinic spaces, preferring instead to talk in more casual ways with patients over time and conducting more extensive interviews only later and outside the clinic. Yet Dr. Luísa and others had little latitude for managing the circumstances of the conversations they had with patients, even as their attempts to explicitly clarify the stakes of their listening practices invited negative responses. Insisting that patients tell the truth, or bluntly stating that the clinic had few resources to offer, or impressing on patients the need to constructively use the limited services that were available was seen by Laura and her colleagues as unempathetic or uncaring. Even when they tried to act in the best interest of their patients, the clinicians could easily appear to their supervisors to be poor listeners.

Cardiana's Consultation

One of the primary challenges psychologists faced was navigating the limitations of psychological assistance in a context where patients (and often staff as well) were frequently concerned about material or practical assistance rather than therapeutic listening. Cardiana, for instance, attended the clinic regularly. Living with her grandmother, she was raising a young son, Armando. She helped her grandmother with her *machamba* (or fields), but was anxious to get a paying job and hoped that her high school education would help. During one session, Cardiana seemed particularly discouraged, asking Dr. Luísa if she thought that some people were "just born to suffer." Dr. Luísa shook her head sadly, neither agreeing nor disagreeing. "Listen," Dr. Luísa said, "you are young. There is a lot you can do [about this situation]. The child's father has to help you; it's the law that he must help you. Haven't you been to the Tribunal de Menores [Juvenile or Family Court]?" Cardiana sighed and said she didn't like to run after people. Dr. Luísa said she understood that, "and in normal situations, if the parents live together, then you don't have to run after anyone. But then there are other cases . . ." Dr. Luísa paused, and then went on:

> You know, because sometimes men might do this . . . they might trick you or they might, well, not trick you but they might get involved with you and then they might also be . . . might also have other women, other children, and maybe they would explain that they can't be involved with you. And you can say, "OK, fine [tudo bem]." Now you know the situation. But they still have responsibilities to the child, that doesn't stop being their responsibility. And the reason, well, when things are normal they care for their responsibilities but when they are not, that's why the Tribunal exists. So I know you don't want to run after people, but in this case it is the responsibility of the father to help with his children even if he's not working—uh—regularly, you know, whatever thing that he can contribute, that's the responsibility of a father to contribute, and also of a mother and that's what—if you go to the Tribunal—they're going to see, you know that also the mother can't just sit with her arms crossed, waiting . . . You need him to pay, and you, too, need to find some little thing you can do.

Cardiana listened politely but without much enthusiasm to Dr. Luísa's lecture, only nodding as Dr. Luísa said she would put her name on the list for the clinic's small and intermittent income-generation projects. Dr. Luísa then mentioned the National Employment Institute and suggested that Cardiana visit their office to find out about any other employment schemes. Finally, Dr. Luísa asked whether Cardiana went to church. Cardiana said that she attended Assembleia de Deus, a Brazilian evangelical church that was rapidly expanding in Maputo (van de Kamp 2016). Dr. Luísa, absentmindedly touching the small crucifix that hung around her neck, nodded as if satisfied. "Ask people to pray for you," Dr. Luísa said, in conclusion. "It will help you stay calm. Everyone has a cross to bear, and each cross has its own weight. It may seem like some people don't have troubles, but every one of us does."

Dr. Luísa's response to Cardiana was lengthier than many consultations but exemplified common interactions in the Psychology Office. Despite drawing on a range of pastoral, therapeutic, judicial, and economic approaches to Cardiana's predicament, Dr. Luísa was able to offer relatively little by way of direct assistance. Her normative framing of family relationships—suggesting that "normal situations" were those in which "parents live together"—overlooked how few clinic patients were living in nuclear households as well as the historical forces, including labor migration, that have shaped domestic living arrangements in Maputo.[5] Drawing on Christian ideals of suffering as a moral challenge and urging clients to pray (or to receive the prayers of others), Dr. Luísa adopted a role that seemed less medical than pastoral, cultivating and caring for a particular kind of inner life among those who attended her consultation sessions.

If these responses were out of keeping with the expectations that the ICHC had for the program, they also extended a disposition that Dr. Luísa had enacted over long years of health work, in which medical and moral authority were mutually reinforcing. Although Dr. Luísa's reply seemed to emphasize advice and admonishment over psychotherapeutic engagement, she was not simply uncaring. Rather, her response to Cardiana mixed moral disapproval with expressions of sympathy and frustration, for in spite of the array of institutions she invoked, the structured social support (from legal assistance to employment) that she recommended was unlikely to take shape.[6] In such a context, it was not clear that it was listening that was desired by either Dr. Luísa or Cardiana.

Moral and Medical Labor

The entanglements of moral and medical work have extensive histories in Mozambique and elsewhere. Medicine has long been on the front lines of efforts to make and remake citizens, and has often reinscribed social and political hierarchies through distinctions between "modern" caregivers and "traditional" patients. But, over a considerable period of time, medical work has also offered important opportunities for social mobility. As in much of colonial Africa, for example, training to be a nurse was one of few avenues to higher education (Prince and Marsland 2014). During the socialist regime that followed independence, health work was lauded as a means of serving the nation, offering unique opportunities for employment, economic stability, and professional advancement in Mozambique. More recently, as socialist policies gave way to a liberal economy and democratic politics, the expansion of higher and private education has also multiplied possible pathways to training in health-related fields. At the same time, the influx of foreign NGOs that has accompanied the global response to AIDS in Mozambique (Matsinhe 2008), and transnational concerns with "global health" have offered some expanded and more lucrative employment opportunities for medical professionals in Mozambique.

These possibilities, however, have coincided with an increasingly restricted public health system, a reduction in public salaries and benefits, and the erosion of some of the prestige associated with public service. Moreover, as possibilities for medical education have expanded (Sherr et al. 2012), older configurations of social class and professional opportunity have been unsettled as increasing numbers of students have entered health care fields. New jobs, organizations, and medical fields—such as medical psychology—have emerged, even as longstanding social and political norms continue to inform how staff interact with one another and with patients, the expectations they bring to bear on their work, and their possibilities for professional success.

These historical and professional shifts were apparent in everyday clinic activities, and in the experiences and professional habitus of the staff that worked there. As new therapeutic and affective imperatives came to characterize medical practice, historically produced repertoires of care contributed to patient well-being. Yet they were also perceived as old-fashioned and moralizing. Successfully inhabiting therapeutic norms was thus not only a concern for patients who wanted to access treatment, food, or therapy, but also for medical professionals who aimed to maintain or improve their professional prospects in a rapidly changing medical landscape (McKay 2016). By more closely considering the professional practices and personal trajectories of staff at Clínica 2, I aim to show how elite medical workers navigated the rapid transformation of public medicine in Maputo. The opening of professional opportunities, I suggest, could also entail professional loss and stoke feelings of anger, resentment, and nostalgia. Ultimately, it was often members of the staff already occupying positions of privilege who were best able to take advantage of the possibilities that transnational care afforded.

The professional trajectory of Dr. Carolina, who was in her late twenties when I met her, exemplified this. Raised in an elite, politically connected family, she had attended a South African university and had returned to Maputo in 2001. On her return, she worked for a time at Maputo Central Hospital's child psychology unit while also holding a lectureship at a nearby university, a position she continued to hold. In 2005, she moved to Clínica 2, where she was head psychologist, and worked closely not only with other clinic staff but also with ICHC advisers such as Laura. In addition to continuing her work at the university, she had a small practice at a private clinic, where she worked some afternoons and evenings. Though Dr. Carolina was, for most of the time I conducted research there, the only psychologist at Clínica 2 engaged in diverse public and private work practices, such combined career strategies were not uncommon among the doctors, for whom private, paying clients offered an important additional source of income.[7] These multiple professional commitments, which indexed the difficulty of fashioning a middle-class livelihood solely as a professor or a public health employee, were a source of grumbled frustration to other staff members, who, with less prestigious degrees and fewer professional connections, were not so easily able to access lucrative outside opportunities for employment, or who did not desire them.

Partly because of Dr. Carolina's competing commitments, much day-to-day work at Clínica 2 was managed by Dr. Luísa and Dr. Felícia, under Dr. Carolina's supervision. Both older than Dr. Carolina, Dr. Luísa and Dr. Felícia had trained and worked as nurses prior to studying psychology. In her late fifties when I first met her, Dr. Luísa sometimes seemed a quintessential public health employee—businesslike and practical, yet warm and often funny. Although Dr. Felícia, who was in her late thirties when we met, was markedly younger than Dr. Luísa, her experience paralleled Dr. Luísa's in many ways. She, too, had worked as a nurse before returning to college, a move made possible by her connection with the National AIDS Council. Dr. Felícia had completed her degree in psychology a few months before beginning work at the Psychology Office, making her Dr. Luísa's senior when my research started.

Along with the women in the Psychology Office, and the doctors, nurses, clerks and janitorial staff who were employed by the Serviço Nacional de Saúde (SNS), Clínica 2 staff incorporated ICHC personnel, including Laura and four or five rotating medical doctors from Spain, the United States, Morocco, Chile, and Brazil. The ICHC also paid the salaries of a data entry clerk, a young Mozambican man named Celso, and of some SNS staff members. As a result, within a single clinic, some of the staff were employed by the Ministry of Health, some by the ICHC, and some by both. Differences in employer entailed differences in salary, schedule, and professional trajectory, and frequently reflected differences in race, class, age, and social identity. For instance, while many doctors employed by the Ministry of Health earned from US$500 to US$600 per month, some ICHC doctors earned five times as much, in addition to benefits such as housing allowances, paid trips home, education supplements, and more (see also Mussa et al. 2013). Many ICHC staff also drew from experiences and opportunities to conduct and publish research in ways that would boost their employment trajectories once they returned to their countries of origin or moved to new positions in Maputo, Geneva, New York, or Atlanta. With some important exceptions, most members of the Clínica 2 staff returned to public service.

Despite the unequal opportunities, working at Clínica 2 was desirable for many staff members, including Dr. Luísa and Dr. Felícia, both of whom lived in central Maputo. Though it was north of the city center, the clinic's location made for a much shorter commute than the daily trek to the larger and more peripherally located hospitals and treatment sites where they might otherwise work. In addition, the presence of ICHC resources at Clínica 2 facilitated their work in ways unavailable in public spaces without nongovernmental assistance. For example, consultation spaces were comfortable, and the psychologists benefited from ICHC-provided resources such as a computer, access to literature and training materials, and a variety of activities and interventions (including the weekly coffee hour) that Laura organized. The attractiveness of these positions was reflected in the psychologists' diverse but privileged social status. In different ways, Dr. Carolina, Dr. Luísa, and Dr. Felícia were all well connected to the Ministry of Health and able to access different forms of political and social authority, such as party connections and institutional longevity. Even so, the Psychology Office was divided by tensions, especially between Dr. Carolina and the staff she supervised. These tensions most often centered on the work given to different members of the staff, as well as the ways in which each had been trained in, and inculcated with, changing regimes of expertise and professional opportunity.

Care in Translation

In the context of Maputo's economic and political transformation, as increasing opportunities for medical education and for employment with foreign organizations coincided with increasing economic inequality, some of the staff—like Dr. Luísa—struggled to listen and to be seen by colleagues as empathetic. Others, such as Dr. Carolina, were described by patients and colleagues as "excellent" and compassionate listeners, despite drawing on an equally wide range of therapeutic practices. And some doctors were demonstrably *un*-empathetic without being subject to censure. What accounts for these differences? How and when were counselors able or unable to listen?

Attending to the disparate ways in which health staff literally could and could not hear patients helps to make clear how relations and practices of distinction shaped clinic practice. Although most hospital business was conducted in Portuguese, many patients preferred speaking Changana or Ronga,[8] common first languages in Maputo. While Dr. Carolina spoke Changana as a second language, other staff members spoke Portuguese and Changana interchangeably among themselves, slipping in and out of languages with ease. Yet despite the wealth of linguistic facility in the office, a premium was placed on the use of Portuguese. Not only were Portuguese-speaking patients considered more likely to comply with their treatment, but Portuguese also marked professional practice. Thus, while psychologists were equally able to offer counseling in Changana and Portuguese, much of their willingness to do so was contextual. Happy to speak Changana in the closed confines of the counseling room, Dr. Luísa and Dr. Felícia were sometimes reluctant to do so in front of supervisors or in front of visiting medical students.

Arriving at the clinic one August morning, for instance, I was waved into the Psychology Office. A middle-aged woman sat at the table with her teenage niece. When they didn't reply to my "*bom dia!*" I tried addressing the older woman in Changana: "*Dzixile, mamana.*" At that moment, Dr. Luísa walked in with Laura and a university student intern. Dr. Luísa made general introductions but, as she spoke, it became clear that the women at the table were not following the conversation. Dr. Luísa asked, still in Portuguese, "What language do you . . . that is, what is your preferred language?" Softly, the older woman replied, "Changana." "Ah, OK," Dr. Luísa said. "I see. But you speak Portuguese?" Still softly, the woman replied in Portuguese, "I don't." "Ahhh . . ." Dr. Luísa replied. Now she looked at us, "You don't speak . . . ?" This was partly a rhetorical question. Though Dr. Luísa knew that I spoke Changana hesitantly, she also knew that I frequently sat through (or excused myself from, as appropriate) Changana-language consultations with her. My identity as a student of anthropology made this easier, since Changana conversation offered an opportunity to practice my language skills along with the lessons I took in the evenings, since anthropology seemed to signal an interest in "culture" that meshed easily with linguistic diversity in the clinic and since, from the outset, the clinic director (and I) had made it clear that my presence in the clinic was possible only if I was careful not to detract from care.[9] I replied, "For me, it's fine." The intern, too, said, "I understand." "The thing is," Dr. Luísa said, "for me, also, *dialecto custa um pouco*" (dialect takes a little work). Though she continued the consultation in Changana, this interlude gave her code-switching a dramatic flair that was not usually present.

The busy consultation room, full of students, anthropologists, and supervisors, belied the claim that these encounters were aimed at creating intimate, empathetic, and deeply therapeutic possibilities for listening. In this case, I soon left the room, uneasy with the ethics of observation in such a crowded and already-fraught context. As I waited down the hall, I reflected on Dr. Luísa's suggestion that speaking Changana was a departure from both regular clinic practice and her own comfort zone. At first, her response struck me as disingenuous, for neither of these were exactly true. But I also came to appreciate her dilemma. For Dr. Luísa, to have included Laura, the intern, and me as equals in her consultation would have meant excluding the very patients she was supposed to assist. Yet the alternative—speaking openly with a patient in Changana or Ronga—excluded visitors and supervisors, and meant forgoing an opportunity to demonstrate her professional practice in ways that mattered for her own career. In some ways, it seemed impossible for Dr. Luísa to "listen" in ways at once legible—or audible—to both patients and ICHC staff.

These uncomfortable tensions were most keenly felt by Dr. Luísa and Dr. Felícia, who had neither the credentials of a medical doctor nor the elite connections of Dr. Carolina to distinguish them. Yet a related set of negotiations involved foreign doctors. Most spoke Portuguese, though none spoke local languages. Some foreign medical staff were struggling to learn Portuguese, fluent instead in Spanish (most frequently) or, occasionally, French. For these doctors, the Psychology Office became a site of translation as they called on the psychologists to explain treatments and go over clinical indicators with patients. Psychologists, keenly attuned to the distribution of professional tasks, understood these requests as doctors "asking us to do their job for them." (Foreign doctors, in turn, heard this resentment as part of what they described as the "xenophobia" that contributed to professional dysfunction at the clinic.) Yet, while an inability to speak Portuguese was a technical and logistical challenge, it also marked expatriate staff as elite and mobile members of a transnational global health community.

Language and translation thus made visible differences in class and social status between different workers. For instance, when I accompanied some of these doctors to work at other clinical sites, I noticed that, in clinics with a smaller medical and psychological staff, doctors called on custodial workers to serve as translators, marking Portuguese as the language of biomedicine (Langwick 2007) and associating Changana with the most menial forms of clinic labor. Even for bilingual psychologists, demonstrating a discomfort with local languages marked a middle-class professional status distinct from patients (and some workers) they saw as poor, "vulnerable," or "traditional." Staff members in the employ of SNS, including Dr. Luísa and Dr. Felícia, rightly perceived that the well-paid foreign doctors working at the clinic enjoyed privileged standards of living from which they were excluded, even as the foreign doctors relied on local staff, especially psychologists, to facilitate the treatments they provided. Linguistic practices such as insisting on Portuguese was one way of signaling membership in an ostensibly transnational—but in practice, exclusive—community of global health workers whose provincial cosmopolitanism recognized only limited forms of belonging. In fact, it was Dr. Carolina, herself from a far more elite background than the rest of the clinic staff and least fluent in Changana, who was most comfortable speaking "in dialect" in front of supervisors, doctors, medical students, and others.

Although other staff members were less concerned than Dr. Luísa with marking the linguistic differences between themselves and the patients they served, class distinctions between patients and workers were nevertheless made visible in telling ways. Middle-class medical students expressed shock and unease when confronted with patients and their stories, frequently commenting on the small size of some children, on the lack of employment among parents, and on the predicaments facing families in which many members were ill (see also Wendland 2010). On a few occasions, students left the room to avoid emotional reactions inappropriate to a consultation room, such as tearful responses to patient narratives.

For the most part, psychologists' greater familiarity and experience with patients' difficult circumstances made them less expressive than students, but practices of differentiation were nevertheless clear. After one consultation, for instance, Dr. Carolina moved to open the door, saying that she needed fresh air because of "the smell of those people." "Don't you smell it?" she asked me. In fact, I always found the smell of the hospital, a combination of disinfectant and sick bodies, a little unnerving. She continued, "*That* is not from riding the bus. That is from not washing. From not taking a bath . . . for days! And that is just the mother. Really, with her level of education, this treatment is going to be so difficult for her." Such comments were not infrequent, as both Mozambican health workers and foreign doctors marked the difference between educated and non-educated bodies, car drivers and bus riders, and so on. Yet although Dr. Carolina made these comments behind closed doors, she worked hard to present an open, nonjudgmental front to patients, and was quick to remind other staff and students to behave similarly, for instance, by saying to Dr. Luísa: "Empathy, doctor, empathy. I think the doctor [Luísa] is judging a lot instead of listening." The performance of empathy and of listening was therefore a key marker of professional habitus, one explicitly articulated by clinic staff and supervisors, and inculcated in students and subordinates.

Limitations or failures of empathy were also understood differently across the staff. For example, the clinic director, Dr. Joana, was known to occasionally lose her cool during consultations. In one such instance, for example, a mother and her young daughter were sent to the counseling office after a meeting with Dr. Joana, who described herself as "furious" about the daughter's worsening health, which Dr. Joana believed was due to the mother seeking help from local healers rather than the clinic. When the mother burst into tears, Dr. Joana had shouted exasperatedly at her, "Tears? These are crocodile's tears!" Later Dr. Joana acknowledged that her response was harsh, a result of her concern about the child and frustration with the mother: "She is spending so much time making this child look pretty, doing her braids, dressing her up like that. She doesn't understand: you don't see this disease!" A refusal of empathy, then, as with "not listening," could mark both one's professional dedication and one's professional limitations; berating patients could be taking them seriously or not taking them seriously enough.

In fact, in spite of yelling or lecturing, elite and foreign doctors were sometimes seen as particularly empathetic. Dr. Joana's outburst, like Dr. Carolina's, mixed judgment and concern in an expression understood to be full of passion and care rather than lacking professionalism. If "not listening" was sometimes considered disparaging to patients and detrimental to the provision of care, similar affects could also be seen as an expression of care. For example, instances of yelling, lecturing, and "not listening" were common when psychologists or doctors surmised that patients were not taking the terms of their treatment seriously. In some cases, ostensibly "unempathetic" attitudes might be described as being "in the patient's best interest," which I came to understand through conversations with Dr. Valentina, one of the Spanish doctors who saw patients at the clinic. One afternoon, after speaking harshly to a family, she turned to me with an embarrassed but amused expression and said, "Sometimes I just have to yell or they don't take this seriously!" Yet she was never accused by the other staff of being unempathetic—in fact, she was singled out for special praise by an American "partner," who commented, "It is only Dr. Valentina who talks to children about school, about how they feel, about emotional things. Most doctors just talk about clinical stuff. They don't ask about psychological issues. Dr. Ana also is a bit like this—today she took this child on her lap and held her, but most doctors don't do this."

Finally, if an apparent lack of empathy marked lower levels of training or unsophisticated counseling techniques, it also blurred into a (sometimes racialized) discourse on modern subjects (Macamo 2005), as foreign counselors, supervisors, and even patients regarded lack of empathy as a particularly Mozambican trait. (Some patients who had been treated in Malawi, for instance, described the nurses there as "nice" and "kind"—"when they draw blood, they say, 'I'm sorry this will hurt,' and afterwards they say, 'I'm sorry I hurt you'"—which they distinguished from the behavior of Mozambican nurses.) Other patients and staff, on the other hand, characterized these interactions differently—commenting that foreign doctors "didn't understand" what life was like in Maputo neighborhoods and held naively sympathetic or even stereotypical views of the patients they served. If harsh words sometimes marked professional failure, at other times they underscored "seriousness" of treatment and dedication to care. Struggles over language and comportment thus indexed both the divisions and the dynamism of social positions in the clinic, as expatriate and elite staff members more easily embodied "caring" dispositions.

Therapeutic Biographies

It was perhaps unsurprising that Dr. Luísa, who had the most difficulty in the Psychology Office, was the staff member with the longest public health career. In fact, it was because of her long experience that I particularly enjoyed talking with her. She had trained as a nurse in the 1970s, just at the end of the colonial regime, when nursing was one of few avenues for higher education and professional advancement open to Mozambicans (Newitt 1995). Dr. Luísa had excelled in her training, and although family commitments had kept her from further study as a young woman, her career had been successful nonetheless. Posted to rural Gaza province in the 1980s, she earned awards and recognition for her contributions to the new nation. Later, even as armed conflict and processes of neoliberal reform weakened the country's public health system, Dr. Luísa became a head nurse at Maputo's Central Hospital and eventually took up a supervisory position in the Ministry of Health.[10] Long involved in the ruling Frelimo party's women's organization, OMM (the Organização da Mulher Moçambicana or Organization of Mozambican Women), she was also a founding member of one of Mozambique's earliest health NGOs. Shaped by the historical moment in which she came of age, Dr. Luísa's diverse career experiences reflected personal accomplishment as well as public and party ideals of medical work in the service of the state.

After some years petitioning the Ministry of Health, Dr. Luísa had been awarded a university scholarship and given paid leave from her work at the ministry in 2003. She matriculated at the Pedagogical University, where she majored in educational psychology. It was this training that facilitated her move to Clínica 2, but the transition had not been without challenges. When I met her, she was writing her senior thesis, which focused on learning disabilities in children. Ostensibly based on experience she was gaining through her work at the clinic, in practice this was a struggle, as long days at work left little time for study and writing. Equally frustrating were her efforts to engage the kinds of empathetic norms that ICHC programs emphasized—norms that seemed to contradict the dispositions and politics of health that had shaped her career before she joined the Psychology Office.

Even so, she often expressed a sense of commitment to and gratitude for her work. She had enjoyed and benefited from being a public servant, and seemed to appreciate the ways in which the state had supported her. Describing her repeated applications for a scholarship, for instance, she acknowledged that "I had to ask them every single year—but in the end, I had my opportunity!" She mentioned the name of a mutual acquaintance who had had a similar experience, working his way up from nurse to an administrator for the city health department. "There are quite a few of us like this," she said. "He doesn't like to remember how we started but I do." Dr. Luísa's reflection on her career helped me to see the Psychology Office as a space of both aspiration and frustration. Drawing from resources provided by a Portuguese-speaking, Catholic, and educated upbringing, by her integration into both party politics and the Ministry of Health, Dr. Luísa had slowly achieved some of the upward professional mobility to which she had aspired at the beginning of her career.

Nevertheless, achieving mobility was not easy. It been a long slog to complete her BA, and it was now difficult to engage in the kinds of continuing education courses that would open up additional professional opportunities. One afternoon, as I talked with Dr. Luísa in the office, her colleague Dr. Vanda stopped by. Dr. Vanda and Dr. Luísa were school friends, and both were participating in a voluntary counseling project helping residents in a neighborhood recently damaged by an explosion. Dr. Vanda mentioned a course that she was taking, a continuing training session on "psycho-drama." Dr. Luísa shook her head, no, I'm not participating. After Dr. Vanda left, she turned to me and said vehemently, "That course—it's 2,400 MT for only ten sessions [approximately US$10/session]. Who needs psycho-drama? This is our work here. *This,*" she gestured to the stack of clinical files she was filling out, "not psycho-drama."

Professional Multiplicity

Anthropologists have shown how humanitarian and development interventions, even those aimed at ameliorating social inequality, are often founded on unequal relations between local staff and expatriate or foreign experts (Fassin 2007; Hindman 2013; Redfield 2013). Some ICHC staff in Maputo earned six-figure salaries and received subsidized housing, often in luxurious buildings; some received tuition assistance for children in Maputo's private schools, and most took annual paid trips back to the United States, Europe, or Latin America. These perks stood in sharp contrast to the salaries and benefits available to public sector staff that worked in the clinic, including Dr. Carolina, Dr. Luísa, and Dr. Felícia. The differences were reflected in the micropolitics of work at the clinic: foreign staff rarely socialized with colleagues in the break room, and Mozambican staff almost never joined ICHC staff on weekend trips to the beach.[11]

The disparate class and social locations of the staff at Clínica 2—and their struggles—reflected broader economic and political transformations in Maputo, where more opportunities for medical education and employment with foreign organizations have coincided with growing economic inequality. Like Dr. Luísa, who had completed her nurses' training during the earliest period of socialist rule, a number of other staff had many years of service in the public sector. Nurse Elsa, whose tall, energetic figure gave her the appearance of someone much younger, had trained during the colonial period and had worked her way up through the SNS during and after the war. She was now head nurse, an important position that reflected her experience, authority, and privilege within hospital hierarchies. Despite their accomplishments, Dr. Luísa and Nurse Elsa were not nearly as well compensated as staff members brought in by foreign organizations. Still, both lived in apartments that had been reserved for state workers in the 1980s and had been given to them by the state. Centrally located, in neighborhoods that had once been the common and comfortable home of midlevel public employees, such apartments were increasingly expensive. Though these buildings were far from the luxurious apartments along Julius Nyerere Avenue where ICHC staff lived, they were also more and more out of reach of younger SNS staff, who no longer received state-sponsored housing. As a result, younger staff were housed neither in luxury buildings downtown nor in centrally located and increasingly expensive, if less luxurious, neighborhoods such as Malhangalene, where Dr. Luísa lived. Dr. Carolina, whose husband worked as an executive at a bank, commuted daily from a large house in Matola, a rapidly growing neighboring city. Others, from cleaning staff to young employees, lived in more affordable suburbs farther afield. Many patients lived in areas more peripheral still, sometimes traveling for hours to get to the clinic in the city.

In everyday ways, then, Dr. Luísa's experiences and frustrations with Clínica 2 revealed middle-class medical work to be both a privileged and precarious position. Over the years that I have known her, Dr. Luísa, like many Maputo residents, has complained more vocally about the increased prices of basic goods such as bread and petrol, and about the appropriation of public resources including coal and health services by elite and transnational actors. Her relatively low salary, and rapidly rising prices in Maputo, meant that— among other consequences—Dr. Luísa was not able to retire as early as she had hoped. These problems were particularly aggravating given Mozambique's natural resource boom, plus the highly visible market in luxury housing and goods available to the small but growing group of locals and expatriates with access to foreign capital and "global" salary scales. As Dr. Luísa saw the situation, "It seems the government is just filling their own pockets without any plan for distributing this wealth."

Yet differently situated workers navigated these transformations in different ways. By 2011, Dr. Carolina had left Clínica 2. As ICHC support to Clínica 2 came to an end, and as PEPFAR and other agencies promoted the transfer of transnational projects to local NGOs, a number of small, Maputo-based organizations emerged to carry out projects previously implemented by international organizations such as the ICHC. These new entities were, in many cases, staffed by the same health workers who had previously implemented these projects in public clinics. Dr. Carolina, for instance, joined an organization founded by former ICHC employees and partners to carry out counseling interventions in ways that met funding requirements. Thus, Dr. Carolina, along with a small group of Clínica 2 doctors and practitioners, was able to channel her success at Clínica 2 into a much more lucrative position at a nongovernmental organization, one that expanded her access to salary and travel, and increased her opportunities for research and study. Ironically, transnational efforts to ensure project sustainability by embedding "global health" in Mozambican organizations also created avenues for the most gifted public practitioners to leave the public health service. For Dr. Luísa, left for a time as the lone Clínica 2 psychologist, such departures showed how forms of education, disposition, and connection once rewarded were now superseded by a professional habitus that elite workers like Dr. Carolina seemed to embody more easily. These changes threw the meaning and value of health work open to question; they also transformed the actors, professional trajectories, and medical circuits through which the work of public medicine is enacted. As a result, the work of constituting public health came to depend on the transnational circuits in which particular clinics were enmeshed.

Lusophone Circuits

At Clínica 2, these circuits were significantly informed by the financial, material, and political assemblages of global health, but they were informed as well by the connections linking Mozambique to other health spaces and places. Many of the expatriate staff working at Clínica 2 and other ICHC projects came from Lusophone countries, primarily Brazil.[12] Though the number of Brazilian staff in both ICHC and GCF projects in Mozambique was explained in terms of shared language, shared experiences with HIV, and a shared status as citizens of the "global South," such similarities glossed over the divergent forms of opportunity and remuneration accrued to those who qualified as "expatriates" and those who were working "at home." Laura, for instance, explained her arrival in Mozambique in these terms. After having worked for two years in a hospital in Rio de Janeiro, she said, a colleague shared information about an international competition for posts in Mozambique. She attributed her success in this competition to the fact that Brazil "already has a name . . . it's internationally recognized in the area of HIV" and to her Portuguese language skills. Other Brazilian staff members I spoke with echoed these perceptions, emphasizing how shared language and shared experiences in "developing countries" made them well suited for work in Mozambique despite the dramatic differences between Brazil, with one of the largest economies in the world, and Mozambique, one of the poorest.

Laura and fellow Brazilians on the staff believed that their shared position in the margins of global health made them particularly sensitive to the importance of local culture. But if these shared experiences evoked a sense of a unified Brazilian or Lusophone practice, expatriate staff, like local staff, also had diverse trajectories into and through the ICHC clinics. Always colorfully dressed, Laura stood out among the doctors and other workers at Clínica 2 in their white coats and blue uniforms. She had a ready smile and a warm, engaging demeanor that seemed appropriate to a psychologist. She had moved to Mozambique about six months before I met her, and she lived in a comfortable house in the Coop neighborhood of Maputo, on a small street near the

Military Hospital. Despite her proximity to Dr. Luísa's flat, only a few blocks away, Laura's area was much more associated with expatriate residents than Dr. Luísa's, and social distance belied the geographical contiguity of their neighborhoods.

While in interviews or formal conversations her demeanor was relentlessly positive, and although her commitment to "local culture" seemed genuine, Laura did not envision a career in Mozambique. Rather, she imagined herself working for the period of her contract—two years—and then returning to clinical practice in Brazil. Her position was too administrative, she told me, and life in Mozambique was socially and logistically difficult. The expatriate community was small; she was anxious about finding a romantic partner; her work was frustrating as well as rewarding; and she missed her life at home. For Laura, then, working in Mozambique was a relatively short-term experience, albeit a well-paying and intellectually stimulating one.

Other expatriate doctors imagined and lived different trajectories through and beyond Clínica 2. Monique, for instance, was in her early forties when I met her. Educated in France, she had lived for five years in Brazil, where she had completed an internship in the infectious disease program at a São Paulo hospital. She had also completed her master's degree in public health, during which she had participated in a three-month training program in Mozambique. It was on the basis of this experience that she had sought out opportunities to return when she graduated. For Monique, working in Mozambique was not imagined as simply a short-term work experience. She was enthusiastic about her work, welcoming me warmly to Clínica 2, often asking about my observations, and introducing me to other ICHC staff. When her initial contract as a clinical adviser in Maputo ended, she took a related position within the same organization, traveling throughout the country to supervise ICHC projects in the provinces. In fact, we were able to cross paths not only in Maputo but also on excursions to Zambézia, where she conducted intermittent supervisory trips.

For Monique, who was more immersed in the daily practice of the clinic, the administrative frustrations that Laura felt were less pressing. Though Monique often described the clinic as a fraught place, one in which expatriate staff were greeted with skepticism and even hostility by other staff members and by "the Ministry," she made an effort to secure long-term employment in Maputo. Despite her efforts, when ICHC funding for Clínica 2 and other care and treatment sites came to an end, Monique's salary went with it. As a result, after working in Mozambique for almost four and a half years, Monique took a position in the United States, one that provided more stability but also foreshortened the efforts at professional engagement she had worked to craft. Even when motivated to do so, many expatriates struggled to fashion long-term professional commitments. As a result, their trajectories through the clinic were not so much "global" as transnational or translocal, and national origin shaped expatriate experiences in important ways.

Care in the Struggling Public Sector

Anthropologists and others have shown how transnational processes of financing and supporting medical treatment circumvent and, as a result, erode national health systems by luring away qualified workers, creating multiple and competing systems of supplying, managing, and evaluating treatment programs, and by privileging some diagnostic categories and treatments over others. These dynamics were visible in the ways that the ICHC came to physically occupy spaces of public care at Clínica 2 and to extract medical professionals, such as Dr. Carolina, when they left. Exploring the entanglements of NGOs and public medicine through the therapeutic practices and professional biographies of Clínica 2 staff, makes possible insight into additional aspects of medical multiplicity as well.

As Claire Wendland has shown in her ethnography of medical students in Malawi (2010), and as was true of GCF staff and program recipients in Morrumbala, shared national origin does not mean that "local doctors" are socially "close" to the patients that they serve. Moreover, as Nolwazi Mkhwanazi has argued (2016), there is a risk in portraying African health workers as singularly dedicated and self-sacrificing. At Clínica 2, mastering "nongovernmental" habitus entailed both social approximation and social distinction. It meant being both close to and different from patients, in ways that were sometimes more easily enacted by elite or expatriate, highly educated staff members, even if they went home at the end of the day to sea-view apartments or gated homes, far removed from many of the patients they served. In this context, staff improvised to provide care—drawing, sometimes out of necessity, from the variety of psychotherapeutic, medical, pastoral, and moral resources that were available, much as Julie Livingston (2012) has described in Botswana. But while the well-being of patients was at stake in these improvised encounters, so too were the professional and personal fortunes of clinic staff, Mozambican and expatriate alike, as they worked through new therapeutic opportunities and professional demands.

In Mozambique, the implementation of new regimes of care, driven by and financed through the interventions of transnational organizations, are enmeshed with and transformative of long-standing public health sites and practices. As a result, both transnational and public practices of care have come to be organized around concepts, bodies of knowledge, affective dispositions, and medical practices shaped by rationalities of humanitarian biomedicine. For Dr. Luísa, for instance, the presence of NGOs has given rise to new practices of psychosocial support within the public clinic and has helped to constitute psychology as a burgeoning and rewarding field of intervention. In addition to making new practices of care available, these transformations alter the professional and moral economies through which care is delivered, and the relations through which professional life is constituted—relations between patients and providers, between providers themselves, and between providers and institutions. The entangled worlds through which care is delivered not only shape biotechnological and epistemological projects (see Nading 2014) but also give rise to new moral and ethical responsibilities, affective orientations, and professional hierarchies.

Yet, even as the work of public medicine has changed, public spaces and institutions remain important sites of contestation, claims-making, resources, and struggle. This became evident, for instance, in Dr. Luísa's enthusiasm for the striking doctors in 2013. For Dr. Luísa, the predicaments of public labor were not reducible to NGOs alone or to the corrosive dynamics of transnational aid. Rather, the public sector remained an important site of remuneration, labor, and contestation amid new structures of professional advancement and reward, but it was a public sector that was itself in transformation.

CHAPTER 6

Paperwork

Capacities of Data and Care

One morning at Clínica 2, I encountered eighteen-year-old Edilia waiting with her younger sister, Jéssica, for an appointment. I'd known Edilia and Jéssica since their initial interview with the clinic psychology staff, had accompanied community health staff members on a visit to their father's house, and had already seen them at the clinic once that week. The earlier session had been interrupted when Edilia was unable to articulate many details about her sister's health, details that might have been included in Jéssica's clinical file but were absent. As a result, they had been instructed to return with their father (a mechanic who worked in a garage on the outskirts of Maputo), their stepmother (with whom they lived), or another adult relative. If they were unable to return with an adult, they had been told, they should come back with Jéssica's prescription slips so that staff could see which medications she was on. Now, a few hours after saying hello in the hallway, the girls were called into the counseling room. From where I sat talking with one of the psychologists, I could hear Edilia explain that their father had arrived earlier at the clinic, but had left for work after waiting for some time. However, they produced a bundle of prescription slips and the patient ID card that listed Jéssica's previous appointments. Dr. Luísa, the psychologist at the door, took the slips, asking, "No one sent you through when *papá* was here?" Then, after glancing at the papers in her hand, she abruptly handed them back with a loud sigh: "This is from last year, last year, the year before. How are these supposed to help me? How will I know what she is being prescribed if I only have these out-of-date papers? And today I don't have your file here either. You need to come back with the right papers, or with your father."

As described in chapter 2, practices of collecting and collating data were central activities of health volunteers, and a key point of contestation over the value of their labor. Much of what Dr. Luísa and others did every day, too, was to fill out and manage the patient files, *processos clínicos* or *processos*, that accompanied patients as they moved through the clinic. Yet encounters like these, in which exasperated health staff excluded patients from care for lack of information, were one common example of how information management not only facilitated but also complicated patient care. Contributing to worker frustration was the rapid expansion of services that outpaced the bureaucratic infrastructures needed to manage information, data, and documents, which produced challenging gaps in patient care. During my fieldwork, I would often sit in the office at the end of the day, chatting to auxiliary staff such as Olinda, who managed the *arquivo*, or file room, and Mateus, who assisted with the food program, as they sorted out the files of patients "lost to follow up."

Paperwork, and the struggles that it entailed, was a common topic of conversation among the clinicians and nurses that I accompanied, and they had been a common theme of my fieldwork in Morrumbala as well. Still, it was only over time that I realized how documentary practices provided an important window into the conditions of care at Clínica 2. On a visit to the clinic after a year away, I was struck by how quickly its offices had been filled with the binders holding *processos*. Once-ample shelves and cabinets designed to hold these files, consent forms, and other medical documents had been completely filled. In the back room, where *processos* were stored, archival boxes sat piled on top of one another. Binders were stacked from floor to ceiling on extra shelving in the clinic office, while still more were heaped on the floor, interspersed with boxes of mosquito nets for distribution. By 2015, the archive had been moved out entirely, to a partially covered attic storeroom where they sweltered, along with the staff browsing through them, under zinc roofing panels. As documents threatened to take over clinic practice, they made visible how health information was prolific but also marginalized and partial, serving as much to complicate medical care as to facilitate treatment.

The proliferation of paperwork at Clínica 2 was significantly driven by the rapid expansion of antiretroviral (ARV) treatment and by the bureaucratic demands that HIV treatment brought with it. Supported by financial, technical, and logistical resources from transnational agencies, Mozambique's HIV/AIDS program had expanded from a handful of health centers in 2004 to over 200 just six years later. By 2014, there were 412 health centers across the country's 198 districts, encompassing a territory twice the size of California. In 2013, the Mozambican Ministry of Health had 330,000 patients on ARV treatment for HIV/AIDS. Each of these patients was managed entirely through a paper-

6.1 Files and filing cabinets in the clinic attic.

based filing system of which the *processos* that Olinda, Mateus, and others struggled to house were the basis. At the same time, many NGOs—including the ICHC—collected more than one hundred data points on each patient they treated, data that circulated electronically both within NGO offices and to supervisory agencies in Washington, DC and elsewhere.[1] These contradictory means of managing data—paper files encoding patient cases in often-rural districts, and technically sophisticated "patient-level" databases that aggregated information across programs, countries, and world regions—were all the more discordant given that the transnational agencies providing care in Mozambique were working through and within public institutions. These adjacent data-gathering practices were therefore just one example of the institutional multiplicity that existed in the rapidly expanding Clínica 2 files and in the binders that lined the shelves of GCF's district offices.

In the previous chapter, I explored how the psychology staff at Clínica 2 worked to assess and assist patients and to forge their professional paths through the institutional multiplicity of medicine in Mozambique. In this chapter, I consider documentary and bureaucratic (as well as regulatory) practices at Clínica 2 and in Morrumbala.[2] Attention to material and bureaucratic practices in the clinic make clear that multiplicity is not an effect of "local" practices of health and caregiving but, rather, is central to transnational biomedicine. Nongovernmental efforts to standardize care and produce knowledge give rise to ever-increasing demands for documentation. In these documents, relations of care are written into clinic practice even as their centrality to global health is obscured.

This proliferation of paperwork not only challenged and frustrated health staff, but also produced discordant relations of data across multiple state and nongovernmental institutions. Recognizing the problems that institutional multiplicity poses to the provision of care, many NGOs work to create documentary and statistical capacity within the state—to reduce, in other words, the multiplication of medical authority (see also Inguane et al. 2016). Yet by disentangling NGOs from public health practices, such efforts have also displaced transnational responsibility for the predicaments of care that accompany global health. Framing the difficulties of managing data as a problem of state capacity, these efforts reinscribe a presumed need for NGOs and obscure the role of transnational initiatives in co-producing these challenges.

The Daily Life of Documents

The importance of documents to clinic practice was evident in the very organization of work at Clínica 2. Each morning, paperwork began before the first patients were seen, when Nurse Elsa—the head nurse—brought in a tall stack of clinical files. These handwritten *processos clínicos* belonged to patients with scheduled appointments. Some were stored in the Serviço Nacional de Saúde's cardboard folders and others in plastic three-ring binders provided by the ICHC and color-coded according to ICHC research projects. On some days, there were just a few. On others, Nurse Elsa carried an overflowing armful. As the stack dwindled throughout the day, it would be supplemented with files sent over with new patients, with patients who had not scheduled appointments in advance, or with those referred from other departments. Sometimes the stack of files seemed to grow faster than clinicians could keep up. At other times, the pile dwindled and staff read the paper, drank tea in the break room, or caught up on other work. Psychology and medical students on rotation from local universities were also frequently present, and quiet moments were often taken up with the questions and opinions of students (and anthropologists).

As each file rose to the top, the clinician would call the patient's name out in the waiting room. If they were called into the Psychology Office, the patient and any accompanying family members or caregivers were encouraged to sit at the round table in the center of the room; small children were given toys to play with at the little table in the corner, and older children might be asked to wait outside. As the patients waited, the psychologists would read or review the files, skimming past entries and identifying the reason for each patient's visit. Despite the range of potential topics these sessions could address, they most often focused on the administration of intake forms for new patients, follow-up questionnaires for returning patients, and counseling for patients referred by doctors with concerns about medication adherence.

The documents enclosed in the *processos* were not the only important papers at Clínica 2. Recognizing the centrality of documents to accessing treatment, and how files that were incomplete, not located, or unreadable could complicate the provision of services, many patients arrived at the clinic with bundles of medical documents—old prescription slips, ID cards, and even X-rays—to facilitate their visit. Lost or misplaced papers were frequently cited to explain missed appointments, as patients reasoned that they would not be seen if they lacked appropriate documentation (Chapman 2010). This reasoning was borne out by common clinic experiences like the visit of Jéssica and Emilia.

In part to manage and ameliorate these situations, bureaucratic practices aimed at tracking patients, regulating relations between patients and providers, and monitoring nongovernmental and public health interventions were central activities at Clínica 2, and staff devoted significant amounts of time to documentary practices. For instance, the ICHC was preoccupied with measuring the outcomes and impacts of the interventions they sponsored, especially AIDS treatment with antiretroviral medications. Another organization supported pediatric care and social development in the surrounding neighborhood; they shared similar anxieties about measuring the outcomes of their interventions. The Ministry of Health aimed to track the number of patients treated each month, and additional governmental and nongovernmental agencies, from the U.S. Centers for Disease Control to UNICEF, were concerned with tracking flows of blood tests, medications, and test kits through the pharmacy and (often closed) laboratory and with tracing flows of patients through clinical, laboratory, and psychosocial encounters.

The diverse entities involved in Clínica 2 maintained separate practices of measuring, monitoring, enumerating, and evaluating their activities of interest, but much of the information with which they were concerned was collected in the *processos*. Though many public health programs had collected relatively little information on patients, and though patients had often assumed responsibility for collecting and saving medical documents, curating in a way their own "medical histories," the advent of HIV treatment brought new documentary regimes and demands for collecting and storing medical information. As a result, *processos* were opened for each patient receiving treatment there.

Usually covered in a green paper or plastic binder with a smaller, newer manila envelope tucked inside, the *processo* consisted of various intake forms, follow-up questionnaires, notes, and prescriptions. On the cover, the patient's ID number was written in thick black marker. Inside, the bulk of the *processo* was constituted by relatively open-ended kinds of clinical writing. The first page, the intake form, included patient name, identifying number, and address at the top. Below, vertical lines divided the rest of the lightly lined paper into columns marked for clinical observations, diagnosis, prescriptions, and dietary recommendations. While medical information was often noted using abbreviations that could concisely convey information in the moments between consultations, some psychology consultations also produced longer narratives describing not only psychological but also social, financial, or medical circumstances with which patients were confronted. Other forms in the *processo* could include small, rectangular prescription forms; signed informed consent forms on bright white paper; and, frequently, large rectangular X-ray films that stuck out awkwardly. In sum, the files held many kinds of paper, information, and modes of writing. The homogeneous appearance of the green binders belied the heterogeneity of their content. *Processos* included diverse medical, social, and psychological information aimed at tracking clinical histories and regulating (through consent forms and related documents) patient care.

Documentary Histories in Mozambique

A primary effect of the expansion of HIV/AIDS treatment in Mozambique was the enhanced role given to nongovernmental programs and to the bureaucratic and documentary norms and practices that came with them. Central to the implementation of nongovernmental programs by agencies such as the ICHC was an emphasis on transparency, both of agency practice and of patient-provider relations (Epstein 2007; West and Sanders 2003). For instance, in 2006, two years after AIDS treatment was made available in Mozambique, the Mozambican Ministry of Health designed and deployed a new document—

the *consentimento informado,* or informed consent form—that was to be signed by all patients initiating HIV treatment and that would mediate the relationship between patients, providers, and pharmaceuticals. In this, the Ministry of Health followed WHO and UNAIDS guidelines on HIV testing, which sought to integrate human rights principles into public health care by codifying principles of confidentiality, voluntarism, and consent in new documentary and bureaucratic practice (Joint United Nations Programme 2004; CNCS 2008).

The informed consent document is just one example of the expansion of documentary and regulatory practices driven by nongovernmental agencies (Heimer 2012). Even in health centers, such as Clínica 2, that used alternative documents and forms, these global norms were expressed in efforts to track patients, contractualize relations between patient and provider, and audit both public and nongovernmental health programs. Whether standard or uniquely designed, the new forms articulated a vision of the patient as a subject who was informed, rational, and responsible for his or her own health. These forms were therefore meant to instantiate what some have hailed as a new "social contract" for public health by recognizing and codifying relations between providers and responsibilized patient-clients (see Robins 2006). Efforts to encode these new relations were visible in the posters that hung on many clinic walls outlining "patient rights and responsibilities." (At many clinics, only the poster describing responsibilities was displayed.) Posters aside, contractual imaginations of public health were not borne out by the actual politics of care, which had more to do with relational and improvisational claims than with abstractly imagined contracts.

Though the proliferation of paperwork was motivated by concerns with standardizing and protecting patient care, it often had unintended consequences.[3] These consequences were visible in the overflow of clinic files into the hallway and in the frustrations of Olinda and Mateus. They were also evident in everyday interactions between patients, health workers, and caregivers. The increased workload associated with the documentary demands of AIDS treatment, for instance, was cited by nurses as a reason they disliked treating patients with HIV (see also Heimer 2010). As Nurse Elsa put it: "HIV patients are difficult. Not difficult as people but difficult to treat. They are on a lot of strong medications and that's hard to manage. Second, it's a lot of paperwork, and that takes time. Even if it's only fifteen minutes per patient, that adds up." Managerial and documentary demands were cited as examples of the "difficulty" and undesirability of certain patients, constituting patients with HIV as distinct bureaucratic persons as well as unique medical cases (Hacking 1999). Rather than contributing to patient protection, documentary practices diminished the time nurses spent with patients and thereby detracted from the quality of care they received. Moreover, in a context of overwork and increasing documentation, the forms themselves were often filled out only partially or incompletely, rendering moot many clinical and data-gathering functions of the documents.

Documentary expansion thus posed a challenge not only for workers struggling to manage paperwork but also for the ICHC. In recent decades nongovernmental organizations have come to be viewed as needing regulation and oversight, whether by governments, donors, or other nongovernmental actors. For example, since 2000, nongovernmental medical organizations working in Mozambique have signed a Code of Conduct outlining their responsibilities and obligations to patients and to the Mozambican Ministry of Health, their "partner" and host (Pfeiffer et al. 2008). These concerns reflect an awareness of the ways that nongovernmental interventions in health in Mozambique and elsewhere have been held responsible for eroding state capacity, by, for instance, hiring talented and experienced health staff away from the public sector through the promise of higher-paying jobs in the nongovernmental sphere. At the same time, organizations such as the ICHC are also accountable to the documentary regimes of donor governments and of individual donors. These entities have reporting requirements of their own, including an emphasis on increasing (and documenting) access to care and on monitoring the efficacy of interventions and services. As one ICHC supervisor put it, "Most fundamentally, we want to know: How many patients *are* on, and *stay* on, treatment?" Yet the processes put in place to generate this information also proliferated the number of forms in use at Clínica 2, creating new dilemmas of data management, and calling into question the kinds of authority and citizenship enacted through these forms.

Intake Forms

At Clínica 2, standard clinical intake forms were substituted by a questionnaire to be completed on the first visit and, for patients with HIV/AIDS, a series of forms administered in months one, three, six, nine, and twelve of their ongoing treatment. Intake questionnaires were most often administered by counselors and psychologists and occasionally by nurses. Though the forms were official clinic forms, they differed from standardized forms used elsewhere in the hospital; in place of the seal of the Republic of Mozambique or the logo of the public hospital to which the clinic was attached, the forms were adorned with a rainbow logo specific to the clinic and paid for by the international organization that funded it.

Psychologists and others often presented the intake process to patients as "*umas perguntinhas*" or "a few little questions," but both intake and follow-up questionnaires solicited detailed information about patients' medical status, social relations, and financial situations. The body of the form asked for basic information such as the date of the intake interview, the name of the interviewer, the patient's ID number, the date of birth, and HIV status (positive, negative, or unknown) of the patient. The form also asked about the patient's level of education and occupation and whether, for patients with HIV, they had problems taking their medication. On a second page, health workers could note the administration of ARVs and solicit data about "social support." The form then asked about the HIV status of other household members and posed a series of fifteen questions regarding their attitudes and opinions about HIV and the effectiveness of HIV medication. These included: "Do you think you will have trouble taking the medication: yes, or no? What do you think will happen after treatment begins: improve, worsen, become dependent, be cured, or don't know? Have you already taken a long-term treatment, for instance, for tuberculosis?" The last page of the form was reserved for counselors to fill out privately, identifying potential problems from a list that included weak social support, difficulties understanding the medication schedule, lack of motivation or signs of sadness, financial difficulties, marital or family problems, problems at work or school, and fear of side effects. Finally, intake forms also included processes by which patient consent for AIDS treatment was solicited and recorded.

From the point of view of Laura, the ICHC supervising psychologist (or clinical adviser) who had designed and first implemented these forms, psychosocial evaluations were important means of assessing and addressing the diverse needs of patients whose life circumstances varied dramatically—from middle-class families living in downtown Maputo to farming families who commuted to the clinic from towns on the outskirts of the city. For Laura, the extended questionnaires were an integral step in ensuring patients' adherence to treatment. By soliciting information about patients' emotional well-being and the social context of illness, she reasoned, counselors might anticipate adherence problems in advance. Influenced by the emancipatory philosophy of Paolo Freire (2000), Laura told me that she hoped the conversations inspired by the questions would create "a space for solidarity" between health worker and patient. Questions about patient expectations regarding treatment, for instance, might serve as a springboard for a broader discussion of the ways in which patients could effectively incorporate demanding and difficult medical treatments into their daily lives.

Yet putting these strategies into practice was more difficult. Patients and psychologists often felt that these sessions served a gatekeeping function that "triaged" care, in anthropologist Vinh-Kim Nguyen's phrase (2010), by limiting it to those who appeared to be "good" patients—expressive, committed, and willing to produce narratives of themselves and their illness in ways expected and recognized by ICHC program managers. In addition, because psychologists were called on both to empathize with and to evaluate claims to material need, and because they often lacked any substantive resources with which to assist their patients, the line between social and medical work was porous and problematic. As a result, although intake forms and protocols included open-ended questions about feelings, expectations, and past experiences, and solicited information about cultural beliefs and the material conditions in which patients lived, both practitioners and patients understood the forms as serving an evaluative role. Questions about traditional medicine, for instance, evoked not only postcolonial prohibitions on the use of traditional medicine, but also ICHC and other NGO guidelines that described traditional medicine as a potentially dangerous "barrier" to good adherence. Questions about the material circumstances in which patients lived, the family members with whom they shared a home, and other potential sources of social support such as membership in a church or mosque, were also fraught in a context where hospitals were important means of accessing resources.

For the psychologists and nurses who most often administered the forms, the forms were differently engaged and served varied purposes. In filling them out, staff members, including Dr. Luísa and Nurse Elsa, rarely followed the forms exactly. While some lines were completely filled out—most often those soliciting identifying information; information about employment, education, and health status; medical information and information about prior medical treatments—other lines were skipped or left blank. For some staff members, this reflected a hierarchical engagement with clinical data, privileging what some saw as "medical facts" over social experience. Especially for staff trained primarily in nursing, the intake form took on the aspect of a clinical biography rather than a psychotherapeutic tool. Blank spaces and unfilled forms also reflected a reluctance to ask questions to which the answers seemed obvious, irrelevant, or alienating. For instance, questions about expectations regarding the results of treatment ("What do you think will happen to you as a result of this treatment?") were often met with confusion. Dr. Luísa and her colleagues acknowledged that they sometimes skipped questions when they found them "confusing" for patients or "complicated" or "unhelpful" in their own work.

For many psychologists and staff members responsible for administering these documents, the forms also provided an opportunity for a rehearsal of rules regarding medications and served as gatekeeping documents. This was particularly true of questions about patients' "belief" in biomedicine and its efficacy, and about their faith in and use of alternative therapies often glossed as "traditional"(*medicina tradicional*). Superficially simple questions like "Do you use traditional medicine?" gave rise to more complicated negotiations. Though patients often responded with statements of renunciation, such as "No, I used to, but not now," sentiments of that kind were often assumed by psychologists to be insincere. In the years following independence, many Ministry of Health discourses emphasized the dangers and "obscurantism" of beliefs in traditional medicine, discourses that continue to circulate today (Meneses 2004).[4] Patients and health staff alike recognized these as loaded questions, ones to which there were clearly defined right answers ("no"). At the same time, the high stakes of the question meant that these same answers were received with skepticism.

Questions related to the consent process, such as "Do you believe that this [biomedical] treatment will work?," elicited similarly standardized responses, for example: "Yes, I believe this treatment will improve my health." Here, too, psychologists both desired and were dubious of such responses. As a result, although the forms themselves recorded standard information, the solicitation of this information constituted and was produced through complex gendered, generational, and classed social relationships and evaluations. As they filled out intake forms, psychology staff members improvised to solicit and record information they deemed most relevant. While some lines were filled out completely, other parts of the form were left blank. Some questions were ignored, while others—such as those regarding the incompatibility of traditional or indigenous medical treatments with antibiotics and antiretrovirals—were elaborated in pedagogical (if off-script) engagements.[5]

Such complex negotiations of diverse medical practices and traditions were not unusual. Questions of pluralism have long been central to discussions of healing, law, and politics in Mozambique, and diverse accounts of legal and medical pluralism have made clear that the politics of plurality are dynamic, indeterminate, and open to contestation (Whyte 1997).[6] Scholars have used the term *therapeutic pluralism* to describe the diversity of traditional, religious, and spiritual healing practices performed by *tinyanga* (healers), *profete* (prophets), and other Mozambican healers. Many patients moved frequently between various, sometimes interconnected forms of healing, which entailed different political, social, and therapeutic diagnoses and consequences.[7]

One of the motivations for such constrained conversation can be found in the ways that intake forms were deployed. Many psychologists, doctors and nurses considered patient responses to such questions "suitable" or "unsuitable." When clinic workers were confronted with patients who professed skepticism about the usefulness of biomedical treatment, expressed reservations or anxieties about complying with norms of care, refused to "give up" traditional medicine, or offered evidence of poor social support, they referred these patients for further counseling to ensure "readiness" for treatment. Through this referral process, which delayed treatment, many patients abandoned efforts to seek care altogether. The intake form was therefore not only a therapeutic tool but also a site for gatekeeping. It reconstituted longstanding discourses on the dangers of medical pluralism in a biomedical language of treatment readiness. In a context where many patients (and staff members) engaged multiple therapeutic practices in addition to biomedical services, these routine questions and processes of soliciting patient consent both recognized and erased the plurality that marked many patients' medical strategies.

These processes complicated the notion that listening alone was adequate for eliciting information and evaluating patient adherence, understanding patient experiences, or developing a therapeutic plan. Moreover, it was not only the use of traditional medicine that elicited judgment and potential sanction from clinic staff. As they worked between empathy with and evaluation of clinical patients, staff members frequently sought information in ways that exceeded or evaded therapeutic listening. Staff often scrutinized patients' clothes, appearance, and everyday habits. For many clinic practitioners, expensive and fashionable clothing, unruly or cranky children, or lack of education and resources were translated into negative assessments and skepticism. Ultimately, these estimations—along with medical evaluations, doctor's recommendations, laboratory tests, and blood work—shaped decisions about treatment through practices beyond the documentary and narrative encounter of the intake interview.

Filling Out Forms

Though the intake form was designed with psychotherapeutic aims, the consequences of consultations—whether enrollment in treatment or referral for further counseling—appeared to be determined largely by factors external to the documentation process. In keeping with this, many patients seemed to see the forms as one among many bureaucratic and paperwork hurdles they encountered as they moved through the clinical system. For instance, many patients understood submission to various documentary procedures as a prerequisite for access to other kinds of treatment. Maria José, a middle-aged woman whose husband had recently died of hepatitis, told me that she insisted on going to the counseling and testing office before seeking general medical attention because "if I don't bring [a referral slip], they'll just send me back there to get tested first." Paperwork therefore took on various and variable meanings, including being one more bureaucratic obstacle between the patient and her treatment.

Yet even apparently skeptical patients like Maria José carefully collected and carried with them their appointment cards, prescription slips, and X-rays. It was not unusual for patients to produce plastic bags or envelopes containing many years' worth of medical forms in addition to the patient ID card that each was required to present. This was not an unnoticed side effect but a normal aspect of clinic practice. When I commented on the assiduousness with which many patients remembered and asked about blood tests, CD4 counts that tracked antiretroviral treatment (for patients with HIV), X-rays (for tuberculosis patients), and other details of treatment, Dr. Valentina explained that "in the beginning, this doesn't happen. They miss appointments, they don't take their medicine, and when this happens I am really *tough*. I am hard. I shout—you can ask the nurse. Then they learn, and they are more anxious and attentive to make sure they are on track." Grappling with documents and their gaps was thus a necessity and responsibility shared by patients and clinicians in the construction of care. Although the forms appeared to solicit standardized information, to record data in routinized and commensurable ways across national and clinical spaces, and to enact regular forms of patient protection and care, in practice they produced a more varied terrain of data in which the relationship between patients, medicine, and authority was complicated by the form's multiple roles as well as by the aporias that it enabled.

Gathering Data, Enacting Care

Depending on when, how, and by whom they were used, intake forms were alternately psychotherapeutic tools, forms for clinical evaluation, and bureaucratic obstacles. The same forms also enacted a variety of knowledge-gathering goals, such as collecting data for research, performing project management functions, and serving as scripts for medical instruction. The forms therefore represented the many kinds of investigative thinking and knowledge production (such as operations research, pilot projects, logistics monitoring, or student research) that took place every day in the clinic. For instance, demographic data solicited in the forms was used by the ICHC to monitor and evaluate program efficacy. Collected in Maputo and other project sites, the numbers were then aggregated, giving rise to data on the gender and age of patients; on treatment retention; on pregnancy and prenatal care; and on TB and HIV screening across ICHC projects. These data were crucial to program monitoring, for funding applications and reports, and for public health research conducted by program staff and affiliated researchers. Without opportunities for data collection, the ICHC would be unable to provide the support that made HIV treatment and other specialized therapies available.

Routine data collection of the kind included in intake processes was therefore important to the ICHC, which relied on this information for program management and reporting. The emphasis on monitoring and research reflected both ICHC aims and global health investments in entwining research and care. Driven by PEPFAR reporting requirements, the inclusion of monitoring and evaluation projects generating statistical data on treatment outcomes was crucial to the ICHC's ability to secure ongoing financial support. This rich statistical information, however, was not included in Ministry of Health statistics, which contained only data collected by the Serviço Nacional de Saúde itself. Only the number of patients, the prescriptions written, and the numbers enrolled in treatment were collected by the Ministry of Health for aggregate health reporting purposes. This segmentation of data was necessary, since the Ministry of Health could not incorporate data that were not collected nationally nor for which it could not ensure ongoing data collection processes. Yet it segmentation also reflects how transnational agencies and the state were able to make very different use of the information generated in Maputo clinics.

Intake forms were also incorporated into more nuanced efforts to know and represent clinic populations. For instance, by asking about socioeconomic circumstances, they allowed relationships between social context and adherence to medication to be more completely understood. This information was used by Laura, the expatriate psychologist who had designed the forms, in conjunction with her dissertation research on adherence to AIDS therapies in resource-poor settings. Another staff member also used the forms, and the information they provided, in a dissertation on pediatric health in Maputo. The presence of research studies at Clínica 2 had significant repercussions for clinic practice. Clinic support provided by ICHC included salaries for much of the psychology staff, supplemental funding for supplies (including for specialized documents such as the questionnaires), and the presence of clinical supervisors such as Laura, who urged a baseline level of engagement with the details requested by the forms. Intake documents and questionnaires were therefore also experimental tools. In this regard, the forms can again be seen as multiple. Combining registration with investigation, and documentation with instruction, the forms enacted a "diversity of objects" under "a single name" (Mol 2002: 84). Apparently singular objects—intake forms—were multiply constituted by, and productive of information about and relations between, a variety of institutions and actors. The questionnaires made clear how bureaucratic, clinical, regulatory, and experimental practices were at work together, even through the same documentary technology.

Finally, documentary multiplicity at the clinic was dynamic. When the research studies ended, which coincided with the cessation of much of the financial support provided by the ICHC, counseling staff at the clinic was reduced. Specialized office supplies such as questionnaire forms dwindled and were eventually eliminated, and much of the computer equipment was moved to other settings, increasing reliance on *processos* and paper. Two years after the studies were completed, the specialized forms designed to solicit information for them were abandoned, and counselors sought and recorded information free-form, writing longhand in the section for general clinical notes included in the files. Yet even after the studies ended, the red binders that distinguished *processos* included in research from the mass of green-covered files remained visible on hallway shelves. These experimental traces pointed to the ways that clinical, mundane, and knowledge-gathering forms of documentary intervention, from intake forms to plastic binders, contributed to the material practices of care at Clínica 2.

Coordinating States: Documentary Management in Morrumbala

The centrality of collecting and circulating information was not limited to Clínica 2. As in the case of Albertina and the Patients' Association, described in chapter 2, collecting and collating patient information was a key means by which small, local NGOs sought to partner with transnational organizations. At GCF, too, the collection and circulation of recipient information was a central activity of the health program and its volunteers and a key point of relation between public health entities and NGOs. Every month, each volunteer group was to submit a compiled set of papers tallying the number and purpose of community visits conducted. Though these numbers were meant to be updated regularly, most volunteers seemed to do the updates only at the request of their supervisors. The numerical totals were entered into a database on one of GCF's three computers and stored in hard copy in binders organized by neighborhood. In addition, an intake form—briefer than those designed by the ICHC—and a series of evaluative forms were collected for each patient. These forms indicated the overall health of the patient, as evaluated by the GCF supervisor, Violeta, or *her* supervisor, both former public health nurses, along with the patient's "psycho-social state." Patients who received food were to be evaluated at each monthly distribution meeting, though these encounters were frequently perfunctory. Those who no longer received food baskets were evaluated less frequently, both because patients resisted attending evaluative meetings in the absence of services and because program staff saw such evaluations as of lower priority, given the lack of resources with which they could respond to any issues they identified. Even so, binders full of patient profiles took up an entire wall of the community health office in the GCF compound.

The forms and patient profiles generated various sorts of information beyond the evaluation of individual patients. For instance, they were used to measure program impact or scope (such as number of visits conducted), and were supplied to provincial, national, and regional headquarters along with more detailed individual portraits of "needy cases" or "success stories," which were forwarded to donors. Volunteers played key roles in the generation of both forms of data, producing monthly numbers that could be tallied and circulated, and identifying and helping to narrate the portraits that program supervisors requested. Some volunteers, Carlota in particular, were seen as exceptionally skilled at identifying and nurturing these narratives, which were then recounted to program staff and written up in brief portraits. Sometimes these portraits were produced by consultants or visiting provincial staff; on two occasions, I helped to write them.

The information contained in the binders circulated not only within GCF but also to staff at other NGOs in Morrumbala and to public health staff. Each week, Violeta attended a "coordination meeting" at the District Hospital. Hosted by one of the doctors or, more frequently, the hospital's HIV coordinator, Nurse William, the meeting was open to public hospital staff and representatives from all the major health organizations working in the district (including World Vision, Save the Children, the Red Cross, a local patients' association, and GCF). Early each Monday morning, NGO and hospital staff (including members of the AIDS program, the TB and leprosy programs, the laboratory, the pharmacy, and sometimes the head doctor) met to compare and coordinate their activities. Most weeks, I accompanied Violeta. Meetings began with the exchange of information, as each NGO reported the number of visits conducted (information collected from volunteers' worksheets), the overall progress of the program, and details on the patients who had died, moved, or recovered. Hospital staff reported on their activities as well, recounting the number of HIV tests performed on adults and children, the numbers of patients admitted and discharged, and so on. Occasionally, conversation would linger on a particular patient or issue—for instance, to ensure that someone had been seen at the hospital or to request that a discharged patient receive visits from a volunteer. For the most part, however, though the numbers and progress reports were shared and circulated, this part of the meeting was relatively brief.

Discussion then turned to the nitty-gritty of "coordination." The first and most frequent topic was shortages faced by hospital staff, such as a lack of transportation to take blood samples to Quelimane for testing, or lack of petrol to fetch medical supplies. In these cases, NGO staff would volunteer, in rotating order, to buy the petrol or to organize transportation. Yet most weeks, some staff from one or more NGOs were missing because they were at their own staff meetings, traveling to rural areas, or hosting visits from national supervisors or foreign donors. In other cases, cars were already booked up or petrol shortages meant that fuel was not available. When this happened, other NGOs would sometimes take on the role of "partner" for the week; at other times, blood samples simply were not taken, medicines were not picked up, or patients were not transferred to Quelimane's Central Hospital. These negotiations were complicated by the fact that neither health nor NGO staff members who participated in these meetings had control over staff meetings, travel schedules, or even local transportation schedules, all of which were determined in Quelimane or Maputo. At the same time, if "poor coordination" caused too many logistical problems, both hospital and NGO staff would get an earful from the energetic and forceful provincial health director. While the participants in the meeting were all ostensibly colleagues, then, a tense and anxious atmosphere often characterized the conversation.

Meetings like the ones at Morrumbala Hospital made it easy to see how institutional and infrastructural gaps persisted not in spite of but *through* practices of "coordination." In Morrumbala as in Maputo, the circulation of documents and information revealed the forms of "infrastructural violence" through which data structures generated both information and value for NGOs in ways more extractive than caregiving (Appel 2012). Yet close attention to documents—whether registration documents, community maps, medical files, recipient profiles, or weekly patient summaries—also can lead one to see how multiple governmental entities may be entangled and how documents may simultaneously articulate a variety of governmental, bureaucratic, knowledge-producing, and economic aims (Berg and Bowker 1997) as a range of institutions, actors, and agencies come to constitute public health infrastructure, whether in the form of databases or of transportation systems. Even relatively simple and singular forms frequently *worked* in a variety of ways—tracking individual patients, providing data for research, and maintaining continuity across programs spanning multiple countries—depending on the context. For instance, *processos* both documented practices of treatment and generated data for research. The context and content of these documents, however, varied dramatically. Forms used in studies tended to be well organized, relatively well documented, and accessible—clearly visible in their bright red binders. General Clínica 2 files in their green covers, by contrast, were more frequently disorganized and hard to locate, as Edilia and Jéssica discovered. Some elements—such as the patient identification numbers inscribed on clinical files—remained constant across the forms, but other aspects changed from one *processo* to the next.

These documentary gaps intensified when considered across multiple clinical sites and programs, as in Morrumbala. Even when clinics and projects reported patient numbers to the Ministry of Health and to each other, it was impossible to know how many patients had registered in multiple clinics and were double counted. Clinicians and supervisors frequently complained about the number of lost patients, patients with files in multiple health centers, and the difficulties of comparing their own work to work at other clinics.

Problems of managing paperwork and clinic information were frustrating not only for staff who grappled with the material dilemmas of filing, storing, and accessing files but also for those who managed and implemented the procedures. The changeability of forms across contexts led to problems of standardization and comparability as clinical files were not shared across different clinical spaces. Such informational absences were frustrating for patients, who wasted time in fruitless visits to the clinic, as well as for staff and workers. For instance, community staff in Maputo and Morrumbala complained about the difficulties that paperwork produced. Lost paperwork and the length of time it took to obtain, notarize, or get a response to inquiries about paperwork were commonly cited obstacles in the process of accessing social benefits tied to medical conditions. My questions about particular cases in which a patient required services often solicited replies along the lines of "I submitted the paperwork six months ago and since then we've been waiting." Far from inscribing a standardized, universal patient-citizen, documentary practices and data points remained largely localized.

Local Opportunities

While documentary confusion frustrated and impeded services, the informational disarray that complicated patient and health worker experiences at Clínica 2 also opened opportunities. Some of these opportunities, such as the soliciting of bribes by health workers, appeared to be in keeping (if at a smaller scale) with analyses of disorder in postcolonial politics.[8] Yet the opportunities created by documentary difficulties were in fact deployed to diverse ends by a variety of patients and staff members across and around Clínica 2. Most evidently, claims that documentation had been lost provided a common and easy means of displacing responsibility up or down a chain of professional hierarchy—from community health workers to nurses, doctors, and clinic administrators. Those in positions of authority were, to some extent, better able to use documentary practices to their advantage, as in the case of social service officers who blithely lost paperwork or asked for endless forms, signatures, and other documents, creating a series of bureaucratic obstacles as a means of denying claims. However, those in less powerful social positions also deployed different kinds of paperwork to their advantage. In a conversation I had with Mikaela, one of Clínica 2's community workers, she described how patients as well as workers manipulated paperwork and documents to disrupt or elude clinical audit practices: "[Sometimes] patients don't want to work with the community health program anymore. They don't come to get referral slips or anything. . . . And then [my supervisor] gets angry too and says, 'Why aren't there any referrals at the hospital?! Aren't you helping the patients?'" Paperwork could therefore be used to facilitate or disrupt bureaucratic processes in multiple ways. Lost, disorganized, or improperly filed paperwork was a genuine source of frustration, but it also indexed struggles and conflicts over claims-making and claims-denying. Bureaucratic mess was productive, generative, and a site of agentive action—as well as frustrating, disabling, and seemingly intractable. It allowed for claims to be made, or not made, or made only in some cases and not others.

Proliferating papers therefore created particular (and partial) opportunities as well as mundane aggravations. While some opportunities, such as the doubling of intake forms and research tools, benefited ICHC researchers, GCF fund-raisers, and others who generated and made use of data in the clinic, other openings and opportunities were valued by patients. This was particularly visible among patients who were ambivalent about the care provided at Clínica 2 and, especially, for those who combined Clínica 2 treatments with care provided by the traditional healers or spiritual and religious leaders that psychologists warned against. When patients missed appointments, hard-to-locate medical charts made it less likely that staff would contact them by phone, visit their home, or even notice their absence. Abbreviated social evaluations allowed patients latitude in explaining deliberate absences. These documentary gaps allowed some patients to construct the types of care they desired. Informational aporias allowed movement between incommensurate therapeutic spaces as patients both evaded and submitted to multiple forms of medical authority.[9]

These creative means of engaging the aporias of clinic documents were brought to my attention by patients such as Rebekah, an HIV-positive woman whose eight-year-old son was being treated at Clínica 2. I first met Rebekah at her intake interview, during which she described her husband's struggle to find work as a driver, and her conflicts with her sisters- and mother-in-law. Unlike some counseling sessions I observed, which were brief and perfunctory, Rebekah's eloquent narrative lasted for almost an hour. After she left, the two psychologists present acknowledged that this was "a very complicated case." I was surprised then, that they noted only the barest of facts in her *processo*—address, health status, employment and the clinical note, "pretreatment counseling for pediatric TARV [HIV therapy]." Rebekah continued to return with her son, Dercio, on a monthly basis, and I came to know her and her family in and out of the clinic. A dedicated mother, Rebekah actively worked to combine HIV treatment in the hospital with healing practices and treatments offered by the evangelical church she and her husband attended each week. Periods of diligent adherence to the hospital schedule alternated with long absences as Rebekah balanced the financial, emotional, and temporal costs associated with different treatments (see Chapman 2010 for a discussion of Mozambican women's health-seeking strategies). These went largely unnoticed in the general overwork and thin documentation that marked Rebekah's experiences of care at Clínica 2. Documentary gaps became important spaces through which Rebekah managed competing social and therapeutic goals. Yet these opportunities coexisted with costs. When, with Rebekah's permission, I reviewed the *processo* that had been opened on her case, I saw that her son's chart repeatedly noted mild malnutrition over a four-year period, without a referral to the hospital social work office, the food support program, a prescription for multivitamins, or nutritional counseling. The openings provided by the disorganization of files and the lack of patient tracking were inextricable from lapses in care that also made patients hesitant to rely on hospital treatment.

The Proliferation of Paper

Predicaments such as Rebekah's, and the problems with accessing or organizing information that gave rise to them, were common sources of frustration for Clínica 2 and ICHC staff as well. Though some staff members recognized that the bureaucratic exigencies of HIV treatment contributed to Clínica 2's struggles, as well as to the "complicated cases" they encountered, others saw problems of documentation as unavoidable and even natural aspects of practicing medicine in Mozambique. Despite the ways in which both nongovernmental and public health practices were imbricated in these dilemmas, the transnational dimensions of documentary disorder were often overlooked by expatriate health workers for whom confused paperwork conveyed a sense of Mozambique as uniquely chaotic. For instance, Caroline, an American public health consultant at Clínica 2, contrasted her experience in Mozambique with earlier experiences in Zimbabwe, saying: "In Zimbabwe, it was so easy. It was really easy to track patients because each case had a case history that showed who the patient was, where they lived, in what conditions. And it was all organized, so it was really easy to see if their neighbors were getting sick, if others in the house were getting sick. And here it's just like . . . nothing! . . . I've honestly never worked anywhere as disorganized as Mozambique." In Caroline's narrative, the disorganization of information became a national characteristic rather than a feature of the transnational governmentality through which some forms of nongovernmental public health were enacted in Maputo.

Emphasizing "national" disorder, or variable "cultures of organization" (Crane 2010: 852), these narratives obscured how NGOs contributed to confused paperwork by multiplying the institutions and documentary practices through which care was provided, even as they aimed to enhance documentary capacity and transparency. That disorganized files contributed to the exclusion of patients such as Edilia and Jéssica, and to the provision of inadequate care to patients such as Rebekah, was not lost on ICHC staff. Such predicaments motivated core interventions including the provision of computer equipment and the elaboration of new bureaucratic practices. Yet interventions of that sort both ameliorated and contributed to the disorganization of clinic documents and to predicaments of care.

These narratives also overlooked how paperwork and its management were important and productive sites through which the ICHC intervened in the name of documentary organization, with attention to the generation and management of knowledge and data, as well as patient protection and care. For while documentary confusion was frustrating and disabling for the ICHC, it also provided further opportunities for the organization to take on governmental practices. The work of elaborating new intake and registration procedures and of computerizing (if only partially) medical records and clinical files became central ICHC activities. Documentary confusion allowed researchers and clinicians at Clínica 2 to intervene in clinic activities and to produce knowledge that they deployed to multiple ends. Moreover, the generation of what the ICHC described as "patient-level data" was important for an organization that relied on measurable and quantifiable measures of program impact. The importance of these measurements meant that opportunities for intervention, documentation, and research were high-stakes concerns for the ICHC as well as for Clínica 2 patients and staff. These modes of research and intervention produced, along the way, ever more paperwork.

Putting Out Data Fires

Intervention in the management of files thus allowed important clinic practices to continue even as it proliferated the plurality of these interventions and their documentary regimes. Yet the generation of nongovernmental data did not always translate into—and sometimes complicated—the generation of public health information. This was expressed in an interview with the chief of staff in the Monitoring and Evaluation Office of the Ministry of Health's National AIDS Program, a young American man named Brian. An employee of a US-based NGO, Brian and his Ministry of Health colleagues were responsible for collecting statistics from clinics such as City Clinic, aggregating the data, and producing quarterly reports on the expansion of the National HIV/AIDS Program. These numbers were drawn from clinic registers (and in some cases patient charts) and submitted each month by the clinic administrator or head nurse. At Clínica 2, Nurse Elsa provided this information; in Morrumbala, Nurse William.

During our conversation, I mentioned that some clinics seemed to estimate rather than tally each patient and Brian immediately nodded. After a pause and a shrug of his shoulders, he replied that he did not consider this to be a problem. The estimates were usually realistic, he noted. If he had doubts, he could always compare them with numbers produced by other agencies (such as the pharmaceutical distribution system). He said, "They [clinic staff] pretty much know how many people they have, so even if they're just estimating, they're probably pretty accurate.... And, if they were to fill out the forms [patient-by-patient] they would pretty much spend one-twentieth of their time every month—more than a whole day's work—just filling out the reports." While these practices of estimation and documentary improvisation left him unconcerned, however, Brian *was* frustrated by the amount of time spent convincing health centers to provide any data at all. Even worse was the time he spent "putting out fires," as he described last-minute efforts to compile information in response to donor requests. "Sometimes," he said, "I feel like I'm just hanging on." Compounding his dissatisfaction was the fact that, although he was supposed to be building state capacity by training his Mozambican colleagues, he was so busy responding to donor demands for information that he had little time to help them. In the end, it was not accurate numbers that caused Brian anxiety but the work of constructing the state's biostatistical capacity.[10]

The anxiety with which Brian described the challenge of aggregation—as he "put out fires" and tried to "hang on"—contrasted with his rueful but understanding attitude toward the inaccuracies of his data. It seemed that what mattered most was *not* carefully accounting for which patients received treatment but creating a coherent, aggregate portrait of the national HIV program, which could then circulate to other ministry and donor staff. As we spoke, Brian bemoaned how problematic these arrangements were. He was unable to analyze data (and therefore to intervene in its production) with the care that he would like and was unable to train his civil servant counterparts in ways that would let them take up the work of aggregation and analysis. Instead, Brian produced numbers for consumption by donors and "partners." Though he aspired to (and was tasked with) "building capacity" in monitoring and evaluation, he noted that his Mozambican counterparts had worked in the monitoring and evaluation office through his predecessor's tenure and much of his own without any of them ever having time or breathing room for comprehensive training.

Attention to the digital form of Brian's spreadsheet shows how the unequal relations of governmental multiplicity are constructed. Managing spreadsheets requires technical know-how and material capacity—training, computers, and software. Yet these skills and this know-how are not equally available to *all* governmental actors. It was relatively easy for Brian, who had advanced degrees in epidemiology and public health, to access and use diverse forms of statistical data and software packages, and to construct spreadsheets and circulate them; it was harder (in his recounting) for his counterparts. This disparity not only reflected the privileged position of transnational agencies and actors but also helped ensure it. As Brian (or his NGO-employed predecessor) managed national data year after year, the material or digital form of the spreadsheet not only responded to but also helped to constitute these unequal relations and to multiply medical information.[11]

Conclusion: Data and Capacities of Care

Documentary medical practices are sites in which unequal labor relations come to the fore. As such, they make clear how complex medical and human experiences are transformed into data and surveillance points, evaluative tools, and fund-raising techniques. As biomedicine shapes and transforms contemporary citizenship projects, the material and digital management of information illustrates how practices of medical governance, and the possibilities for livelihood, care, and citizenship that they enable, are marked by multiplicity. Patients not only accessed clinical care in ways simultaneously public and nongovernmental; they also made use of the openings constituted by such multiplicity in order to construct the plural forms of care they desired. At the same time, as they created documentary records, staff like Dr. Luísa and her colleagues "not only generat[ed] knowledge about their clients but also produce[d] a record of their own performance, a record that [could] raise or lower their professional status and determine the trajectory of their career" (Drybread 2016). Similarly, institutions such as the ICHC and GCF intervened in documentary multiplicity in ways that simultaneously aimed to ameliorate disorganization and created conditions for its perpetuation, allowing for knowledge-production and intervention into the tracking of patients as well as the auditing of services and the surveillance of community staff.

Yet attention to clinic paperwork also shows that medical multiplicity is not an aberration of Mozambican medicine; rather, as attention to infrastructures of data and information make clear, it is integral to and produced by transnational biomedical practice itself. Following the circulation of medical data and documents across clinical and ministry spaces draws attention to how some state capacities were constituted by way of a rotating but constant cast of expatriates. Mundane processes of collecting and managing data, through singular documentary efforts in the same clinics, with the same providers and patients, simultaneously gave rise to both the state (experienced as an inadequate and undercapacitated statistical office) *and* a detailed, demanding, and sophisticated transnational health apparatus. As information moved from paper-based lists and files into the digital values of an Excel chart, social relations, professional values, and moral economies were transformed into numerical values that could be entered into the neat boxes of a spreadsheet. In the process, the conditions and relations that enabled patients to seek care, the professional negotiations through which patient narratives were heard and recognized or dismissed and ignored, fell out of the very processes designed to record them. At the same time, these processes stabilized interventions by generating statistics that circulated across the public health service and through nongovernmental organizations. Attending to how paper-based and electronic statistical data, patient information, and programmatic documents circulate through overlapping but unequal practices and channels shows how the multiplicity of caregiving strategies, regulatory authorities, and documentary processes emerges not in spite of but through transnational intervention.

Afterword

Critique and Caring Futures

In this book, I have explored how practices of treating and managing disease have shaped the landscape in which patients and health workers seek and provide medical care and the forms of politics and labor that are associated with these interventions. Attending to the daily work through which transnational medical projects are implemented, I have showed how new regimes of medical governance are articulated with long-standing practices of public health, development, and humanitarian assistance in ways that challenge and enable the relations (professional, personal, and in between) through which medical goods are made into medical care. In a context of multiple, often rapidly changing interventions, the work of nourishing and extending relations, whether as patient or caregiver, professional or volunteer, becomes an important means through which caring futures are constituted. This relational work is shaped by NGOs and public health systems, as well as by the political affiliations, class positions, gendered subjectivities, and historical experiences that make care possible and meaningful but also unequal.

I came to this project because I wanted to understand the mechanisms and effects of large-scale transnational funding flows as they enabled and transformed medical experience. I wanted to understand how care was made when goods, knowledges, and practices were shaped by a multiplicity of interventions, involving diverse actors, aims, and temporalities, all deployed to a variety of ends. Over the course of my fieldwork, I found a particular kinship, intellectual and social, with the mainly women health workers (Mozambican and expatriate) in my study who were navigating this terrain. Their experiences and observations ultimately informed my focus on time, politics, and labor. I have tried to keep their perspectives and experiences in mind while writing, considering how ethnographic depictions of health and medicine in Mozambique not only represent but also help to constitute some of the broader context of instability and multiplicity in which they and their colleagues work.

I began my research by moving in and out of the public health system and NGO offices, talking with patients, drivers, logisticians, nurses, psychologists, technicians, and volunteers about their experiences. As I did so, I was struck by the enthusiasm with which the news that I was an anthropologist was greeted by many expatriate medical workers in Mozambique. Where I had anticipated skepticism or hesitation, NGO staff responded to my introductions with sometimes uncertain but most often friendly statements such as "An anthropologist? Great! You can tell us what is really going on!" I was pleased and grateful for this warm reaction, yet also sometimes puzzled; I was just beginning my research and often hoped that they would tell *me* what was going on.

Over time, I became more interested in the kinds of goings on that different interlocutors found compelling. For clinical actors and program directors at NGOs, it seemed that "tell us what is really going on" was often linked to a desire to generate "better metrics" (Adams 2016), seen as a means of more accurately assessing whether patients were "*really* taking their medicines," whether community health workers were "*really* visiting patient homes," or whether recipients "*really* needed" their food baskets.[1] In this view, my role as ethnographer offered the promise of rendering visible, and even surveilling, a "real world" outside the clinic in ways that could inform or refine programmatic notions of success or failure.

When I introduced myself to public health workers, by contrast, they were more likely to direct my attention to institutions and agencies than to patients. Dr. Joana, the director of Clínica 2, for instance, told me in an interview:

> *Olha* [Look], if you want to know what I think, what the *true* scandal is, it's the NGOs. They just come here and suck up the resources—the scarce resources—that we have; they pay their staff more than we can pay; they suck the human resources out of the system by paying Mozambican staff just *slightly* more than we can pay—but not a wage a foreigner would work for. And when there's no more money left in AIDS, they will leave and we will be weaker, and have fewer resources, than we did before they arrived.[2]

After a pause, she reflected, "It's a shame. The attitudes that they come with, the territoriality, the ways they relate to each other . . . It's neocolonial!" Her comments brought to mind the language I often heard as NGO workers described their areas of intervention, phrases like "Clínica 25 de Setembro is *ours*" or "We *have* Bairro Ferroviario." Dr. Joana's words were also informed by the dynamics of hiring, employment, and care that some critics have described as an "internal brain drain" (Sherr et al. 2012). Most importantly, her comments articulated a critique in which the eventual departure of newly arrived organizations, then so highly visible, was a taken-for-granted public health future.

Beyond deflecting my attention to other subjects—after all, my interlocutors also participated in my interviews, facilitated my ethnographic engagements in their clinics and offices, and introduced me to other participants—such responses helped me understand how differently positioned actors understood and narrated the story of medicine in Mozambique as a new era of increased possibilities for care or a brief moment of plentitude in a history of extraction. Such conceptualizations of transnational medicine not only raised questions for me about where to direct my ethnographic attention—to the "real world" of care or the "true scandal" of NGOs—but they also prompted reflection about the work that ethnographic narratives do to articulate a vision or critique of transnational medicine. What makes representations of patients and illness compelling or "real," even in ethnographies critically attuned to the governmental practices and economic structures through which global health projects have come to be? What makes attention to NGOs more "scandalous"—or, at least, critical—than descriptions of patient illness and well-being?

Such questions are more urgent considering the ways that anthropological and pedagogical attention to global health has flourished as funding for it has increased (Institute for Health Metrics and Evaluation 2015). Global health programs have emerged at many universities and colleges in North America (Crane 2013; Erikson and Wendland 2014; Locke 2014; Sullivan 2016), and concerns with global health and development have reached popular audiences through articles by journalists such as Nicholas Kristof. In some cases, ethnographic and anthropological accounts have been incorporated into global health training itself (for instance, see Farmer et al. 2013; also Hahn and Inhorn 2008; Nichter 2008; Singer and Erickson 2013). Many ethnographers have also turned a critical eye on global health initiatives, elucidating how and why nongovernmental organizations have become key actors in the management of health and the provision of care (Singer and Castro 2004), or tracing how humanitarian logics and rationalities may harm as well as help (as shown in Bornstein and Redfield 2011 and Fassin 2011). Yet even critical ethnographies of global interventions may deploy representations of suffering, where pain is not alleviated and is perhaps even exacerbated by the shortcomings of nongovernmental interventions, in order to articulate and make clear what is at stake. As Leslie Butt has noted, the figure of the suffering patient is often the grounds from which critique can be articulated (2002), suggesting that ethnographic realism and political critique may sometimes be two sides of the ethnographic coin.[3]

The convergence between descriptive-ethnographic, critical, and "applied" perspectives on NGOs may be particularly sharp in Mozambique, where a postsocialist history lends particular immediacy to claims (or suspicions) that NGOs and donors threaten state sovereignty. This history has helped to generate a robust critical discourse among observers and medical practitioners alike (for instance, Hanlon 1991; Pfeiffer 2004: 213; Sherr et al. 2012). From national directors to NGO administrators, there seemed to be widespread agreement in Maputo on the value of the public system and the ambivalent effects of nongovernmental assistance, agreement that sometimes echoed the critiques of anthropologists and others.[4] For instance, a director at the World Bank, a Mozambican national with many years of experience in the public sector, remarked to me that the conversation about the weakness or incapacity of public institutions was long-standing and difficult. He argued that "the government *should* direct things . . . in the sense that it's necessary to make plans, to strategize, to have the capacity to say 'no' to unwanted projects," even as he acknowledged that this was often not the case. Critical views of NGOs thus circulated widely in Mozambique even at agencies, such as the World Bank, that promoted them. Discourses on respecting and even strengthening public or state institutions often seemed central to the everyday work of NGOs themselves, as shown in chapter 2.[5] The dream of "2030," recounted in the introduction, seemed to be broadly compelling.

These critical views informed my own ethnographic interests and practice. Yet over time I came to wonder about the convergence between critical representations and those deployed by NGOs themselves. This shared critical perspective suggests that medical ethnographies may not only represent but also help to constitute and stabilize global health as a field of intervention, by underscoring a universalized and humanistic sense of vulnerable bodily subjects (Robbins 2012) *and* by reiterating the utopian aspirations that often animate humanitarian and development interventions. While depictions of illness illustrate the need for intervention, critiques of intervention suggest a need for "better" modes of intervening, however that improvement is defined. Yet this "will to improve" (Li 2007), reflected in ethnographic accounts and NGO reports alike, also works to stabilize global health even as it is part of what makes such projects so tenuous begin with.

These dynamics of improvement and critique have been particularly visible in many ethnographies of African medicine. As African patients, health workers, and health systems have become emblematic of global health efforts, encapsulated in the familiar imagery of celebrity philanthropists posing with African patients, they have also been central to ethnographic attempts to unpack these representational, financial, medical, and infrastructural practices. The centrality of African examples to global health both as a therapeutic project and as a critical-analytical object reflects how Africa, as Achille Mbembe has written, "constitutes one of the metaphors through which the West represents the origin of its own norms, develops a self-image, and integrates this image into the set of signifiers asserting what it supposes to be its identity" (2001: 2). In this case, such examples give rise to narratives of a caring West, even as they also describe "a world apart . . . for which we are hardly responsible" (Mbembe 2016: 49). Thus global health stories about Africa, driven by health indicators and depictions of disparity, are integral to projects of Western—including ethnographic—knowledge production and self-fashioning. Within an "affective economy" (Hardt 1999, Muehlebach 2012) depictions of Africa—and of African illness—are sites for generating racialized symbolic and economic value (Pierre 2013).

In other words, while critical ethnographies of health and health systems have attended to how such value is produced, ethnographic critiques of global health, too, gain critical currency from illustrating the shortcomings of Western and transnational institutions through depictions of abject African patients (Benton 2016). Though critical narratives may problematize the role played by transnational NGOs, they sometimes do so by reinforcing larger narratives of racialized misery. The convergences between ethnographic and humanitarian representational strategies, and the wide-ranging circulation of utopian critique, thus seem to mark out a field in which the predicaments of the ethnographic endeavor and the challenge of narrating "Africa" from the West become particularly salient.[6] Indeed, one social scientist has suggested that, in Mozambique, "the most intriguing problem faced by the social sciences is not so much the inability to produce a critical theory [of aid and development], but rather its uselessness" so long as the violent processes through which structural adjustment was produced and stabilized remain unaccounted for (Macamo 2003). As the violence of structural adjustment has given way to new (but also violent) crises of debt, aid, and political legitimacy, the relation of theory and ethnography remains important.

How, then, can ethnographic accounts engage these political and critical processes and attend to realities of care without also stabilizing intervention as a field of practice? In seeking to respond to this challenge, this book has tried to attend to the social life of critique in the field, showing how critique is not only the outside stance of an observer looking in but also helps to constitute the object of study. Recent accounts of humanitarianism have called for a "critical thinking located 'at the frontiers'" (Fassin 2011: 245). Building on these efforts, I have attempted to straddle "inside" and "outside" but also to attend to how ethnographic critique *participates* in the construction of these frontiers (Latour 2004). One of my aims has been to show how critique itself becomes part of the transnational currency (medical-humanitarian or ethnographic) that enables intervention.

It is in this spirit that I have tried to attend to not only the criticisms of World Bank directors and clinic managers, but also the everyday observations of expatriate as well as Mozambican health workers, as they navigate the aspirations and limitations of the projects they enact. When Brian shares his frustration with the shortcomings of statistical capacitation, for instance, he at once articulates a poignant critique of his work *and* reinforces a narrative in which states and other entities can and *should* be disentangled. Even as ethnographic critiques describe important problematics, they may also work to stabilize and render self-evident development processes themselves. To offer another example, in recent years, much transnational attention has shifted to concerns with "health systems strengthening"—itself a response to critiques, articulated by anthropologists and others, that narrow and vertically focused interventions (for instance, on HIV alone) may weaken and damage health services more broadly. But this shift in resources, even if well intentioned and important, has hastened the rapidity with which the projects I followed came to an end.

By contrast, in the recollections of Susana or in the frustrations of Pastor Tomás or Dr. Luísa, it is possible to see not only a critique of NGO practice but an insistence on the long historical processes through which Mozambican patients, workers, and families have been unequally situated but centrally located participants in the production of global goods, knowledge, and value. Attending to the "agency of local actors" as it is "bound to preexisting forms of exchange, politics, and desires" (Biehl and Petryna 2013: 14) makes clear that the power of critique may not be in disentangling public and humanitarian futures, but rather in demanding more equitable and even reparative modes of current and future engagement. Thus, throughout this book, I have aimed to trace how ethnographers, workers, practitioners, and patients articulate and enact critical views—sometimes in ways more complex, and more profoundly critical, than totalizing narratives might suggest. In the course of doing so, I have attended to how people work *anyway,* in the space between the critical view of what could be and the pragmatic sense of what is—to how they work in the meantime.[7]

To say that transnational medical regimes in Mozambique and the therapeutic and life strategies that they enable are marked by a politics of multiplicity, then, always keeps the "meantime" within view. It seeks to account for the histories and economies in which patients, clients, doctors, and volunteers are incorporated into global health projects—whether they involve TB treatment, adherence research, or food support—and through which they incorporate projects into their lives and relations. By showing how medical goods can give rise to a diversity of life possibilities and can be the basis for historical and political critique, their examples suggest the flip side of ethnography's role in stabilizing "global health." Like the patients, doctors, and health staff whose experiences appear in these pages, then, perhaps ethnographers too can articulate a critical understanding of health that makes room for and recognizes the complex and multiple investments of workers, patients, caregivers, and families in fashioning tenable forms of life. Beyond advocating for access to medical technologies or for more capacious public modes of care, I hope that ethnographic work can also be a force for enduring engagements with and across the articulations of inequality that make global modes of caregiving at once necessary, troubling, and precarious. Alongside critique, ethnographic or otherwise, attention to the work that happens *in the meantime* points to the futures of care and justice that enduring if troubled relations might enable.

NOTES

Introduction

1 The names of all organizations, clinics, and individuals, as well as some geographical indicators and locations, have been changed to ensure the confidentiality of the people I spoke with, the patients they served, and the families and communities with whom they worked.

2 Mirroring these entanglements, studies in anthropology, critical development, and related fields have emphasized how transnational investment in medicine has transformed the provision of public health, the development of public capacity, and the meanings of health and citizenship, as the nation-state (for instance, the Serviço National de Saúde) overlaps with the transnational (such as foreign NGOs) (e.g., Hanlon and Smart 2008; Pfeiffer 2013; Geissler 2015). Scholars have raised important questions about what these overlapping and unequal medical regimes mean for citizenship, rights, and politics (Nguyen 2010); about how humanitarian approaches to care can also produce new exclusions (Fassin 2011); and about how global circulations of medical technologies shape and produce new ethical dilemmas (Redfield 2010).

3 Variants of this photo—the (young, white) American woman with (young, cute) African patients—are today banal commonplaces, and a frequent target of pointed humor. For instance, an article at the satirical news site *The Onion* jokes about "6-Day Visit to Rural African Village Completely Changes Women's Facebook Profile Picture." The apparent familiarity of global health spaces is important to keep in mind, since it helps to stabilize assumptions about what health *is*, emphasizing some aspects of clinical care and obscuring the racialized inequalities through which care is assembled (see also Benton 2016).

4 I thank João Biehl for his observations on this point.

5 In order to protect the anonymity of my informants, I use pseudonyms for both organizations and individuals described in this book. I have also changed identifying details and some descriptive passages are drawn from general observations rather describing specific places and individuals.

6 As Lisa Stevenson notes, "Shifting our understanding of care away from its frequent associations with either good intentions, positive outcomes, or sentimental responses to suffering allows us to nuance the discourse on care so that both the ambivalence of our desires and the messiness of our attempts to care can come into view" (2014: 3).

7 There is also a rich anthropological literature on multivocality and polysemic meaning, informed by the work of Victor Turner (e.g., Turner 1967) and elaborated on to describe how symbols, places, and practices may be interpreted, explained, or made meaningful in multiple and even competing ways. Central to Turner's symbolic analysis is attention to the ambiguity, dynamism, and complexity of symbols as well as to their interconnection with a variety of processes. Many of the practices and objects I describe *are* polysemic—for instance, the photograph—and I have endeavored to bring this attention to ambiguity and change into my analysis as well. Nevertheless, my emphasis is on how singular practices may do (and be intended to do) different things for different actors, rather than on meaning or interpretation.

8 Literature on the historical longevity and complexity of medical practice and research in Africa (including Comaroff and Comaroff 1991; Flint 2008; Fullwiley 2011; Hunt 1999; Iliffe 1998; Livingston 2012; Marks 1994; Tilley 2011; Wendland 2010) clearly shows that care-giving practices are always moral and political endeavors, shaped not only by scientific knowledge and medical norms but also by social, political, and economic relations.

9 When some clinics were built by NGOs without "coordination" with the Ministry of Health, they sat empty and unused (de la Fuente 2014).

10 There is a rich anthropological literature on "states of emergency" and humanitarian intervention (Fassin and Pandolfi 2010a; Bornstein and Redfield 2011). Moreover, consideration of emergent short-term temporalities is not restricted to humanitarian action alone. Janet Roitman, for instance, has recently unpacked the temporal and political dimensions of "crisis" (2013). Exploring macroeconomic and prophetic doctrines in Africa, for instance, anthropologist Jane Guyer (2007) has outlined the convergence of "fantasy futurism and enforced presentism," showing how "the near future may be evacuated" (410) as time comes to be structured around "an instantaneous present and an altogether different distant future" (417). Of course, she notes, the near future "is still—and newly—inhabited. The ethnographic and comparative analytical question is, how?" (410).

11 Global health and humanitarian medical projects are frequently motivated by temporal notions—for instance, by "emergencies" that connote a sense of urgency around the need for immediate action (Redfield 2013; Scherz 2014); other projects may be motivated by eradicating diseases understood to be anachronistically persistent in a modern world. Humanitarian projects, unlike development initiatives (Calhoun 2010), are often assumed to be fleeting and transitory.

12 As a site of nostalgic, contested, or ambivalent memory (Geissler 2015; Mbembe and Roitman 1995; Tousignant 2013; Droney 2014), and of practice, professional aspiration, and even stability, the state remains an important site of medical work and care (Whyte 2014). Some have suggested that these political formations constitute a "para-state," to capture how "the state, albeit changed or in unexpected ways, continues to work as structure, people, imaginary, laws, standards, and so on (Geissler 2015: 1), even as others have described nongovern-

mental actors as humanitarian "para-infrastructures" that provide state-like services (Biehl 2013).

13 The document both confirmed and confounded analyses of interventions that have emphasized the evacuation of the state by transnational institutions.

14 The revelation, in early 2016, that the Mozambican government had contracted nearly $2 billion worth of undisclosed loans from Credit Suisse and the Russian bank VTB complicated these triumphant narratives. The so-called secret debt led the IMF and major European donors to freeze all future lending; it also highlighted just how compelling narratives of unrivaled growth had been.

15 Initially an acronym for the *Frente de Libertação de Moçambique (Mozambican Liberation Front)*, FRELIMO refers to the organization prior to independence and to the party following independence through 1992. Initially named the Mozambique National Resistance, later Resistência Nacional Moçambicana, RENAMO similarly refers to the organization between 1976 and 1992. Following the signing of peace accords and adoption of a multi-party democratic system in 1992, the parties became Frelimo and Renamo, respectively. Use of earlier names and orthography thus refers exclusively to events prior to 1992.

16 By some estimates, 85 percent of the medical staff and resources developed by the colonial state remained in three major urban areas (Maputo, Beira, and Nampula), where they had served the white colonial population almost exclusively (Vio 2006).

17 Even as Portugal consolidated political control in the nineteenth century, colonial authorities continued to lease large tracts of land, and cede responsibility for administering these lands, to private concessionary companies under the control of Portuguese, British, and other European directors. Portuguese rule, through the mid-1970s, was rooted in practices of forced labor (Isaacman 1996), coercive labor migration (Lubkemann 2008), and a plantation-based agricultural economy (Vail and White 1980). In central Mozambique, including Morrumbala, nonstate authorities—from the owners of *companhias* to the traditional authorities known as *mfumos* and *regulos*, often installed and backed by the colonial state—were responsible for much of the political administration in the territory. Complexly entangled relations between private, often transnational, entities and the state thus have a long history.

18 Despite important historical and contextual differences, Alex Nading (2014) and P. Sean Brotherton (2012) have explored similar revolutionary and counterrevolutionary dynamics in Nicaragua and Cuba, respectively, showing how these legacies continue to shape and inform the practice of global health.

19 Although global politics profoundly shaped RENAMO's emergence, the armed campaign also captured the disappointment of rural citizens subjected to disruptive and exploitative development plans (West 2005), excluded from development and government (Adam 2005, Dinerman 2006) and frustrated with local hierarchies of authority (Geffray 1990). Relying heavily on forced conscription as well as on resentment of the government's antipathy to long-standing religious,

political, and social formations, antigovernment opposition escalated into a brutal civil war throughout the early 1980s.

20   Of the 1.5 million refugees outside Mozambique's borders, at least one million went to Malawi. By 1990, Mozambican refugees constituted one-tenth of Malawi's population, then the largest refugee population in Africa and the third largest in the world (UNHCR 1996). Those who remained in Morrumbala District were concentrated in the district capital. Those who crossed to Malawi were received by UN agencies together with twenty-two implementing partners, including the Malawian Red Cross and local and international NGOs.

21   For instance, Marta, a retired nurse who now volunteers for a community health program in the Maxaquene neighborhood of Maputo, recounted how an Italian doctor had trained her to handle high-risk pregnancies and deliveries, so that she could better assist pregnant women in Zambézia during the war.

22   Since the late 1980s, processes of political and economic reform driven by international agencies such as the International Monetary Fund and the World Bank, global governing bodies including the UN, and transnational actors including both NGOs and corporations have dramatically impacted the development of policy and the delivery of public goods and services in states around the world. These processes have been particularly evident in poor countries, where access to funds, including international loans, has often been contingent on the adoption of policies and governmental practices developed and enacted by transnational actors. As NGOs became increasingly powerful actors over the 1980s, 1990s, and 2000s, scholars pointed out the political ambiguities that resulted, as responsibility for core governmental functions became vested in transnational agencies.

23   To many, NGOs appeared to arrive in Mozambique as part of a package that included economic and political changes with often dire public health consequences. Observers described "swarms of new 'non-governmental organizations' . . . taking advantage of the shift in donor policies that moved funding for projects away from mistrusted state bureaucracies and into what were understood as more 'direct' or 'grassroots' channels of implementation" (quoted in Ferguson 2006: 38). As state functions were outsourced to NGOs, skilled state functionaries left the public sector for more lucrative private sector or nongovernmental employment, compounding the devastation of public services.

24   Examples of global health agencies include the Gates Foundation; GAVI, the Vaccine Alliance; and the Global Fund for AIDS, TB, and Malaria.

25   Today, many public health initiatives, especially in fields that garner international attention, are enacted through "partnerships" between foreign organizations and the Ministry of Health. Yet despite the mutually supportive connotations of the term, critics have pointed out that the unequal institutional and political relations through which partnership is often enacted frequently evokes long-standing colonial legacies of inequality and even exploitation (Crane 2013).

26   The disjuncture between situated conditions of care and broadly defined global health targets was not restricted to his project (see also Pfeiffer 2004) or to

Mozambique. One study of PEPFAR across three countries suggested that funding allocations were "remarkably consistent" across diverse epidemiological conditions and health systems, "suggest[ing] that global earmarks and donor conditionalities were driving funding allocations regardless of countries' diseases, health needs, and priorities" (Biesma et al. 2009; Oomman et al. 2007).

27 How medicine intersected with race, class, gender, or national origin shaped the relations of care available in different places. It also impacted the kinds of subject positions available to me as an ethnographer; see chapter 4.

Chapter 1: Governing Multiplicities

1 There are many evocative accounts of the Mozambican war (e.g., Finnegan 1992), and some portray in clear and occasionally dramatic terms the forms and effects of violence that the war entailed (Nordstrom 1997).

2 In contesting Paula's right to the house, Paula's in-laws cited both local tradition, through which the house would pass to Castigo's family, and only recently overturned property laws, written by the Portuguese, under which women could not own personal property (Obarrio 2014).

3 Paula's experience serves as a reminder that there are many forms of care, and many "saviors," in Morrumbala that exceed therapeutic or biological forms of government and are thus concerned not only with bodily suffering.

4 "Unlike the concept of citizen," Chatterjee (2004) notes, "the concept of population ... does not carry a normative burden. Populations are identifiable, classifiable, and describable by empirical or behavioral criteria and are amenable to statistical techniques such as censuses and sample surveys" (34). Chatterjee describes membership in such populations as a form of political society, partly facilitated by "the rise to dominance of a notion of governmental performance" whether enacted by the nation-state or by international agencies "that emphasize the welfare and protection of populations" (47).

5 Extending this approach, anthropologist Austin Zeiderman has described a *biopolitics of the governed*, in which being identified "as vulnerable lives at risk and in need of protection" becomes a necessary precursor to "becom[ing] rights-bearing citizens" (Zeiderman 2013: 82). For instance, Zeiderman shows that for the Bogotá residents he studied to "demand ... rights to protection, housing, food, and employment ... [they] first had to be recognized as belonging to the population guaranteed entitlements on account of their vulnerability" (79).

6 This approach importantly points to diversity within political domains commonly marked as "formal" or "modern" (Santos 2006: 63), a perspective that I extend to consider biopolitical dimensions of government. Rather than the *disarticulation* of plural orders, however, I am concerned with the interconnections and productivity of multiple biopolitical forms at work in community health.

7 This was not true of everyone. For instance, one of the GCF volunteers whom I knew best had initially lived in nearby Tete Province, near his wife's family, who

stipulated that they could marry only if they lived close by. It took some years, in his recounting, for his wife's parents to "trust" him enough to let them move farther away. Even so, they only moved as far as Morrumbala, some fifty kilometers away, so that his wife could continue to see her family with regularity.

8 While my arrival together with Felisardo might have shaped some of the responses I received, I had by this point had enough critical conversations with Tomás, Mavote, and others, that I hesitate to discard these responses merely because they failed to match my expectations. Moreover, other participatory practices—as we shall see below—did not always proceed along the lines laid out by GCF staff.

Chapter 2: Making Communities

1 In addition, GCF ran projects in a neighboring district as well as in the provinces of Nampula and Inhambane.

2 These included USAID, the Red Cross, Family Health International, and UNAIDS among other transnational organizations, as well as RENSIDA (the National AIDS Network), the Foundation for Community Development (a large foundation headed by former first lady Graca Machel), legal NGOs such as Gender and Women in Southern Africa, and the Mozambique Nurses Association.

3 In distinguishing the peripheral grassroots from the better connected and better established organizations whose participants were included in the process, Sandra's words brought to my mind descriptions of the postcolonial masses proudly declaring themselves members of FRELIMO, only to be told that FRELIMO had become a vanguard party, open only to the few (Ottaway 1988).

4 In some GCF workshops I attended, goods provided by donors were presented as charitable gifts to be treasured and valued but not expected. For instance, in training sessions with Dr. Felix, he often said: "If your bicycle breaks, you must fix it—not ask the donor for a new one! If your uncle gave you a shirt, would you expect him to give you the soap to wash it with? Or to fix the buttons when they fall off?"

5 Examples of these approaches include Brown and Prince 2015, and Muehlebach 2012.

6 These distinctions, however, between voluntary labor (as freely given) and paid labor (as materially motivated) obscure the value attached to voluntary labor within an "affective economy" that invests community commitments with moral value, that transforms volunteer work into a "valued status symbol" (Brown and Prince 2015: 36), and that offers volunteers an opportunity for demonstrating moral worth (Muehlebach 2012). Frequently, volunteer work becomes a means by which to develop not just moral but professional value, as volunteers acquire skills, connections, and experiences that can be translated into educational or employment opportunities (Erikson and Wendland 2014). By the same token, working for pay does not negate the real moral commitments that motivate care

in fields such as medicine, social work, or other forms of caregiving labor (Brodwin 2013; there is a rich feminist literature on the relationship between care and paid labor, including Hochschild 2003). Community and volunteer work are thus historically situated concepts, the meanings of which are shaped by transnational circuits and by specific historical, economic, and political contexts.

7 Maes and Kalofonos 2013 and Maes 2014 provide a broader discussion of community health work in Mozambique and Ethiopia, describing some of the commonalities in community health projects and showing how the use of volunteers, activitists, or community health workers has become a key, widely circulating, global health technology. Brown and Prince 2015 highlight how voluntary, or unpaid labor, has roots in colonial modes of rule.

8 The continuities between contemporary governmental practices and older political processes and actors has been explored in a rich literature on state-making, tradition, and legal authority in Mozambique (Kyed 2007; Kyed and Buur 2006; Obarrio 2010; West 2005; West and Kloeck-Jensen 1999). Because, as Matsinhe shows (2005), medical and humanitarian constitutions of community are shaped by similar donor agendas, these insights inform my analysis of the processes through which decentralized and local service delivery has become central to health provision.

9 See for instance Burr and Kyed 2006; Bertelsen 2009; Gonçalves 2006; Obarrio 2014. Anthropologist Bjorn Bertelsen demonstrates, for instance, that residents of poor neighborhoods inhabit "complex sediments of overlapping and conflicting state and non-state authority structures" (2009: 126) that not only provide for political representation but may also introduce violence and insecurity into marginal neighborhoods. Bertelsen shows that for residents of many Mozambican *bairros* [neighborhoods], processes of restructuring authority have not only divided power between a variety of community-based, "traditional," and state-affiliated authorities. In addition, the restructuring of power over the decades since independence has shaped and destabilized residents' political allegiances. In the neighborhoods Bertelsen describes in Chimoio, in central Mozambique, he illustrates how, "as a consequence of its perceived FRELIMO link, a great number of inhabitants neither consult nor trust these purportedly community representatives. Instead, they may address representatives of the opposition RENAMO party, criminal networks, traditional authorities, or other formations of authority with their diverse problems and preoccupations" (2009: 126).

10 These included World Vision International and Family Health International, as well as other local and national NGOs.

11 They also show how community volunteer work was seen not only as an altruistic or moral enterprise, but also as a means of inhabiting "the margins of the development establishment" (Brown and Green 2015: 65).

12 Therapies for the treatment of AIDS had arrived in Mozambique through transnational mechanisms largely disconnected from the activities or experiences of most GCF volunteers.

13 The language of fatness and eating that Pastor Tomás used has been theorized in a rich literature on the politics of the belly (Bayart 2009; see also Kalofonos 2010). This is discussed in more detail in chapter 5.

14 Pfeiffer (2003: 733) writes: "The per diem problem was intensified by the proliferation of seminars and training for health workers in the annual provincial plan; training usually designed to upgrade skills for involvement in foreign agency projects. Health workers eagerly supported seminars that required travel since one week of per diems at a seminar was worth more than a month's salary. This proliferation of seminars was jokingly referred to by planners as *seminarite* in Portuguese (or seminaritis). There was little incentive to reduce the number of training sessions since seminars allowed agencies to claim that they were 'capacity building,' while the per diems provided crucial salary augmentation for local workers. The seminars also pulled workers away from their routine duties leading to major gaps in key activities such as patient consultation, data collection, supervision visits, and reporting."

15 Increasing attention to NGO efficiency was reflected in (and to some extent also served to drive) the increasing use of metrics and strategies of transparency, highlighted by the emergence of websites like Charity Navigator that aim to quantify the efficacy and impact of NGOs. Recently, Charity Navigator (and other aid evaluation services) have responded to arguments that expenditures on infrastructure and overhead (salaries, phone lines, office space) are also integral to effective NGO practice and have modified their strategies of evaluation. Nevertheless, amid these new modalities of aid evaluation, workshops became an "ideal vehicle for development interventions," as Nguyen has argued (2010: 41): "They were far less expensive than programs that directly addressed the material needs of target populations. Limited to the cost of airfares, consulting fees, per diems, and hotels, workshops generated few unexpected expenses and once they were finished, they did not require any ongoing costs. Furthermore, workshops contributed to development agencies' credibility in two ways. First, they were counted as 'program outputs.' . . . Second, workshops helped development agencies collect more qualitative evidence of program success . . ." (Nguyen 2010: 41).

16 In his discussion of the "per diem problem," Pfeiffer (2004) quotes a frustrated department head in a Provincial Health Department saying, "Nothing gets done without per diems anymore. People won't even show up for a training at their own health post if there isn't a per diem attached."

17 Leslie Butt, in her article "The Suffering Stranger" (2002), provides an in-depth critique of the work such representations may do.

18 For instance, writing about NGO workshops in Malawi, anthropologist Harri Englund notes that "despite its promise of dialogue and empowerment, civic education on human rights in Malawi contributed to making distinctions between the grassroots and those who were privileged enough to spread the messages" (2006: 70); the work of making these distinctions, he shows, happens through "certificates, closed workshops, common appearance and . . . jargon (often in

English)" (2006: 71). Though Englund was writing about a neighboring country and an unrelated topic, these observations might equally describe how class, professional level, and interpersonal relationships imposed a hierarchical and depoliticizing frame on the workshop in Quelimane, despite a proliferation of discourses of activism, equality, and liberation. Workshops are thus key sites of anthropological critique and ethnographic description.

19 Since the 1970s, anthropology has moved away from the concerns with "traditional peoples" and "primitive cultures" that characterized the founding of the discipline. "Anthropologists today are expected," Ferguson wrote in 1997, "to address questions of the transformation of local communities and of linkages with wider regional and global processes." But, he goes on to point out, "it remains the case that it is a particular *kind* of people we are interested in seeing change, and a particular kind of local community that we seek to show is linked to the wider world." As a result, Ferguson argues, anthropology is perpetually shadowed by anxieties over finding and locating the field and determining how and by whom it is populated. This anxiety keeps the discipline locked in a "strange, agonistic" embrace with development, which simultaneously reifies and threatens the notions of locality that anthropology both disavows and fetishizes.

Chapter 3: Afterlives

1 As I have shown, in certain governmental arenas, GCF has for many years been a more visible presence than many of the state agencies with which it "partners" in Morrumbala. GCF's mandate is not, as has been described of other organizations, aimed at "the temporary administration of survival" (Redfield 2005), and anxieties regarding long-term intervention are less visible among GCF staff than in other accounts of humanitarian action (Redfield 2010). Nevertheless, GCF activities today privilege aid to specific populations meeting biological conditions of vulnerability, particularly patients with HIV/AIDS, tuberculosis, and other illnesses in the newly powerful category of "chronic disease." Temporal and moral arguments regarding appropriate forms of care and help, fears of cultivating "dependent" subjects, and economic constraints on an organization funded largely by charitable donations all shape the capacity of GCF to intervene in lives in short- and long-term ways.

2 Like Paula, Susana's experiences showed how women's worlds were often constituted in circulation; unlike Paula, however, Susana was better positioned to take advantage of the supports available to her in this rural town.

3 In his study of the Zambian copperbelt, Ferguson (1999) shows how development efforts have long assumed that African workers can simply go "back to the land" in times of need, regardless of environmental conditions or individual experiences with, aptitude for, or interest in farming (see 123–25; see also Li 2014).

4 If wartime experiences have profoundly shaped conceptions of humanitarian governance in Morrumbala, residents were also careful to note that humanitarian

assistance accessed during the war was not in itself a motivation to leave. As one returnee and local community leader explained in an interview: "Before when a person fled from here to there, he didn't say, 'I'm going there, I'm going to receive, I'm going to be helped.' He just ran, he was running from the war—and when you arrived there, the people began to come and you received. They [in Malawi] also suffered a food crisis, too, during a whole year. Because in the previous years when the refugees were already multiplying, there were many there in Malawi, they weren't raising their own food. It was the government that helped, the Malawian government, or the Mozambican government helped, or the foreigners that supported the refugees—it's when they began to help people, because they saw that we were suffering too much."

5 Refugee camps have often been sites for exploring the dangers of identity reduced to biological being—from Hannah Arendt's theorization of the fragility and danger of universalist conceptions of humanity ([1951] 1973) to Georgio Agamben's discussion of "the camp" as the limit concept of the nation-state and thus of the rights-bearing citizen (Agamben 2005). Recent critics (e.g., Weheliye 2014) have contested Agamben's avoidance of race in the constitution of the human and of bare life.

6 Strikingly, the discourses I encountered in Morrumbala stand in vivid contrast to sentiments described in neighboring Tete Province in the early 1990s. At that time, anthropologist Harri Englund recounts, displaced Mozambicans nostalgically longed for home, "the place where maize stalks were recalled to grow like trees and where only big granaries could contain the impressive harvests that the land yielded. Tiny granaries and meager harvests, on the other hand, defined the landscape of 'Malawi'" (2001: 165). Yet once returned home, Englund shows, residents whose hopes for development were deflated also invoked, with similarly nostalgic gloss, the days of the Portuguese. As Englund argues, the invocation of the past "emerged in the conditions of perceived impoverishment" of their return, as development projects failed to materialize. "In their post-war frustration, . . . villagers drew on their most compelling images of development" (1996:167). These nostalgic contemplations are best seen, Englund suggests, as "expectations of remembered performance" though which the "hope of return" to different conditions is expressed (1996: 169). This view of nostalgia as a compelling expression of expectation points to how Morrumbala residents articulated memories of Malawi in a context of "perceived impoverishment." Moreover, the relation between memory and politics in Mozambique has not necessarily emphasized the narration of violent events as in contexts marked by formal processes of reconciliation (Wilson 1992); instead, legacies of violence have often been addressed through mediations with spirits of the dead (Honwana 2002) or through managing the past with care and discretion (Shaw 2007). Here, I have focused not on discussions of past violence but on remembered and politicized experiences of aid.

7 Historian Allen Isaacman recounts that, in nineteenth-century Morrumbala, residents had to produce "one hundred kilograms of cotton in order to purchase a single 'capulana' [a length of printed cloth]" (Isaacman 1996: 239). Working conditions improved in the late colonial period, and cotton production became an avenue for the modest accumulation of wealth. By the 1970s, the district was producing almost 15,000 tons of cotton annually.

8 Strikingly, if in some ways unsurprisingly, Dunavant Enterprises traces the company's origins back to the end of the American Civil War, and the company website traces their rise "from a small scale Memphis cotton trader/merchant into a leading global cotton enterprise" (Dunavant 2017).

9 That relations of dependence and distribution are politically complex is also suggested by feminist theory. In a classic essay, for instance, Nancy Fraser and Linda Gordon show how "dependency" served as a "political keyword" of welfare reform in the United States in the mid-1990s, figuring poor and racialized welfare recipients as not only impoverished but also pathological and, simultaneously, at risk of being harmed by governmental intervention, by dependency itself. In such a context, limiting welfare benefits was presented not as an intensification of the suffering of poor women and children, but as an act undertaken for their own benefit. So, too, in ethnologized discourses on *tambira* or the insistence that food support was merely to "lend a hand," the restriction of material assistance was itself portrayed as a positive contribution to patient recuperation and a strategy for facilitating the development of modern and independent political subjects.

10 Anthropologist Peter Redfield has termed such expectations "biopolitical imaginar[ies]" (2011) to capture how political theorists, following Foucault, have envisioned and imagined governmental responsibilities for fostering the life of populations.

11 These modernist conceptions of political economic change were teleological, conceiving development as a singular and inevitable path forward through time and upward economically. They were also hierarchical; poor countries were not only poor but "behind," "backwards"—"naturally, perhaps even racially, *beneath* [the West]" (Ferguson 2006: 190)

12 Such temporal orientations not only shaped large-scale conceptions of development but also impacted everyday experiences of medicine and medical labor. For example, post-independence medicine, in many African states, was seen as a stable and rewarding profession, one shaped by "more continuous and certain trajectories" than health work today as well as a space of "expansive and inclusive progress" (Geissler et al. 2013).

Chapter 4: Nourishing Relations

1 In fact, the archetypal quality of Sr. Francisco's predicament is reflected in the similarity it bears to the struggles of the main character, Joaquim, in the film *A Miner's Tale*, directed by Nic Hofmeyr and renowed Mozambican filmmaker

Gabriel Mondlane. Similar stories circulate in occasional media reports on global HIV/AIDS, such as a PBS *NewsHour* "Global Health" report on Mozambique (Suarez 2010).

2 Explorations of gendered practices of labor and migration, especially to South Africa's mines and industries, have constituted some of the classic social science understandings of southern Africa since the colonial period (Moodie et al. 1988; Packard 1989). Much of this attention has focused on migration to the South African mining and agricultural industries that, beginning in the nineteenth century, drew from labor "reserves" across southern Africa, including the countries we now call Lesotho, Swaziland, Botswana, and Mozambique, as well as from peripheral areas and apartheid-era "Bantustans" within South Africa itself. In this model of labor recruitment and migration, men from around the region traveled to South African mines, where they lived in single-sex hostels (Harries 1994; Donham 2011).

3 With few exceptions, 80,000–90,000 workers a year had labor contracts in South Africa through most of this period (Lubkemann 2008; Penvenne 1995). Even when mine-recruiting agencies were disbanded in the 1960s and 1970s, high rates of migration continued. By the late 1960s, "it was estimated that although only 80,000 Mozambicans were working on official contracts in South African mines, there were altogether 300,000 workers in South Africa and a further 150,000 in Rhodesia [now Zimbabwe]" (Newitt 1995: 498). These workers sought employment in service jobs and domestic work, agriculture, and construction, and increasingly they included women looking to be household or domestic workers like servants or nannies, or who supported themselves through cross-border trading and other forms of informal work (Lubkemann 2008). As migration to the mines reinforced networks and connections between South Africa and Mozambique, migrants also traveled clandestinely, without formal contracts to South Africa, Zimbabwe, and Malawi.

4 The scope and the precariousness of Mozambican migration to South Africa became particularly clear in 2008, when xenophobic riots broke out in South African cities, prompting thousands of Mozambicans to cross the border back into Mozambique. So many laborers returned that the Mozambican government organized buses to carry them from the border to their homes in the southern and central part of the country.

5 Although the image of the male migrant remains a salient cultural imaginary, migration has long been important to women as well (Penvenne 2015).

6 Like the WFP guidelines, Ministry of Health guidelines (under review in 2007–2008) also emphasized BMI or rapid weight-loss as important criteria of eligibility along with vaguer references to "socio-economic criteria (fragile)." Thus, in the clinic, struggles over entry into the program were mediated by the measure of patients' height and weight, with priority going to low BMI patients (16–18.5 kg/m^2) who had recently started on HIV treatment and to pregnant women. Exit crite-

ria were also technically determined. Food support for almost all patients was stopped after six months. (In a very few cases, such as malnourished, pregnant or lactating, HIV-positive women, food aid could be extended until the beneficiary's BMI exceeded 18.5 for two consecutive months.) While a range of additional factors is mentioned as criteria for inclusion (from nutritional status to socioeconomic characteristics), clinic staff were given few means by which socioeconomic characteristics could be determined. Community volunteers were tasked with visiting patients' homes, where socioeconomic characteristics could be observed, but how they might evaluate "the most vulnerable" was still left unclear.

7   The cycles of obligation and giving that illness entailed were not only material but also spiritual or social. For instance, patients might later make an effort to attend the churches of neighbors who visited and prayed for them when they were sick, or to reciprocate with social visits once they were well.

8   This perception was not mistaken. Some staff did consider that women with boyfriends were both less vulnerable and also less compliant with the norms of the program, which emphasized celibacy or safe sex for AIDS patients and which counseled against drinking, carousing, staying up late, and other activities that "having a boyfriend" was assumed to imply. The criticism of "boyfriends" and "girlfriends" was present in both public health discourses on risk and promiscuity and in Malthusian discourses on the poor as overly procreative, unable or unwilling to limit the number of their children. In Morrumbala, program supervisors lectured patients about the importance of birth control and on multiple occasions asked me what I thought could be done "to make them understand: they can't have any more children!" Yet for many patients, the life of celibacy that these discourses implied was untenable and antisocial, an added indignity and a further constraint on their ability to support themselves and their households.

9   Such ambiguity is well-established in studies of healing in Africa (Feierman and Janzen 1992; Vaughan 1994) as well as of Western biomedicine (e.g., Jain 2013).

10 Writing in a different context, Hannah Landecker (2013) has described what she terms "postindustrial metabolism." She argues that metabolism works as a "conduit between economic and biological domains" (497). Landecker is concerned with the new science around obesity, diabetes, and related diseases, and discusses a "fat knowledge" of "food, time, and biology." At Clínica 2, concerns with diabetes, obesity, and weight were subsumed by the apparent emergencies of poverty and AIDS, even as linkages between diabetes and tuberculosis (itself linked to HIV infection) went unexplored and despite the long and fraught entanglements of health, nutrition, politics, and HIV in southern Africa. Landecker's linking of food, time, and the body is productive, however, showing that biology, pharmacology, and economy are connected to each other in humanitarian responses to the "metabolic demands" of new pharmaceuticals.

Chapter 5: The Work of Health in the Public Sector

1 Damien Droney (2014) has also explored how jokes and irony express perceptions of temporal and geographical disjunctures around medical and scientific work in Africa.

2 Whether these connections conveyed a sense of appreciation and care or of alienated alternative imaginations of childhood and child-rearing was less evident from the patients who sat quietly in the spacious waiting room each morning, or from the brisk, even hassled, efficiency with which nurses directed flows of mothers, fathers, children, grandmothers, and aunts in and out of examination rooms.

3 These historical legacies are clearly demonstrated in Nguyen 2010; I thank Didier Fassin for bringing to my attention the importance of these histories.

4 This emphasis on conduct has informed analyses of therapeutic projects as forms of governmentality—that is, a form of government oriented toward the "conduct of conduct" (Foucault 1991; Rose 2006). Yet my emphasis here is less on expectations of patient conduct than on complexly imbricated professional and therapeutic practices, which were harder to map onto notions of governmentality.

5 An important body of literature on labor, migration, and gender in Mozambique—including Webster 1978; Penvenne 1995; Harries 1994; and Gengenbach 2005—has shown how such family expectations have been historically and economically conditioned. Julie Archambault (2013) discusses how the demise of both "traditional" and nuclear family arrangements created new forms of precarity for women but also enabled the evasion of restrictive household dynamics.

6 Frustration with the limited conditions of their own work was expressed not only in psychologists' sometimes brusque responses, but also at other moments. One morning, for instance, Dr. Felícia picked up a copy of the daily paper, which had a large, close-up photograph of the minister for women and social affairs emblazoned on the front. Dropping the paper back on the table, Dr. Felícia said loudly, to no one in particular, "Ah! That woman just wants us to do her job for her." "Mmmm," Dr. Luísa agreed with a sardonic raise of her eyebrow, "*that* one . . ." That they were often called on to respond to social predicaments and economic constraints alongside or even more than the treatment of medical conditions was a widely recognized condition and challenge of their work at Clínica 2.

7 While such moonlighting has provoked contentious reactions, it is generally accepted and was, for a time, built into National Health policy when the government opened "Clínicas Especiais"—or Special Clinics—for paying clients within National Health institutions. These clinics were modeled on IMF recommendations and in operation from 1998 to 2005, when they were closed because they were regarded as detracting from care available in regular health units.

8 Changana and Ronga, closely related languages, are spoken by close to two million people across southern Mozambique and eastern South Africa.

9 As I describe later in this chapter, I frequently excused myself—or was asked to excuse myself—from consultations. There were certain kinds of consultations

that I never attended, including cases of (suspected or reported) sexual assault, most consultations in which children were present, all consultations involving adolescents, all consultations in which patients were not adhering to treatment, and any instances in which I did not have confidence that patients could consent to my presence. Most consultations I observed were with patients whom I had met previously, and a majority of the interactions I observed were "maintenance" consultations, often those used to complete paperwork or to address routine tasks. Because my interest focused on the politics and institutional dynamics of care, rather than on a comprehensive portrait of patient experience, and because routine appointments constituted a majority of consultations at the clinic, I was able to develop a multifaceted perspective on the professional practices of clinic staff.

10 As detailed in the introduction, neoliberal reform entailed processes of democratization and governmental decentralization promoted by World Bank and IMF policies.

11 Importantly, such distinctions were shaped more by national identity than race. When the sister of a staff member died in a car crash, for instance, Mozambican staff of all races attended the funeral services and visited her family at home; few foreign staff, many of whom juggled busy ICHC schedules, participated in these expressions of sympathy.

12 The Lusophone (or Portuguese-speaking) countries are made up of Portugal, Brazil, Mozambique, Angola, Cabo Verde, São Tome and Principe, and Guinea-Bissau. Portuguese is also one of the official languages of Equatorial Guinea, East Timor, and Macao.

Chapter 6: Paperwork

1 Such data were aggregated by program and country, and were also provided to the U.S. Global AIDS Program, a Washington, DC-based agency that manages, monitors, and evaluates PEPFAR partner programs.

2 Documents and bureaucratic writing have been rich sites of anthropological investigation (Hull 2012b; Feldman 2008; Hetherington 2011; Herzfeld 1993; Riles 2000 and 2006; on medical records and documents in particular, see work by anthropologists and sociologists such as A. Jones 2009; Risse and Warner 1992; Timmermans and Berg 2003; Mol 2002; Whyte et al. 2013). In another context, anthropologist Matthew Hull has demonstrated the importance of attending to material and bureaucratic forms of government to better understand the daily workings of the state (2012). In his account, Hull shows that documents help us to see the state not as a unified entity but as a set of practices (see also Abrams 1988; Mitchell 1991). Similarly, materialist accounts of medical documents have shown how medical records enact multiple and different bodies, bodies politic, and bodies of knowledge in ways that open up "organizational multiplicity" (Berg and Bowker 1997: 523).

3 This is not only true of Mozambique but has also been documented in many other African medical spaces (Geissler et al. 2008). As Carol Heimer shows, the expansion of documentary practices in the name of patient care has often, perversely, eroded the time available for health workers to engage with patients (Heimer and Petty 2010).

4 Combined with the clinical skepticism regarding traditional medicine that marked care provided by the International Center for Health Care, these encounters constrained possibilities for empathetic engagement and "solidarity" at Clínica 2.

5 Discussing practices of "bad" form-filling elsewhere, anthropologist Adam Reed notes that in some cases "it matters little which sections of the document are filled in or left blank. . . . In a sense their answer is already there, forecast in the design of [the document]" (Reed 2006: 168). Here, too, the event of filling out the form, and the information that was conveyed around it, appeared to be as significant as the content contained in the form and its responses.

6 For legal contexts, see Buur and Kyed 2006 and Santos 2006. For accounts of healing practices that are pluralistic as well as dynamic and sometimes contested or experimental, see Langwick 2011 and Meneses 2004.

7 The geographical, epistemological, and etiological trajectories traveled by patients in search of traditional or religious therapies have been described by many recent scholars including Granjo 2009; Luedke 2006; Luedke and West 2006; Meneses 2004; Langwick 2011; Schuetze 2010; West 2005.

8 Among the best known of these analyses is Chabal and Daloz (1999).

9 Strategies of moving between and avoiding diverse modes of medical authority in Mozambique have been described by Chapman (2010) and Granjo (2009) and elsewhere by Langwick (2011) and Stevenson (2014).

10 In his discussion of population statistics and poverty alleviation in India, anthropologist Akhil Gupta distinguishes the work of biopolitics from the work of state representation, arguing that "for biopolitics, the accuracy of the data does indeed matter, whereas for representing the state as singular, accuracy is not necessarily important but aggregation of the data is critical" (2012: 49). Although Gupta is concerned with representations of state singularity (also Hull 2012a: 167), this distinction between accuracy and aggregation is a helpful means of understanding the stakes of information management. In Gupta's example, the aggregative work of statistics makes visible the singularity of the state; here it highlights the unequal heterogeneity of governmental practice.

11 In an essay on the anthropology of documents, Matthew Hull (2012) notes that while scholars have paid increasing attention to paper materials, we have paid less attention to "electronic forms of documentary life." He urges us to bring electronic and paper-based documentary forms into the same "analytic frame." Bringing the struggles of patients like Rebekah, staff members like Dr. Luísa and Nurse William, and nongovernmental actors like Brian into the same frame helps to show how documentary regimes of transnational intervention shape

patient and provider experiences of care, and also how the informational gaps that characterize documents in the clinic travel into public databases and practices of governance.

Afterword

1 Ironically, as João Biehl and Adriana Petryna have recently argued, ethnographic evidence most often "dies" in the metric-driven contexts of evaluation and assessment that often characterize global health analysis (2013: 16).

2 See similar comments in Mussa et al. (2013).

3 More recently, Joel Robbins (2013) has described contemporary ethnographic concerns more broadly as enamored of the "suffering slot." He deploys the term to describe "a way of writing ethnography in which we do not primarily provide cultural context so as to offer lessons in how lives are lived differently elsewhere, but in which we offer accounts of trauma that make us and our readers feel in our bones the vulnerability we as human beings all share." The power of vulnerability, as both an object and an analytic, is partly that it captures so well this shared humanistic view. Yet *vulnerability* is merely one term among others (such as *community* and *patient*) in which ethnographic frames and global health analytics may sit very close to one another.

4 In this, the strangeness of the critical project may again mirror the strangeness of the aid project itself. Confronted with the unequal social relations (and uncomfortable philosophical implications) of aid work, many humanitarian and medical actors have elaborated a rich repertoire of cynical or ironic jokes, parodies, satires, and comments on the aid world, as Peter Redfield has described in his ethnographic account of Médecins Sans Frontières (MSF) (2013). And, as Didier Fassin has shown (2007), MSF has also institutionalized practices of self-evaluation and critique aimed at producing forms of accountability and reflection that go beyond the forms of quantitative assessment that often govern global health projects. These humorous and self-critical repertoires may even generate reflection and description that mirror ethnographic observation.

5 These critical circulations may reflect growing popular discourses on the critique of development, as found in works by authors like Dambisa Moyo, William Easterly, and even Jeffrey Sachs, who explain why aid fails or (in the case of Sachs) how to do it better (see also Munk 2013). The shortcomings of development are often most highly visible to those tasked with the work of enacting these projects (Mosse 2005).

6 In his classic essay, "Anthropology and the Savage Slot," Michel-Rolph Trouillot (2003) offers a powerful historical account of the philosophical formation and disciplinary structures of anthropology. He also suggests a number of potential, partial ways forward, including an insistence on the specificity of otherness, a reassessment of methodological specificity, new theories of ethnography that question the symbolic world on which native-ness is premised, and an insistence

on historicity as a "two-pronged historicization" of both the West and anthropology that puts interrogation of the place of fieldwork within Western and transnational formations at the heart of critical and historical analysis (see also Hankins 2014). My thanks to Joe Hankins and Jeff Flynn for our reading group discussions in 2014.

7 I am grateful to David Valentine for our conversations on this point.

WORKS CITED

Abrams, Phillip. 1988. "Notes on the Difficulty of Studying the State." *Journal of Historical Sociology* 1 (1): 58–89.

Adam, Yussuf. 2005. *Escapar Aos Dentes Do Crocodilo E Cair Na Boca Do Leopardo: Trajectoria de Mocambique Pos-Colonial (1975–1990)*. Maputo: Promedia.

Adams, Vincanne, ed. 2016. *Metrics: What Counts in Global Health*. Durham, NC: Duke University Press.

Adams, Vincanne, Michelle Murphy, and Adele E. Clarke. 2009. "Anticipation: Technoscience, Life, Affect, Temporality." *Subjectivity* 28 (1): 246–65.

AFP. 2013a. "Mozambique Doctors March for Higher Wages." *Mail & Guardian*, June 5. Accessed May 16, 2017. https://mg.co.za/article/2013-06-05-mozambique -doctors-march-for-higher-wages.

AFP. 2013b. "Mozambique Riot Police, Army Deploy amid Medics' Strike." Accessed May 28, 2016. http://www.google.com/hostednews/afp/article/ALeqM5hzDUy sm3NrT9zN97vbaUTdACwo9Q?docId=CNG.643d728ea763c1cbe8a536a441b5 d5f8.91.

Agamben, Giorgio. 2005. *State of Exception*. Translated by Kevin Attell. Chicago: University of Chicago Press.

Agier, M. 2002. "Between War and City: Towards an Urban Anthropology of Refu-gee Camps." *Ethnography* 3 (3): 317–41.

Anand, Nikhil. 2011. "Pressure: The PoliTechnics of Water Supply in Mumbai." *Cultural Anthropology* 26 (4): 542–64.

Appel, Hannah. 2012. "Walls and White Elephants: Oil Extraction, Responsibility, and Infrastructural Violence in Equatorial Guinea." *Ethnography* 13 (4): 439–65.

Araujo, Manuel. 2009. "Promoting Employment through Foreign Direct Investment: The Case of the Cotton Sector (Dunavant) in Morrumbala District." Conference Paper No. 4. Maputo: Instituto de Estudos Sociais e Económicos. http://www. iese.ac.mz/lib/publication/II_conf/CP4_2009_Araujo.pdf

Archambault, Julie Soleil. 2013. "Cruising through Uncertainty: Cell Phones and the Politics of Display and Disguise in Inhambane, Mozambique." *American Ethnologist* 40 (1): 88–101.

Arendt, Hannah. (1951) 1973. *The Origins of Totalitarianism*. New York: Harcourt, Brace, Jovanovich.

Ashforth, Adam. 2005. *Witchcraft, Violence, and Democracy in South Africa*. Chicago: University of Chicago Press.

Baily, Moya, and Whitney Peoples. 2017. "Towards a Black Feminist Health Science Studies." *Catalyst: Feminism, Theory, Technoscience* 3 (2).

Barad, Karen. 2007. *Meeting the Universe Halfway: Quantum Physics and the Entanglement of Matter and Meaning.* Durham, NC: Duke University Press.

Barrett, C. B., and D. G. Maxwell. 2005. *Food Aid after Fifty Years: Recasting Its Role.* New York: Routledge.

Bayart, Jean-Francois. 2009. *The State in Africa: The Politics of the Belly.* Cambridge, MA: Polity.

Benton, Adia. 2012. "Exceptional Suffering? Enumeration and Vernacular Accounting in the HIV-Positive Experience." *Medical Anthropology* 31 (4): 310–28.

Benton, Adia. 2016. "Risky Business: Race, Nonequivalence, and the Humanitarian Politics of Life." *Visual Anthropology* 29 (2): 187–203.

Berg, Marc, and Geoffrey Bowker. 1997. "The Multiple Bodies of the Medical Record: Toward a Sociology of an Artifact." *Sociological Quarterly* 38 (3): 513–37.

Bertelsen, Bjorn Enge. 2009. "Multiple Sovereignties and Summary Justice in Mozambique: A Critique of Some Legal Anthropological Terms." *Social Analysis* 53 (3): 123–47.

———. 2016. *Violent Becomings: State Formation, Sociality, and Power in Mozambique.* New York: Bergahn Books.

Biehl, João. 2005. *Vita: Life in a Zone of Social Abandonment.* Berkeley: University of California Press.

———. 2007. *Will to Live: AIDS Therapies and the Politics of Survival.* Princeton, NJ: Princeton University Press.

———. 2013. "The Judicialization of Biopolitics: Claiming the Right to Pharmaceuticals in Brazilian Courts." *American Ethnologist* 40 (3): 419–36.

Biehl, João, and Ramah McKay. 2012. "Ethnography as Political Critique." *Anthropological Quarterly* 85 (4): 1209–28.

Biehl, Joao, and Adriana Petryna, eds. 2013. *When People Come First: Critical Studies in Global Health.* Princeton, NJ: Princeton University Press.

Biesma, Regien G, Ruairí Brugha, Andrew Harmer, Aisling Walsh, Neil Spicer, and Gill Walt. 2009. "The Effects of Global Health Initiatives on Country Health Systems: A Review of the Evidence from HIV/AIDS Control." *Health Policy and Planning* 24 (4): 239–52.

Biruk, Crystal. 2012. "Seeing like a Research Project: Producing High Quality Data in AIDS Research in Malawi." *Medical Anthropology* 31 (4): 347–66.

Boltanski, Luc. 1999. *Distant Suffering: Morality, Media, and Politics.* Cambridge: Cambridge University Press.

Borges Coelho, João Paulo. 1998. "State Resettlement Policies in Post-colonial Rural Mozambique: The Impact of the Communal Village Programme on Tete Province, 1977–1982." *Journal of Southern African Studies* 24 (1): 61–91.

Bornstein, Erica. 2005. *The Spirit of Development: Protestant NGOs, Morality, and Economics in Zimbabwe.* Stanford, CA: Stanford University Press.

Bornstein, Erica, and Peter Redfield. 2011. *Forces of Compassion: Humanitarianism between Ethics and Politics*. Santa Fe, NM: SAR Press.

Bourdieu, Pierre. 1997. *Pascalian Meditations*. Stanford, CA: Stanford University Press.

Brada, Betsey Behr. 2016. "The Contingency of Humanitarianism: Moral Authority in an African HIV Clinic." *American Anthropologist* 118(4): 755–771.

Brodkin, Karen, Sandra Morgen, and Janis Hutchinson. 2011. "Anthropology as White Public Space?" *American Anthropologist* 113 (4): 545–56.

Brodwin, Paul. 2013. *Everyday Ethics: Voices from the Front Line of Community Psychiatry*. Berkeley: University of California Press.

Brotherton, P. Sean. 2012. *Revolutionary Medicine: Health and the Body in Post-Soviet Cuba*. Durham, NC: Duke University Press.

Brown, Hannah, and Maia Green. 2015. "At the Service of Community Development: The Professionalization of Volunteer Work in Kenya and Tanzania." *African Studies Review* 58 (2): 63–84.

Brown, Hannah, and Ruth Prince. 2015. "Introduction: Volunteer Labor—Pasts and Futures of Work, Development, and Citizenship in East Africa." *African Studies Review* 58 (2): 29–42.

Brugha, Ruairí, Martine Donoghue, Mary Starling, Phillimon Ndubani, Freddie Ssengooba, Benedita Fernandes, and Gill Walt. 2004. "The Global Fund: Managing Great Expectations." *The Lancet* 364 (9428): 95–100.

Buse, K., and G. Walt. 1997. "An Unruly Mélange? Coordinating External Resources to the Health Sector: A Review." *Social Science and Medicine* 45 (3): 449–63.

Butt, Leslie. 2002. "The Suffering Stranger: Medical Anthropology and International Morality." *Medical Anthropology* 21 (1): 1–24.

Buur, Lars. 2010. "Xiconhoca: Mozambique's Ubiquitous Post-Independence Traitor." In *Traitors: Suspicion, Intimacy, and the Ethics of State-Building*, edited by Sharika Thiranagama and Tobias Kelly. Philadelphia: University of Pennsylvania Press.

Buur, Lars, and Helene Maria Kyed. 2006. "Contested Sources of Authority: Re-Claiming State Sovereignty by Formalizing Traditional Authority in Mozambique." *Development and Change* 37 (4): 847–69.

Cabot, Heath. 2013. "The Social Aesthetics of Eligibility: NGO Aid and Indeterminacy in the Greek Asylum Process." *American Ethnologist* 40 (3): 452–66.

Calhoun, Craig. 2010. "The Idea of Emergency: Humanitarian Action and Global (Dis)Order." In *Contemporary States of Emergency: The Politics of Military and Humanitarian Interventions*, edited by Didier Fassin and Mariella Pandolfi. New York: Zone Books.

Carr, E. Summerson. 2010. *Scripting Addiction: The Politics of Therapeutic Talk and American Sobriety*. Princeton, NJ: Princeton University Press.

Castro, Arachu. 2005. "Adherence to Antiretroviral Therapy: Merging the Clinical and Social Course of AIDS." *PLoS Medicine* 2 (12): e338.

Chabal, Patrick, and Jean-Pascal Daloz. 1999. *Africa Works: Disorder as Political Instrument*. Bloomington: Indiana University Press.

Chapman, Rachel. 2010. *Family Secrets: Risking Reproduction in Central Mozambique*. Nashville, TN: Vanderbilt University Press.

Chatterjee, Partha. 2004. *The Politics of the Governed: Reflections on Popular Politics in Most of the World*. New York: Columbia University Press.

Chichava, Sergio. 2013. " 'They Can Kill Us but We Won't Go to the Communal Village': Peasants and the Policy of 'Socialisation' of the Countryside in Zambezia." http://www.scielo.org.za/pdf/kronos/v39n1/06.pdf.

Chingono, Mark. 1996. *The State, Violence, and Development: The Political Economy of War in Mozambique, 1975–1992*. Aldershot, UK: Avebury.

Choy, Timothy. 2011. *Ecologies of Comparison: An Ethnography of Endangerment in Hong Kong*. Durham, NC: Duke University Press.

Cliff, J., and A. R. Noormahomed. 1988. "Health as a Target: South Africa's Destabilization of Mozambique." *Social Science Medicine* 27 (7): 717–22.

———. 1993. "The Impact of War on Children's Health in Mozambique." *Social Science Medicine* 36 (7): 843–48.

Cohen, Lawrence. 2012. "Making Peasants Protestant and Other Projects: Medical Anthropology and Its Global Condition." In *Medical Anthropology at the Intersections: History, Activisms, and Futures*, edited by Marcia C. Inhorn and Emily A. Wentzell. Durham, NC: Duke University Press.

Cole, Jennifer, and Lynn M. Thomas, eds. 2009. *Love in Africa*. Chicago: University of Chicago Press.

Collier, Paul. 2007. *The Bottom Billion: Why the Poorest Countries Are Failing and What Can Be Done About It*. New York: Oxford University Press.

Comaroff, Jean. 1993. "The Diseased Heart of Africa: Medicine, Colonialism, and the Black Body." In *Knowledge, Power, and Practice: The Anthropology of Medicine and Everyday Life*, edited by Shirley Lindenbaum and Margaret Lock, 305–29. Berkeley: University of California Press.

———. 2007. "Beyond Bare Life: AIDS, (Bio)Politics, and the Neoliberal Order." *Public Culture* 19 (1): 197–219.

Comaroff, Jean, and John L. Comaroff. 1991. *Of Revelation and Revolution, Volume 1*. Chicago: University Of Chicago Press.

Comaroff, Jean, and John L. Comaroff, eds. 2001. *Millennial Capitalism and the Culture of Neoliberalism*. Durham, NC: Duke University Press.

Conselho Nacional de Combate ao HIV/SIDA em Moçambique (CNCS). 2008. "Universal Declaration of Commitment on HIV and AIDS: Mozambique Progress Report for the United Nations General Assembly Special Session on HIV and AIDS, 2006–2007." Maputo: CNCS (National AIDS Council).

Conteh, Lesong, and Patricia Kingori. 2010. "Per Diems in Africa: A Counter-Argument." *Tropical Medicine & International Health* 15 (12): 1553–55.

Crane, Johanna. 2010. "Adverse Events and Placebo Effects: African Scientists, HIV, and Ethics in the 'Global Health Sciences.' " *Social Studies of Science* 40 (6): 843–70.

———. 2013. *Scrambling for Africa: AIDS, Expertise, and the Rise of Global Health Science*. Ithaca, NY: Cornell University Press.

Crisp, Jeff, and Andrew Mayne. 1996. "Evaluation of UNHCR's Repatriation Operation to Mozambique." EVAL/02/96. UNHCR. http://www.unhcr.org/research /RESEARCH/3ae6bcf90.html.

Crush, Jonathan, Alan Jeeves, and David Yudelman. 1991. *South Africa's Labor Empire: A History of Black Migrancy to the Gold Mines*. Vol. 10. Cape Town: Westview Press.

Cruz e Silva, Teresa. 2001. *Protestant Churches and the Formation of Political Consciousness in Southern Mozambique (1930–1974)*. Basel: P. Schlettwein.

Cueto, Marcos. 2004. "The Origins of Primary Health Care and Selective Primary Health Care." *American Journal of Public Health* 94 (11): 1864–74.

Cunguara, Benedito, and Joseph Hanlon. 2012. "Whose Wealth Is It Anyway? Mozambique's Outstanding Economic Growth with Worsening Rural Poverty." *Development and Change* 43 (3): 623–47.

Das, Veena. 2011. "State, Citizenship, and the Urban Poor." *Citizenship Studies* 15 (3–4): 319–33.

Deaton, Angus. 2013. *The Great Escape: Health, Wealth, and the Origins of Inequality*. Princeton, NJ: Princeton University Press.

Declaration of Alma Ata: International Conference on Primary Health Care, Alma Ata, USSR, Sept 6–12, 1978. 2000. http://www.euro.who.int/__data/assets/pdf _file/0009/113877/E93944.pdf?ua=1.

"Diagnosis of HIV Infection in Infants and Children | Pediatric ARV Guidelines." 2015. *AIDSinfo*. Accessed July 7. http://aidsinfo.nih.gov/.

Dinerman, Alice. 2006. *Revolution, Counter-Revolution, and Revisionism in Postcolonial Africa: The Case of Mozambique, 1975–1994*. New York: Routledge.

Donham, Donald. 2011. *Violence in a Time of Liberation: Murder and Ethnicity at a South African Gold Mine*. Durham, NC: Duke University Press.

Donzelot, Jacques. 1979. *The Policing of Families*. Baltimore, MD: Johns Hopkins University Press.

Drèze, Jean, and Amartya Sen. 1991. *The Political Economy of Hunger, Volume 1: Entitlement and Wellbeing*. Oxford: Oxford University Press.

Droney, Damien. 2014. "Ironies of Laboratory Work during Ghana's Second Age of Optimism." *Cultural Anthropology* 29 (2): 363–84.

Drybread, Kristen. 2016. "Documents of Indiscipline and Indifference: The Violence of Bureaucracy in a Brazilian Juvenile Prison." *American Ethnologist* 43: 411–23.

Duffield, Mark. 2001. *Global Governance and the New Wars: The Merging of Development and Security*. New York: Zed Books.

———. 2007. *Development, Security, and Unending War: Governing the World of Peoples*. Cambridge: Polity Press.

Dumit, Joseph. 2012. *Drugs for Life: How Pharmaceutical Companies Define Our Health*. Durham, NC: Duke University Press.

Easterly, William. 2006. *The White Man's Burden: Why the West's Efforts to Aid the Rest Have Done So Much Ill and So Little Good*. New York: Penguin Press.

Elyachar, Julia. 2005. *Markets of Dispossession: NGOs, Economic Development, and the State in Cairo*. Durham, NC: Duke University Press.

Englund, Harri. 2001. *From War to Peace on the Mozambique-Malawi Borderland*. Edinburgh: Edinburgh University Press.

———. 2006. *Prisoners of Freedom: Human Rights and the African Poor*. Berkeley: University of California Press.

Epstein, Steven. 2007. *Inclusion: The Politics of Difference in Medical Research*. Chicago: University of Chicago Press.

Erikson, Susan. 2012. "Global Health Business: The Production and Performativity of Statistics in Sierra Leone and Germany." *Medical Anthropology* 32 (4): 367–84.

Erikson, Susan, and Claire Wendland. 2014. "Exclusionary Practice: Medical Schools and Global Clinical Electives." *BMJ: The British Medical Journal* 22 (g3252).

Escobar, Arturo. 1995. *Encountering Development: The Making and Unmaking of the Third World*. Princeton, NJ: Princeton University Press.

Evans-Pritchard, E. E. 1976. *Witchcraft, Oracles, and Magic among the Azande*. Abridged edition. Oxford: Oxford University Press.

Fabian, Johannes. 2014. *Time and the Other: How Anthropology Makes Its Object*. New York: Columbia University Press.

Farmer, Paul. 2004. *Pathologies of Power: Health, Human Rights, and the New War on the Poor*. Berkeley: University of California Press.

Farmer, Paul, Jim Kim, Arthur Kleinman, and Matthew Basilico. 2013. *Reimagining Global Health: An Introduction*. Berkeley: University of California Press.

Fassin, Didier. 2007. "Humanitarianism as a Politics of Life." *Public Culture* 19 (3): 499–520.

———. 2009. "Another Politics of Life Is Possible." *Theory, Culture and Society* 26 (5): 44–60.

———. 2011. *Humanitarian Reason: A Moral History of the Present*. Berkeley: University of California Press.

Fassin, Didier, and Mariella Pandolfi, eds. 2010. *Contemporary States of Emergency: The Politics of Military and Humanitarian Interventions*. New York: Zone Books.

Feierman, Steven, and John M. Janzen, eds. 1992. *The Social Basis of Health and Healing in Africa*. Berkeley: University of California Press.

Feldman, Ilana. 2008. *Governing Gaza: Bureaucracy, Authority, and the Work of Rule, 1917–1967*. Durham, NC: Duke University Press.

Ferguson, James. 1994. *The Anti-Politics Machine: Development, Depoliticization, and Bureaucratic Power in Lesotho*. Minneapolis: University of Minnesota Press.

———. 1999. *Expectations of Modernity: Myths and Meanings of Urban Life on the Zambian Copperbelt*. Berkeley: University of California Press.

———. 2006. *Global Shadows: Africa in the Neoliberal World Order*. Durham, NC: Duke University Press.

———. 2013. "Declarations of Dependence: Labour, Personhood, and Welfare in Southern Africa." *Journal of the Royal Anthropological Institute* 19 (2): 223–42.

———. 2015. *Give a Man a Fish: Reflections on the New Politics of Distribution.* Durham, NC: Duke University Press.

Ferguson, James, and Akhil Gupta. 2002. "Spatializing States: Toward an Ethnography of Neoliberal Governmentality." *American Ethnologist* 29 (4): 981–1002.

Finnegan, William. 1993. *A Complicated War: The Harrowing of Mozambique.* Berkeley: University of California Press.

Fisher, William F. 1997. "Doing Good? The Politics and Antipolitics of NGO Practices." *Annual Review of Anthropology* 26 (1): 439–64.

Flint, Karen E. 2008. *Healing Traditions: African Medicine, Cultural Exchange, and Competition in South Africa, 1820–1948.* Athens: Ohio University Press.

Foley, Conor. 2007. "Mozambique : A Case Study in the Role of the Affected State in Humanitarian Action." HPG (Humanitarian Policy Group) Working Paper. London: Humanitarian Policy Group and Overseas Development Institute.

Foley, Ellen. 2009. *Your Pocket Is What Cures You: The Politics of Health in Senegal.* New Brunswick, NJ: Rutgers University Press.

Foucault, Michel. 1991. "Governmentality." In *The Foucault Effect: Studies in Governmentality,* 87–104. Chicago: University of Chicago Press.

Fraser, Nancy, and Linda Gordon. 1994. "A Genealogy of Dependency: Tracing a Keyword of the U.S. Welfare State." *Signs* 19 (2): 309–36.

Freire, Paulo. 2000. *Pedagogy of the Oppressed: 30th Anniversary Edition.* Translated by Myra Bergman Ramos. New York: Bloomsbury Academic.

Fuente, Raul de la. 2014. *A Luta Continua.* Medicus Mundi Catalunya and Kanaki Films.

Fullwiley, Duana. 2011. *The Encultured Gene: Sickle Cell Health Politics and Biological Difference in West Africa.* Princeton, NJ: Princeton University Press.

Garcia, Angela. 2010. *The Pastoral Clinic: Addiction and Dispossession along the Rio Grande.* Berkeley: University of California Press.

Geffray, Christian. 1990. *La cause des armes au Mozambique: Anthropologie d'une guerre civile.* Paris: CREDU.

Geissler, Paul Wenzel. 2013. "Public Secrets in Public Health: Knowing Not to Know while Making Scientific Knowledge." *American Ethnologist* 40 (1): 13–34.

———, ed. 2015. *Para-States and Medical Science: Making African Global Health.* Durham, NC: Duke University Press.

Geissler, P. Wenzel, Ann H. Kelly, Babatunde Imoukhuede, and Robert Pool. 2008. "'He Is Now like a Brother, I Can Even Give Him Some Blood'—Relational Ethics and Material Exchanges in a Malaria Vaccine 'Trial Community' in The Gambia." *Social Science and Medicine* 67 (5): 696–707.

Geissler, P. Wenzel, Ann H. Kelly, John Manton, Ruth J. Prince, and Noemi Tousignant. 2013. "Introduction: Sustaining the Life of the Polis." *Africa* 83 (4): 531–38.

Gengenbach, Heidi. 2005. *Binding Memories: Women as Makers and Tellers of History in Magude, Mozambique.* New York: Columbia University Press.

Gonçalves, Euclides. 2006. "Finding the Chiefs: Political Decentralisation and Traditional Authority in Mocumbi, Southern Mozambique." *Africa Insight* 35 (3): 64–70.

———. 2013. "Orientações Superiores: Time and Bureaucratic Authority in Mozambique." *African Affairs* 112 (449): 602–22.

Good, Byron J. 1994. *Medicine, Rationality, and Experience: An Anthropological Perspective.* Cambridge: Cambridge University Press.

Good, Mary-Jo DelVecchio, Sandra Hyde, Sarah Pinto, and Byron J. Good, eds. 2008. *Postcolonial Disorders.* Berkeley: University of California Press.

Granjo, Paulo. 2009. "Saúde, Doença, E Cura Em Moçambique." In *Migração, Saúde, E Diversidade Cultural,* edited by Elsa Lechner, 249–74. Lisbon: Imprensa de Ciencias Sociais.

Grépin, Karen A. 2012. "HIV Donor Funding Has Both Boosted and Curbed the Delivery of Different Non-HIV Health Services in Sub-Saharan Africa." *Health Affairs* 31 (7): 1406–14.

Gupta, Akhil. 2012. *Red Tape: Bureaucracy, Structural Violence, and Poverty in India.* Durham, NC: Duke University Press.

Guyer, Jane. 2004. *Marginal Gains: Monetary Transactions in Atlantic Africa.* Chicago: University of Chicago Press.

———. 2007. "Prophecy and the Near Future: Thoughts on Macroeconomic, Evangelical, and Punctuated Time." *American Ethnologist* 34 (3): 409–21.

Hacking, Ian. 1999. "Making Up People." In *The Science Studies Reader,* edited by Mario Biagioli, 161–71. New York: Routledge.

Hahn, Robert, and Marcia Inhorn. 2008. *Anthropology and Public Health: Bridging Differences in Culture and Society.* Oxford: Oxford University Press.

Hall, Margaret, and Tom Young. 1997. *Confronting Leviathan: Mozambique since Independence.* Athens: Ohio University Press.

Han, Clara. 2012. *Life in Debt: Times of Care and Violence in Neoliberal Chile.* Berkeley: University of California Press.

Hankins, Joseph. 2014. *Working Skin: Making Leather, Making a Multicultural Japan.* Berkeley: University of California Press.

Hanlon, Joseph. 1991. *Mozambique: Who Calls the Shots?* Bloomington: Indiana University Press.

———. 2003. *Peace without Profit: How the IMF Blocks Rebuilding in Mozambique.* Portsmouth, NH: James Currey.

———. 2007. "Is Poverty Decreasing in Mozambique?" Maputo: Instituto de Estudos Sociais e Económicos. Accessed May 19, 2010. http://www.iese.ac.mz/lib/publication/Hanlon,Joseph_Poverty.pdf

Hanlon, Joseph, and Teresa Smart. 2008. *Do Bicycles Equal Development in Mozambique?* Woodbridge, UK: James Currey.

Hardt, Michael. 1999. "Affective Labor." *Boundary* 2 (summer): 89–100.

Harries, Patrick. 1994. *Work, Culture, and Identity: Migrant Laborers in Mozambique and South Africa, C. 1860–1910.* Portsmouth, NH: Heinemann.

Harvey, David. 2007. *A Brief History of Neoliberalism.* Oxford: Oxford University Press.

Hecht, Gabrielle, ed. 2011. *Entangled Geographies. Empire and Technopolitics in the Global Cold War.* Cambridge, MA: MIT Press.

Heimer, Carol. 2012. "Inert Facts and the Illusion of Knowledge: Strategic Uses of Ignorance in HIV Clinics." *Economy and Society* 41 (1): 17–41.

Heimer, Carol, and JuLeigh Petty. 2010. "Bureaucratic Ethics: IRBs and the Legal Regulation of Human Subjects Research." *Annual Review of Law and Social Science* 6: 601–26.

Herzfeld, Michael. 1993. *The Social Production of Indifference*. Chicago: University of Chicago Press.

Hetherington, Kregg. 2011. *Guerrilla Auditors: The Politics of Transparency in Neoliberal Paraguay*. Durham, NC: Duke University Press.

Hindman, Heather. 2013. *Mediating the Global: Expatria's Forms and Consequences in Kathmandu*. Stanford, CA: Stanford University Press.

Hochschild, Arlie. 2003. *The Managed Heart: Commercialization of Human Feeling*. Berkeley: University of California Press.

Holston, James, ed. 1998. *Cities and Citizenship*. Durham, NC: Duke University Press.

———. 2009. *Insurgent Citizenship: Disjunctions of Democracy and Modernity in Brazil*. Princeton, NJ: Princeton University Press.

Honest Accounts. 2017. "How the World Profits from Africa's Wealth." London: Global Justice Now.

Honwana, Alcinda Manuel. 2002. *Espiritos Vivos, Tradicaes Modernas: Possessao de Espiritos E Politicas Culturais No Sul de Mocambique*. Maputo: Promedia.

Hull, Matthew S. 2012a. *Government of Paper: The Materiality of Bureaucracy in Urban Pakistan*. Berkeley: University of California Press.

———. 2012b. "Documents and Bureaucracy." *Annual Review of Anthropology* 41 (1): 251–67.

Human Rights Watch. 2016. "Mozambique: Opposition Group Raids Hospitals." Johannesburg: Human Rights Watch. Accessed May 17, 2017: https://www.hrw.org/news/2016/08/24/mozambique-opposition-group-raids-hospitals

Hunt, Nancy Rose. 1997. "Condoms, Confessors, Conferences: Among AIDS Derivatives in Africa." *Journal of the International Institute* 4 (3): 15–17.

———. 1999. *A Colonial Lexicon: Of Birth Ritual, Medicalization, and Mobility in the Congo*. Durham, NC: Duke University Press.

Hunter, Mark. 2010. "Beyond the Male-Migrant: South Africa's Long History of Health Geography and the Contemporary AIDS Pandemic." *Health and Place* 16 (1): 25–33.

Hussein, Karim. 1995. "The Nutrition Crisis among Mozambican Refugees in Malawi: An Analysis of the Response of International Agencies." *Journal of Refugee Studies* 8 (1): 26–47.

Iliffe, John. 1998. *East African Doctors*. Cambridge: Cambridge University Press.

Inguane, Celso Azarias, Stephen Gloyd, João Luis Manuel, Charlene Brown, Vincent Wong, Orvalho Augusto, Wisal Mustafa Hassan, et al. 2016. "Assessment of Linkages from HIV Testing to Enrolment and Retention in HIV Care in Central Mozambique." *Journal of the International AIDS Society* 19 (5Suppl 4). doi:10.7448/IAS.19.5.20846.

Institute for Health Metrics and Evaluation (IHME). 2015. *Financing Global Health 2014: Shifts in Funding as the MDG Era Closes*. Seattle, WA: IHME.

Isaacman, Allen. 1996. *Cotton Is the Mother of Poverty: Peasants, Work, and Rural Struggle in Colonial Mozambique, 1938–1961*. Portsmouth, NH: Heinemann.

Israel, Paolo. 2014. *In Step with the Times: Mapiko Masquerades of Mozambique*. Athens: Ohio University Press.

Jacob, Marie-Andrée, and Annelise Riles. 2007. "The New Bureaucracies of Virtue: Introduction." *PoLar: Political and Legal Anthropology Review* 30 (2): 181–91.

Jain, S. Lochlann. 2013. *Malignant: How Cancer Becomes Us*. Berkeley: University of California Press.

James, Erica. 2010. *Democratic Insecurities: Violence, Trauma, and Intervention in Haiti*. Berkeley: University of California Press.

Janes, Craig R., and Kitty K. Corbett. 2009. "Anthropology and Global Health." *Annual Review of Anthropology* 38 (1): 167–83.

Janzen, John M., Charles Leslie, and William Arkinstall. 1982. *The Quest for Therapy: Medical Pluralism in Lower Zaire*. Berkeley: University of California Press.

Johnson, Paul. 2009. "Abuse of HIV/AIDS-Relief Funds in Mozambique" *The Lancet* 9 (9): 523–24.

Joint United Nations Programme on HIV/AIDS (UNAIDS)-WHO. 2004. "Policy Statement on HIV Testing." Geneva: UNAIDS and WHO.

Jones, Aled. 2009. "Creating History: Documents and Patient Participation in Nurse-Patient Interviews." *Sociology of Health and Illness* 31: 907–23.

Jones, Sam. 2009. *Whither Aid? Financing Development in Mozambique*. Copenhagen: Danish Institute for International Studies.

Joyce, Patrick. 2002. *The Social in Question*. New York: Routledge.

Junod, Henri A. 2012. *The Life of a South African Tribe*. London: Forgotten Books.

Kalofonos, Ippolytos Andreas. 2010. "All I Eat Is ARVs": The Paradox of AIDS Treatment Interventions in Central Mozambique." *Medical Anthropology Quarterly* 24 (3): 363–80.

Kaminski, M. 2007. "Editorial Board: The Mozambique Miracle." *Wall Street Journal*, April 7 edition.

Kew, Janice. 2015. "Mozambique Millionaires Seen Leading Growth of Africa's Rich." *Bloomberg News*, August 2. Accessed May 17, 2017. https://www.bloomberg.com/news/articles/2015-08-02/mozambique-millionaires-seen-leading-growth-of-africa-s-rich.

Kyaddondo, David, and Susan Reynolds Whyte. "Working in a Decentralized System: A Threat to Health Workers' Respect and Survival in Uganda." *International Journal of Health Planning and Management* 18 (4): 329–42.

Kyed, Helene Maria, and Lars Buur. 2006. "New Sites of Citizenship: Recognition of Traditional Authority and Group-Based Citizenship in Mozambique*." *Journal of Southern African Studies* 32 (3): 563–81.

Laet, Marianne de, and Annemarie Mol. 2000. "The Zimbabwe Bush Pump: Mechanics of a Fluid Technology." *Social Studies of Science* 30 (2): 225–63.

Lagarde, Christine. 2014. "Africa Rising—Building to the Future." Keynote Address. Accessed May 29, 2016. http://www.imf.org/external/np/speeches/2014/052914.htm.

Lakoff, Andrew. 2010. "Two Regimes of Global Health." *Humanity: An International Journal of Human Rights* 1 (1): 59–79.

Landecker, Hannah. 2013. "Post-Industrial Metabolism: Fat Knowledge." *Public Culture* 25 (3): 495–522.

Langwick, Stacey. 2007. "Devils, Parasites, and Fierce Needles: Healing and the Politics of Translation in Southern Tanzania." *Science, Technology, and Human Values* 32 (1): 88–117.

———. 2008. "Articulate(d) Bodies: Traditional Medicine in a Tanzanian Hospital." *American Ethnologist* 35 (3): 428–39.

———. 2011. *Bodies, Politics, and African Healing: The Matter of Maladies in Tanzania.* Bloomington: Indiana University Press.

Latour, Bruno. 2004. "Why Has Critique Run Out of Steam? From Matters of Fact to Matters of Concern." *Critical Inquiry* 30 (2): 225–48.

Lederman, Rena. 2006. "Anxious Borders between Work and Life in a Time of Bureaucratic Ethics Regulation." *American Ethnologist* 33 (4): 277–481.

Le Marcis, F. 2004. "The Suffering Body of the City." *Public Culture* 16 (3): 453–77.

Li, Tania. 2007. *The Will to Improve: Governmentality, Development, and the Practice of Politics.* Durham, NC: Duke University Press.

Livingston, Julie. 2012. *Improvising Medicine: An African Oncology Ward in an Emerging Cancer Epidemic.* Durham, NC: Duke University Press.

Locke, Peter. 2014. "Anthropology and Medical Humanitarianism in the Age of Global Health Education." In *Medical Humanitarianism in States of Emergency,* edited by Sharon Abramowitz and Catherine Panter-Brick. Philadelphia: University of Pennsylvania Press.

Lubkemann, Stephen C. 2008. *Culture in Chaos: An Anthropology of the Social Condition in War.* Chicago: University of Chicago Press.

Luedke, Tracey J. 2006. "Presidents, Bishops, and Mothers: The Construction of Authority in Mozambican Healing." In *Borders and Healers: Brokering Therapeutic Resources in Southeast Africa,* edited by Tracey J. Luedke and Harry G. West, 43–64. Bloomington: Indiana University Press.

Luedke, Tracey J., and Harry G. West, eds. 2006. *Borders and Healers: Brokering Therapeutic Resources in Southeast Africa.* Bloomington: Indiana University Press.

Macamo, Elisio. 2003. "How Development Aid Changes Societies: Disciplining Mozambique through Structural Adjustment." Accessed May 17, 2017. http://www.codesria.org/IMG/pdf/macamo.pdf.

———. 2005. "Negotiating Modernity: From Colonialism to Globalization." In *Negotiating Modernity: Africa's Ambivalent Experience.* London: Zed Books, in association with CODESRIA.

———. 2006. "Accounting for Disaster: Memories of War in Mozambique." *Africa Spectrum* 41 (2): 199–219.

Maes, Kenneth. 2014. "'Volunteers Are Not Paid Because They Are Priceless': Community Health Worker Capacities and Values in an AIDS Treatment Intervention in Urban Ethiopia." *Medical Anthropology Quarterly*, September.

Maes, Kenneth, and Ippolytos Kalofonos. 2013. "Becoming and Remaining Community Health Workers: Perspectives from Ethiopia and Mozambique." *Social Science and Medicine* 87 (June): 52–59.

Malkki, Liisa H. 1995. *Purity and Exile: Violence, Memory, and National Cosmology among Hutu Refugees in Tanzania*. Chicago: University of Chicago Press.

———. 2015. *The Need to Help: The Domestic Arts of International Humanitarianism*. Durham, NC: Duke University Press.

Mamdani, Mahmood. 1996. *Citizen and Subject: Contemporary Africa and the Legacy of Late Colonialism*. Princeton, NJ: Princeton University Press.

Manuel, Sandra. 2009. "Presentes Perigosos: Dinámicas de Risco de Infecção Ao HIV/SIDA Nos Relacionamentos de Namoro Em Maputo." *Physis: Revista de Saúde Coletiva* 19 (2): 371–86.

Marcus, George E. 1995. "Ethnography in/of the World System: The Emergence of Multi-Sited Ethnography." *Annual Review of Anthropology*, 2, 24 (1): 95–117.

Marks, Shula. 1994. *Divided Sisterhood: Race, Class, and Gender in the South African Nursing Profession*. New York: St. Martin's Press.

Marsland, Rebecca. 2012. "(Bio)Sociality and HIV in Tanzania." *Medical Anthropology Quarterly* 26 (4): 470–85.

Marsland, Rebecca, and Ruth Prince. 2012. "What Is Life Worth? Exploring Biomedical Interventions, Survival, and the Politics of Life." *Medical Anthropology Quarterly* 26 (4): 453–69.

Matsinhe, Cristiano. 2008. *Tabula Rasa: Dynamics of the Mozambican Response to HIV/AIDS*. Maputo: Kula.

Matza, Tomas. 2012. "'Good Individualism?' Psychology, Ethics, and Neoliberalism in Postsocialist Russia." *American Ethnologist* 39 (4): 804–18.

Mavhunga, Clapperton. 2014. *Transient Workspaces: Technologies of Everyday Innovation in Zimbabwe*. Cambridge, MA: MIT Press.

Mbembe, Achille. 2001. *On the Postcolony*. Berkeley: University of California Press.

———. 2017. *Critique of Black Reason*. Durham, NC: Duke University Press.

Mbembe, Achille, and Janet Roitman. 1995. "Figures of the Subject in Times of Crisis." *Public Culture* 7 (2): 323–52.

McKay, Ramah. 2016. "The View from the Middle: Lively Relations of Care, Class, and Medical Labor in Maputo." *Critical African Studies* 8(3): 278–290.

Meneses, Maria Paula G. 2004. "'Quando Não Há Problemas, Estamos de Boa Saúde, Sem Azar Nem Nada': Para Uma Concepção Emancipatória de Saúde E Das Medicinas." In *Moçambique E a Reinvenção Da Emancipação Social*, edited by Boaventura de Sousa Santos and Teresa Cruz e Silva, 77–110. Maputo: Centro de Formação Jurídica e Judiciária.

Meyers, Todd, and Nancy Rose Hunt. 2014. "The Other Global South." *The Lancet* 384 (November): 1921–22.

Minter, William. 1994. *Apartheid's Contras: An Inquiry into the Roots of War in Angola and Mozambique*. New York: Zed Books.

Mitchell, Timothy. 1991. "The Limits of the State." *American Political Science Review* 85: 77–96.

———. 2002. *Rule of Experts: Egypt, Techno-Politics, Modernity*. Berkeley: University of California Press.

Mkhwanazi, Nolweni. 2016. "Medical Anthropology in Africa: The Trouble with a Single Story." *Medical Anthropology* 35(2): 193–202.

Mol, Annemarie. 2002. *The Body Multiple: Ontology in Medical Practice*. Durham, NC: Duke University Press.

———. 2008. *The Logic of Care: Health and the Problem of Patient Choice*. New York: Routledge.

Mol, Annemarie, Ingurr Moser, and Jeannette Pols, eds. 2010. *Care in Practice: On Tinkering in Clinics, Homes, and Farms*. Bielefeld, Germany: Verlag.

Mondlane, Eduardo. 1969. *The Struggle for Mozambique*. Baltimore, MD: Penguin Books.

Moodie, T. Dunbar. 1994. *Going for Gold: Men, Mines, and Migration*. Berkeley: University of California Press.

Moodie, T. Dunbar, Vivienne Ndatshe, and British Sibuyi. 1988. "Migrancy and Male Sexuality on the South African Gold Mines." *Journal of Southern African Studies* 14 (2): 228–56.

Mosse, David. 2005. *Cultivating Development: An Ethnography of Aid Policy and Practice*. London: Pluto Press.

Moyo, Dambisa. 2009. *Dead Aid: Why Aid Is Not Working and How There Is a Better Way for Africa*. New York: Farrar, Straus and Giroux.

Muehlebach, Andrea. 2012. *The Moral Neoliberal: Welfare and Citizenship in Italy*. Chicago: University of Chicago Press.

Munk, Nina. 2013. *The Idealist: Jeffrey Sachs and the Quest to End Poverty*. New York: Doubleday.

Mussa, Abdul H., James Pfeiffer, Stephen S. Gloyd, and Kenneth Sherr. 2013. "Vertical Funding, Non-Governmental Organizations, and Health System Strengthening: Perspectives of Public Sector Health Workers in Mozambique." *Human Resources for Health* 11 (1): 26–26.

Nading, Alex M. 2014. *Mosquito Trails: Ecology, Health, and the Politics of Entanglement*. Berkeley: University of California Press.

Newitt, Malyn. 1995. *A History of Mozambique*. Bloomington: Indiana University Press.

Nguyen, Vinh-Kim. 2010. *The Republic of Therapy: Triage and Sovereignty in West Africa's Time of AIDS*. Durham, NC: Duke University Press.

Nichter, Mark. 2008. Global Health: Why Cultural Perceptions, Social Representations, and Biopolitics Matter. Tucson: University of Arizona Press.

Nielsen, Morten. 2014a. "A Wedge of Time: Futures in the Present and Presents without Futures in Maputo, Mozambique." *Journal of the Royal Anthropological Institute* 20 (S1): 166–82.

———. 2014b. "The Negativity of Times: Collapsed Futures in Maputo, Mozambique." *Social Anthropology* 22 (2): 213–26.

Nordstrom, Carolyn. 1997. *A Different Kind of War Story.* Philadelphia: University of Pennsylvania Press.

Obarrio, Juan. 2014. *The Spirit of the Laws in Mozambique.* Chicago: University of Chicago Press.

Olsen, William, and Carolyn Sargent. 2017. *African Medical Pluralism.* Bloomington: Indiana University Press.

Oomman, Nandini, Michael Bernstein, and Steven Rosenzweig. 2007. *Following the Funding for HIV/AIDS: A Comparative Analysis of the Funding Practices of PEPFAR, the Global Fund, and World Bank MAP in Mozambique, Uganda, and Zambia.* Washington DC: Center for Global Development.

Ottaway, Marina. 1988. "Mozambique: From Symbolic Socialism to Symbolic Reform." *Journal of Modern African Studies* 26 (2): 211–26.

Packard, Randall M. 1989. *White Plague, Black Labor: Tuberculosis and the Political Economy of Health and Disease in South Africa.* Berkeley: University of California Press.

Page, Helán E., and Brooke Thomas. 1994. "White Public Space and the Construction of White Privilege in U.S. Health Care: Fresh Concepts and a New Model of Analysis. *Medical Anthropology Quarterly* 8: 109–16.

Penvenne, Jeanne. 1995. *African Workers and Colonial Racism: Mozambican Strategies and Struggles in Lourenço Marques, 1877–1962.* Portsmouth, NH: Heinemann.

———. 2015. *Women, Migration, and the Cashew Economy in Southern Mozambique, 1945–1975.* Suffolk, UK: James Currey.

Peterson, Kristin. 2014. *Speculative Markets: Drug Circuits and Derivative Life in Nigeria.* Durham, NC: Duke University Press.

Petryna, Adriana. 2002. *Life Exposed: Biological Citizenship after Chernobyl.* Princeton, NJ: Princeton University Press.

———. 2005. "Ethical Variability: Drug Development and Globalizing Clinical Trials." *American Ethnologist* 32 (2): 183–97. doi:10.1525/ae.2005.32.2.183.

———. 2013. "The Right of Recovery." *Current Anthropology* 54 (S7): S67–S76.

Pfeiffer, James. 2003. "International NGOs and Primary Health Care in Mozambique: The Need for a New Model of Collaboration." *Social Science & Medicine* 56 (4): 725–38.

———. 2004. "International NGOs in Mozambique: The 'Velvet Glove' of Privatization." In *Unhealthy Health Policy: A Critical Anthropological Examination,* edited by Arachu Castro and Merrill Singer, 43–62. Walnut Creek, CA: Altamira Press.

———. 2013. "The Struggle for a Public Sector: PEPFAR in Mozambique." In *When People Come First: Critical Studies in Global Health,* edited by João Biehl and Adriana Petryna, 166–81. Princeton, NJ: Princeton University Press.

Pfeiffer, James, and Rachel Chapman. 2010. "Anthropological Perspectives on Structural Adjustment and Public Health." *Annual Review of Anthropology* 39: 149–65.

———. 2015. "The Art of Medicine: An Anthropology of Aid in Africa." *Lancet* 385 (May 30): 2144–45.

Pfeiffer, James, Kenneth Gimbel-Sherr, and Orvalho Joaquim Augusto. 2007. "The Holy Spirit in the Household: Pentecostalism, Gender, and Neoliberalism in Mozambique." *American Anthropologist* 10: 688–70.

Pfeiffer, James, Wendy Johnson, Meredith Fort, Aaron Shakow, Amy Hagopian, Steve Gloyd, and Kenneth Gimbel-Sherr. 2008. "Strengthening Health Systems in Poor Countries: A Code of Conduct for Nongovernmental Organizations." *American Journal of Public Health* 98(12): 2134–40.

Pierre, Jemima. 2013. *The Predicament of Blackness: Postcolonial Ghana and the Politics of Race.* Chicago: University of Chicago Press.

Piot, Charlie. 2010. *Nostalgia for the Future: West Africa after the Cold War.* Durham, NC: Duke University Press.

Pitcher, M. Anne. 1998. "Disruption without Transformation: Agrarian Relations and Livelihoods in Nampula Province, Mozambique, 1975–1995." *Journal of Southern African Studies* 24(1): 115–40.

———. 2002. *Transforming Mozambique: The Politics of Privatization, 1975–2000.* Cambridge: Cambridge University Press.

Pitcher, M. Anne, and Kelly Askew. 2006. "African Socialisms and Postsocialisms." *Africa* 76 (1): 1–14.

Prince, Ruth J. 2013. "'Tarmacking' in the Millenium City: Spatial and Temporal Trajectories of Empowerment and Development in Kisumu, Kenya." *Africa* 83 (04): 582–605.

———. 2015. "Seeking Incorporation? Voluntary Labor and the Ambiguities of Work, Identity, and Social Value in Contemporary Kenya." *African Studies Review* 58 (2): 85–109.

Prince, Ruth, and Rebecca Marsland, eds. 2014. *Making and Unmaking Public Health in Africa: Ethnographic and Historical Perspectives.* Athens: Ohio University Press.

Ranger, Terence. 1992. "Plagues of Beasts and Men: Prophetic Responses to Epidemic in Eastern and Southern Africa." In *Epidemics and Ideas: Essays on the Historical Perception of Pestilence*, edited by Paul Slack and Terence Ranger, 241–68. Cambridge: Cambridge University Press.

Redfield, Peter. 2005. "Doctors, Borders, and Life in Crisis." *Cultural Anthropology* 20 (3): 328–61.

———. 2006. "A Less Modest Witness: Collective Advocacy and Motivated Truth in a Medical Humanitarian Movement." *American Ethnologist* 33 (1): 3–26.

———. 2008. "Vital Mobility and the Humanitarian Kit." In *Biosecurity Interventions: Global Health and Security in Question*, edited by Andrew Lakoff and Stephen J. Collier, 147–73. New York: Columbia University Press.

———. 2010. "The Verge of Crisis: Doctors Without Borders in Uganda." In *Contemporary States of Emergency: The Politics of Military and Humanitarian Interventions*, edited by D. Fassin and M. Pandolfi, 173–95. New York: Zone Books.

———. 2013. *Life in Crisis: The Ethical Journey of Doctors Without Borders.* Berkeley: University of California Press.

Reed, Adam. 2006. "Documents Unfolding." In *Documents: Artifacts of Modern Knowledge,* edited by Annelise Riles, 158–80. Ann Arbor: University of Michigan Press.

Rees, Tobias. 2014. "Humanity/Plan; or, On the 'Stateless' Today (Also Being an Anthropology of Global Health)." *Cultural Anthropology* 29 (3): 457–78. doi:10.14506/ca29.3.02.

Riles, Annelise. 2000. *The Network Inside Out.* Ann Arbor: University of Michigan Press.

———, ed. 2006. *Documents: Artifacts of Modern Knowledge.* Ann Arbor: University of Michigan Press.

Risse, Guenter B., and John Harley Warner. 1992. "Reconstructing Clinical Activities: Patient Records in Medical History." *Social History of Medicine* 5 (2): 183–205.

Robbins, Joel. 2013. "Beyond the Suffering Subject: Toward an Anthropology of the Good." *Journal of the Royal Anthropological Institute* 19 (3): 447–62.

Robins, Steven. 2006. "From 'Rights' to 'Ritual': AIDS Activism in South Africa." *American Anthropologist* 108 (2): 312–23.

Robinson, Cedric. 2000. *Black Marxism: The Making of the Black Radical Tradition.* Chapel Hill: University of North Carolina Press.

Roitman, Janet. 2013. *Anti-Crisis.* Durham, NC: Duke University Press.

Rose, Nikolas. 2006. *The Politics of Life Itself: Biomedicine, Power, and Subjectivity in the Twenty-First Century.* Princeton, NJ: Princeton University Press.

Santos, Boaventura de Sousa. 2006. "O Estado Heterogéneo E O Pluralismo Jurídico." In *Conflito E Transformação Social: Uma Paisagem Das Justiças Em Moçambique,* edited by Boaventura de Sousa Santos and João Carlos Trinidade. Vol. 1. Porto, Portugal: Afontamento.

Scherz, China. 2014. *Having People, Having Heart: Charity, Sustainable Development, and Problems of Dependence in Central Uganda.* Chicago: University of Chicago Press.

Schuetze, Christy. 2010. "'The World Is Upside Down': Women's Participation in Religious Movements in Mozambique." Publically accessible Penn dissertations. Philadelphia: University of Pennsylvania. http://repository.upenn.edu/edissertations/101.

Schuller, Mark. 2009. "Gluing Globalization: NGOs as Intermediaries in Haiti." *PoLAR* 32: 84–104.

Schumaker, Lyn. 2001. *Africanizing Anthropology: Fieldwork, Networks, and the Making of Cultural Knowledge in Central Africa.* Durham, NC: Duke University Press.

Seth, Suman. 2009. "Putting Knowledge in Its Place: Science, Colonialism, and the Postcolonial." *Postcolonial Studies* 12 (4): 373–88.

Shaw, Rosalind. 2007. "Displacing Violence: Making Pentecostal Memory in Postwar Sierra Leone." *Cultural Anthropology* 22 (1): 66–93.

Sherr, Kenneth, Baltazar Chilundo, Sarah Gimbel, and James Pfeiffer. 2012. "Brain Drain and Health Workforce Distortions in Mozambique." *PLoS ONE* 7 (4): e35840.

Singer, Merrill, and Arachu Castro. 2004. *Unhealthy Health Policy: A Critical Anthropological Examination.* Lanham, MD: Rowman Altamira.

Singer, Merrill, and Pamela Erickson. 2013. *Global Health: An Anthropological Perspective.* Long Grove, IL: Waveland Press.

Smith, Daniel Jordan. 2003. "Patronage, Per Diems, and the 'Workshop Mentality': The Practice of Family Planning Programs in Southeastern Nigeria." *World Development* 31 (4): 703–15.

———. 2014. *AIDS Doesn't Show Its Face: Inequality, Morality, and Social Change in Nigeria.* Chicago: University of Chicago Press.

Stevenson, Lisa. 2014. *Life Beside Itself: Imagining Care in the Canadian Arctic.* Berkeley: University of California Press.

Strathern, Marilyn, ed. 2000. *Audit Cultures: Anthropological Studies in Accountability, Ethics, and the Academy.* London: Routledge.

Street, Alice. 2014. *Biomedicine in an Unstable Place: Infrastructure and Personhood in a Papua New Guinean Hospital.* Durham, NC: Duke University Press.

Suarez, Ray. 2010. "Reporter's Notebook: A Clinic's Strains in Mozambique." *PBS NewsHour,* Global Health Report. Accessed May 10, 2017. http://www.pbs.org /newshour/rundown/mozambique-clinic/.

Sullivan, Noelle. 2011. "Mediating Abundance and Scarcity: Implementing an HIV/ AIDS-Targeted Project within a Government Hospital in Tanzania." *Medical Anthropology* 30 (2): 202–21.

———. 2016. "Hosting Gazes: Clinical Volunteer Tourism and Hospital Hospitality in Tanzania." In *Volunteer Economies: The Politics and Ethics of Voluntary Labour in Africa.* Portsmouth, NH: James Currey.

Swidler, Ann, and Susan Cotts Watkins. 2009. " 'Teach a Man to Fish': The Doctrine of Sustainability and Its Effects on Three Strata of Malawian Society." *World Development* 37 (7): 1182–96.

Taimo, N. V., and Rachel Waterhouse. 2007. "REBA Case-Study No. 7 of the Food Subsidy Programme of the National Institute for Social Action (INAS)." Regional Evidence Based Agenda Program/Regional Hunger and Vulnerability Programme. Accessed June 20, 2010. http://www.ipc-undp.org/publications/cct /africa/REBACaseStudyPSAOctober07.pdf

Thomas, Deborah. 2011. *Exceptional Violence: Embodied Citizenship in Transnational Jamaica.* Durham, NC: Duke University Press.

Ticktin, Miriam. 2011. *Casualties of Care: Immigration and the Politics of Humanitarianism in France.* Berkeley: University of California Press.

———. 2014. "Transnational Humanitarianism." *Annual Review of Anthropology* 43 (1): 273–89.

Tilley, Helen. 2011. *Africa as a Living Laboratory: Empire, Development, and the Problem of Scientific Knowledge, 1870–1950.* Chicago: University of Chicago Press.

Timmermans, Stefan, and Marc Berg. 2003. "The Practice of Medical Technology." *Sociology of Health and Illness* 24 (5): 550–74.

Tousignant, Noemi. 2013. "Pharmacy, Money, and Public Health in Dakar." *Africa* 83: 561–81.

Trouillot, Michel-Rolph. 2003. *Global Transformations: Anthropology and the Modern World.* New York: Palgrave Macmillan.

Tsing, Anna. 1993. *In the Realm of the Diamond Queen: Marginality in an Out-of-the-Way Place.* Princeton, NJ: Princeton University Press.

Turner, Victor. 1967. *The Forest of Symbols: Aspects of Ndembu Ritual.* Ithaca, NY: Cornell University Press.

Turshen, Meredith. 1999. *Privatizing Health Services in Africa.* New Brunswick, NJ: Rutgers University Press.

UNICEF. 2006. "Childhood Poverty in Mozambique: A Situation and Trends Analysis." UNICEF.

United Nations. 2009. "Human Development Index." United Nations Development Program.

USAID. 2008. Mozambique Country Assistance Strategy 2009–2014. Available online: https://www.usaid.gov/sites/default/files/documents/1860/CAS_%20 2009–14.pdf. Last accessed August 29, 2017.

Vail, Leroy, and Landeg White. 1980. *Capitalism and Colonialism in Mozambique: A Study of Quelimane Distict.* Minneapolis: University of Minnesota Press.

van de Kamp, Linda. 2016. *Violent Conversion: Brazilian Pentecostalism and Urban Women in Mozambique.* Surrey, UK: James Currey.

Vassal, A., J. Shotton, and O. K. Reshetnyk. 2014. "Tracking Aid Flows for Development Assistance for Health." *Global Health Action* 7 (10): 3402.

Vaughan, Megan. 1992. *Curing Their Ills: Colonial Power and African Illness.* Oxford: Oxford University Press.

Vaughan, M. 1994. "Healing and Curing: Issues in the Social History and Anthropology of Medicine in Africa." *Social History of Medicine: The Journal of the Society for the Social History of Medicine / SSHM* 7 (2): 283–95.

Vio, Ferruccio. 2006. "Management of Expatriate Medical Assistance in Mozambique." *Human Resources for Health* 4 (1): 26.

Waal, Alex de, and Alan Whiteside. 2003. "New Variant Famine: AIDS and Food Crisis in Southern Africa." *The Lancet* 362: 1234–37.

Walque, Damien de, Harounan Kazianga, Mead Over, and Julia Vaillant. 2011. "Food Crisis, Household Welfare and HIV/AIDS Treatment: Evidence from Mozambique." Washington, DC: The World Bank, Development Research Group, Human Development and Public Services Team.

Walt, Gill. 1993. "WHO Under Stress: Implications for Health Policy." *Health Policy* 24: 125–44.

———. 1998. "Globalization of International Health." *The Lancet* 351 (February 7): 434–37.

Walt, Gill, and J. Cliff. 1986. "The Dynamics of Health Policies in Mozambique 1975–85." *Health Policy and Planning* 1: 148–57.

Walt, G., and A. Melamed. 1983. *Toward a People's Health Service*. London: Zed Books.

Watkins, Amy Kaler, and Susan Cotts. 2001. "Disobedient Distributors: Street-Level Bureaucrats and Would-Be Patrons in Community-Based Family Planning Programs in Rural Kenya." *Studies in Family Planning* 32 (3): 254–69.

Webster, David. 1978. "Migrant Labour, Social Formations, and the Proletarianisation of the Chopi of Southern Mozambique." *African Perspectives* 1: 151–74.

Weheliye, Alexander. 2014. *Habeus Viscus: Racializing Assemblages, Biopolitics, and Black Feminist Theories of the Human*. Durham, NC: Duke University Press.

Wendland, Claire. 2010. *A Heart for the Work: Journeys through an African Medical School*. Chicago: University of Chicago Press.

———. 2012a. "Moral Maps and Medical Imaginaries: Clinical Tourism at Malawi's College of Medicine." *American Anthropologist* 114 (1): 108–22.

———. 2012b. "Animating Biomedicine's Moral Order." *Current Anthropology* 53 (6): 755–88.

West, Harry G. 1998. "'This Neighbor Is Not My Uncle!': Changing Relations of Power and Authority on the Mueda Plateau." *Journal of Southern African Studies* 24 (1): 141–60.

———. 2001. "Sorcery of Construction and Socialist Modernization: Ways of Understanding Power in Postcolonial Mozambique." *American Ethnologist* 28 (1): 119–50.

———. 2005. *Kupilikula: Governance and the Invisible Realm*. Chicago: University of Chicago Press.

West, Harry G., and Scott Kloeck-Jensen. 1999. "Betwixt and Between: 'Traditional Authority' and Democratic Decentralization in Post-War Mozambique." *African Affairs* 98 (393): 455–84.

West, Harry G., and Todd Sanders, eds. 2003. *Transparency and Conspiracy: Ethnographies of Suspicion in the New World Order*. Durham, NC: Duke University Press Books.

Whyte, Susan Reynolds. 1997. "Misfortune and Uncertainy." In *Questioning Misfortune: The Pragmatics of Uncertainty in Eastern Uganda*. Cambridge: Cambridge University Press.

———, ed. 2014. *Second Chances: Surviving AIDS in Uganda*. Durham, NC: Duke University Press.

Whyte, Susan Reynolds, Michael Whyte, Lotte Meinert, and Jenipher Twebaze. 2013. "Therapeutic Clientship: Belonging in Uganda's Projectified Landscape of AIDS Care." In *When People Come First: Critical Studies in Global Health*, edited by João Biehl and Adriana Petryna, 140–65. Princeton, NJ: Princeton University Press.

Whyte, Susan Reynolds, Michael Whyte, and David Kyaddondo. 2010. "Health Workers Entangled: Confidentiality and Certification." In *Morality, Hope, and*

Grief: Anthropologies of AIDS in Africa, edited by Hansjorg Dilger and Ute Luig. New York: Berghahn Books.

Williams, Raymond. 1985. *Keywords: A Vocabulary of Culture and Society.* New York: Oxford University Press.

Wilson, Ken. 1992. "Cults of Violence and Counter-Violence in Mozambique." *Journal of Southern African Studies* 18 (3): 527–82.

World Bank. 2015. "Net Official Development Assistance and Official Aid Received." *World Bank Open Data.* http://data.worldbank.org/indicator/DT.ODA.ALLD .CD?contextual=region&locations=MZ.

Yach, Derek, and Douglas Bettcher. 1998. "The Globalization of Public Health." *American Journal of Public Health* 88: 735–41.

Zeiderman, Austin. 2013. "Living Dangerously: Biopolitics and Urban Citizenship in Bogotá, Colombia." *American Ethnologist* 40 (1): 71–87.

economic growth in Mozambique, 14–15

emergencies. *See* states of emergency

empathy, 154, 157–58

ethnography, global health, 13, 22–24, 85–87, 194

evidence-based medicine, 20–21

food support programs: at Clínica 2, 114–15, 121–25, 136, 139; contesting, 133–35; critique of, 96–99, 134–35; debates on, 105; distribution practices, 88–93, 105, 107–9, 115–16, 121–22; exchange practices, 132–33; gendered relations and, 135–37; in global health, 92, 114–15; for HIV/AIDS patients, 34–37, 92, 95, 114, 134; patient truthfulness and, 129–31; policies, 34–37, 95–96, 116, 122–23, 210–11n6; poverty/illness and, 113–14, 128–33, 135–36; social justice and, 122–24; as therapeutic aid, 113–14, 134–35, 138; vulnerability and, 42–43

FRELIMO/Frelimo, 15, 38, 74, 89, 99, 159, 201n15

Gates Foundation, 4

Global Children's Fund (GCF), 7, 23, 29–31, 111; community participation with, 49–50, 62–64; data collection, 66–68, 182–85; entanglements, 31, 56; food support, 133–35; history in Morrumbala, 38–40; initiatives, 64–65; per diem economies, 79–80; principal cases, 34–37; rewards promised by, 75–77; support for children, 51–53, 55; volunteer benefits, 30, 57–58, 60, 73–74; volunteers, locating, 32–34; volunteers' backgrounds, 71–75; volunteer training by, 68–71, 77–80

Global Fund for AIDS, Tuberculosis, and Malaria, 4

global health, 7, 20–23, 24, 38–39; African representations of, 12; caregiving strat-

egies, 144–46; ethnography of, 85–87, 196–98; food support programs, 92, 114–16; funding for, 3–4, 38–39, 138; futures of care and, 20–22; HIV/AIDS interventions, 39, 65, 86, 114, 115, 151–52; infrastructures of, 10–11; training, 194. *See also* public health

Guebuza, Armando, 105

health care. *See* caregiving; global health; public health

health career trajectories, 145, 151–54, 160, 161–65

HIV/AIDS: access to medication, 4, 14, 148; documentary practices for, 172–74; food support programs, 34–37, 92, 114, 134; funding for, 4, 20, 83; global health interventions, 39, 65, 86, 114, 115, 151–52; programs for, 14, 61, 65, 111, 146–48, 168–69; therapeutic citizenship and, 41–42; volunteer programs, 32–34. *See also specific programs*

Human Development Index, 113

ICHC. *See* International Center for Health Care (ICHC)

IMF. *See* International Monetary Fund (IMF)

INAS. *See* National Social Welfare Institute (INAS)

International Center for Health Care (ICHC), 7, 13, 23, 112, 144–45, 161, 162, 165, 171, 181, 191

International Monetary Fund (IMF), 14, 19, 20, 38, 201n14, 202n22, 212n7, 213n10

interventions: for HIV/AIDS, 39, 65, 86, 114, 115, 151–52; by NGOS, 20–21, 39, 109–10, 193; from transnational funding, 4, 16, 22–23, 49, 86, 111, 114, 138, 145–46, 191, 192, 199n2, 214–15n11

Isaacman, Allen, 104, 209n7

Kristof, Nicholas, 194

language, 154–59
listening, 146–49, 158
Lusophone countries, 163–65, 213n12

Machel, Samora, 16–17
Mail and Guardian (newspaper), 1
malaria, funding for, 4, 13
Malawi, comparison to, 96–99, 104, 105
malnutrition, 91–92, 98, 116, 134
mapping: in Maputo, 48–49, 50, 51; of
    vulnerability, 45–48, *48*
Maputo, 8; as ethnographic location,
    22–24; food distribution in, 121–22;
    public health services in, 1
Mbembe, Achille, 196
medical multiplicity: in caregiving,
    10–13, 145–46, 165–66, 190–93; docu-
    mentary, 181, 189–91, 213n2; politics
    of, 31; in transnational funding,
    26–27, 169–70, 192; use of term, 10
medical pluralism, 11, 177–78
Millennium Development Goals
    (MDGS), 20
mining, 118–19, 210n2
Ministry of Health, Mozambique, 3,
    5, 13–14, 16; APE program, 64; data
    collection, 48–49, 67, 168–69, 171, 180,
    184–85, 188–90; documentary prac-
    tices, 172–74, 184–85; donor manage-
    ment, 20–21; employment policies,
    153, 160; food support policies, 34–35,
    116, 210–11n6; health policies, 23, 30,
    129, 202n25; on traditional medicine,
    177; volunteer programs, 48–49,
    59, 67; workshops, 68–69. *See also*
    Clínica 2 (pseud.)
Ministry of Women, Children and
    Social Action, 38. *See also* National
    Social Welfare Institute (INAS)
Morrumbala District, 7, 8, 29; agricul-
    tural production in, 102–3; commu-

nity leadership in, 63; displacement
    and violence in, 19, 38, 92; as ethno-
    graphic location, 7–8, 22–24; food
    distribution in, 121–22; NGO histories
    in, 38–40; politics of vulnerability
    in, 40–43; postwar developments,
    101–4; villagization in, 99–101. *See also*
    Global Children's Fund (GCF)
Mosse, David, 46
multiplicity: defined, 53; documentary,
    181, 189–91, 213n2; governmental, 54,
    190; institutional, 53–54, 56, 169–70,
    213n2; medical, 10–13, 26–27, 145–46,
    165, 169–70, 190–93; politics of, 31,
    198; professional, 161–63; of sover-
    eignty, 42; use of term, 10

National AIDS Council, Mozambique, 116
National Health Service, Mozambique,
    114, 116
National Social Welfare Institute (INAS),
    35, 37, 52, 55, 61, 73
NGOs (nongovernmental organizations),
    4, 7, 13–14, 17; critiques of, 110;
    entanglements, 4, 6–7, 24–25, 31, 53,
    56, 91, 111, 165; evaluation of, 206n15;
    histories in Morrumbala, 38–40;
    interventions, 20–21, 39, 109–10, 193,
    202nn22–23; per diem economies,
    79–80; transnational governmentality
    of, 55. *See also specific organizations*
Nguyen, Vinh-Kim, 79
Nsanje, 99–101

Oikos, 51–52, 135
OJM (Organization of Mozambican
    Youth), 72
OMM (Organization of Mozambican
    Women), 72, 73, 159

Packard, Randall, 118
PEPFAR (President's Emergency Plan for
    AIDS Relief, U.S.), 4, 23, 121, 162, 180

politics: biopolitics, 51, 111, 203nn5–6, 214n10; of multiplicity, 31, 98; of time, 13; of vulnerability, 40–43
Project RITA, 51–52
psychology, 143–44
Psychology Office, 4–5, 142, 145, 146–47, 149–51, 153–54, 153–56, 159–60, 170–71
public health: access to care, 4, 27, 30–31, 38, 41–43, 131–33; closure of services, 1; community histories, 64–66; glory days of, 16–19; labor migration and, 119–21; neoliberal reform in, 138, 159, 213n10; relations and, 11; remaking policies, 19–20; socialist vision of, 16, 19; state role, 55–56; WHO commitment to, 38. *See also specific organizations*

Quelimane, 57–58

racial capitalism, 103
Red Cross, Mozambique, 65
relations: caregiving and, 11, 116–17; dependent, 106–9; of exchange, 131; food support and, 135–37, 139–41; nourishing, 192; in political belonging, 58–59
RENAMO/Renamo, 15, 19, 38, 57, 201n15, 201n19

Save the Children, 51–52
Serviço Nacional de Saúde (SNS), 153; data collection, 180; strike, 1–3, 166
Sisters of Charity, 112
SNS. *See* Serviço Nacional de Saúde (SNS)
South Africa, labor migration to, 118, 119–20, 124–25, 210nn2–4
states of emergency, 110, 114, 128, 200nn10–11
Strategic Plan for HIV/AIDS, Mozambique, 13–14, 16

strikes, 1–3, 76, 166
suffering slot, 215n3

tambira (to receive), 105–6
therapeutic citizenship, use of term, 41–42
therapeutic pluralism, use of term, 178. *See also* medical pluralism
time: caregiving and, 7, 12, 13–15, 31; ethnographic practice and, 12, 192, 200n10; in food distribution, 88, 96, 121–22; historical, 110; of length of support, 126; politics of, 13; punctuated, 110; in relational practices, 107
traditional medicine, 71–72, 176, 177, 178, 214n4
transnational funding: for Clínica 2, 3, 4–7, 12–14, 112, 145, 146, 165–66; interventions from, 4, 16, 22–23, 49, 86, 111, 114, 138, 145–46, 191, 192, 199n2, 214–15n11; medical multiplicity and, 26–27, 169–70, 192
Trouillot, Michel-Rolph, 215–16n6
tuberculosis, funding for, 4, 13

UNAIDS, 1, 173
UNICEF, 145
United Nations High Commission on Refugees (UNHCR), 101–2
USAID (United States Agency for International Development), 15, 58

volunteer programs, 32–34; benefits, 30, 57–58, 60, 73–74; data collection, 48–49, 67, 167–68; expansion of, 20; in food support, 134; genealogies of, 62–64, 65–66; for HIV/AIDS, 32–34; lack of rewards, 75–77; personnel background, 71–75; political belonging in, 58–59; role of, 48–49, 65–66; task force on, 59–62; training, 68–71, 77–80. *See also specific organizations* vulnerability: gendered relations and, 136–37; mapping, 45–48, *48*; politics of, 40–43; registering, 49–53; representing, 43–48, 123; use of term, 215n3

WFP. *See* World Food Programme (WPF)
World Bank, 20, 195, 202n22, 213n10

World Food Programme (WFP), 111, 121, 123–24, 126–27, 145
World Health Organization (WHO), 17, 38, 64, 173
World Vision, 40, 51–52

Zambézia Province, 57, 93–96